Celtic: Keeping the Faith

Celtic: Keeping the Faith

Richard Purden

FREIGHT BOOKS

First published 2015

Freight Books
49–53 Virginia Street
Glasgow, G1 1TS
www.freightbooks.co.uk

A CIP catalogue reference for this book is available from the
British Library.

ISBN 978-1-910449-53-0
eISBN 978-1-910449-54-7

Typeset by Freight in Tiempos
Printed and bound by Bell and Bain, Glasgow

the publisher acknowledges investment from
Creative Scotland toward the publication of this book

For Christina Doreen Purden

RENFREWSHIRE COUNCIL	
243178021	
Bertrams	30/10/2017
796.334	£8.99
REN	

Acknowledgments

My sincere thanks to all the Celtic supporters and former players and managers I've interviewed over the years.

To Louise, Ryan and Christina for love and light.

To my parents, wee Nana, Jenny Wren, Terry Bhoy and all the wider family.

At the end of a long journey thanks to Suzanne Lofthus, Bob, Stan, Jonathan Taylor, Julian Flanders and Adrian Searle.

Thanks to Andy, Ronnie, Paul Dykes and all the friends who have walked with me over the course of the two books.

These two books wouldn't have been possible without the grace, love and energy of others – thank you all for your kind support.

Contents

001 **Chapter 1**

The Croy Express

Ex-miners from Croy discuss how their ancestors built community around work, Celtic, faith and family life in the aftermath of the Irish famine.

017 **Chapter 2**

Five Years

Martin O'Neill made Celtic one of the most invincible clubs in Europe, heralding the end of a transitional spell when he arrived in 2000. He provides a fascinating insight into his illustrious five years, which remain among supporters' most cherished memories.

045 **Chapter 3**

Cliftonville Skyline

Outside Glasgow, Belfast arguably contains the highest concentration of Celtic supporters who regularly journey across the water to support the team. Cliftonville F.C. chairman Gerard Lawlor, acclaimed author and playwright Padraig Coyle and principal of St Mary's University College Peter Finn discuss what Celtic means to supporters in the city.

067 **Chapter 4**

Streams of Whisky

The story behind Shane MacGowan's trilogy of Celtic songs: 'Tomorrow Belongs to Me', 'Road to Paradise' and 'The Celtic Song'. The late Philip Chevron also reflects on The Pogues relationship with Celtic supporters over the last thirty years.

'My theme is how you live, how an average person, not as extreme as, say, St Francis but how an average person can live a saintly existence. 'We still exist; therefore, there must be a road for us to follow, for the layman to follow, the Catholic layman.'
Martin Scorsese

'I have fought the good fight, I have finished the race, I have kept the faith.'
2 Timothy 4:7

Foreword

In November 2014 I received a late night message from a friend inviting me to the unveiling of a new painting by Glasgow based artist Peter Howson of Celtic's founding father Brother Walfrid. On the afternoon of the event it was a pleasure to meet many fellow Celts including Matt McGlone and former player Frank McAvennie celebrating this powerful new work. There was also a showing of the documentary Brother Walfrid: The Founder. It's fair to say you could feel the emotions in the room shift as the trauma of the famine years and its deeper causes were narrated by actor Peter Mullan and discussed by the likes of Sir Tom Devine and Professor Joe Bradley. Also at the event was the publisher of my first book (We Are Celtic Supporters) Bob McDevitt. Bob has since left publishing but I'd like to thank him for pursuing that book and introducing me to Adrian Searle of Freight Books who got this edition off the ground. That morning led to a chain of events that one year on have resulted in the publication of Celtic: Keeping the Faith. Emma O'Neill has allowed the use of Peter Howson's traumatic yet moving portrait for the cover of this special edition which comes 100 years after the death of the man whose spirit remains at the core of Celtic Football Club. Emma's passion for the Walfrid story was clear and there was a certain synchronicity and organic quality in the latent parts of this edition coming together. I am extremely grateful to her for allowing me to use this image of Brother Walfrid.

Introduction
A Sort of Homecoming

A FASCINATING ASPECT of the Celtic support, which also captures something of the joy of being a fan, is the culture of pilgrimage that has grown around the club's history. Aside from travelling to the games themselves, thousands of supporters have embarked on journeys to the Estádio Nacional in Lisbon, to America to join the New York Celts on St Patrick's Day and more recently to visit the bronze statue of Henrik Larsson in Helsingborg. Closer to home the Brother Walfrid memorial in Sligo and Andrew Kerins' final resting place in Dumfries have become sacred journeys. Another addition has been the Jimmy Johnstone statue and memorial garden in his home village of Viewpark. Each trip has a different meaning for the traveller, but we've all made them, often for reasons beyond a passion for the game. With an international support that spans generations many have discovered Celtic when searching for an ancestral link to the Irish famine and its aftermath, something many readers will still only be one or two generations away from. Often it's just a name, a genetic feature or information passed on from parents and grandparents that sparks a search through the past.

Celtic Park has come to stand as a positive beacon for Irish-derived people not just in Scotland but around the globe. For many, this football intuition continues to offer a sense of place while piecing together an unknown personal history that can often seem just out of reach. For others without an Irish or Catholic link, the social values and inclusion of the excluded are often equally attractive reasons to support the team. The David and Goliath-style triumph over Barcelona at Celtic Park in the Champions League will be the overriding memory of the 2012–13 season. It is occasions such as this that turn legions of neutrals across the globe into Celtic fans because no matter what the odds are we all want to believe we can triumph in the face of adversity. If ever a football club has become symbolic of that then it is Celtic.

The journey of this book began around a table in the heart of Glasgow at the Babbity Bowster on Blackfriars Street with one of those supporters who bought into this ideal. The bar/restaurant is a regular watering hole for Benny Krieger, a farmer from Israel who regularly travels to watch Celtic.

Benny's story captures many of the reasons why Celtic are a special club. Sitting with his Pogues tattoo, a pint, a green and white scarf, and denims, he looks every inch the typical Celtic supporter, but his excursion to the East End is less ordinary. Krieger has worked in agriculture since he was a boy, growing oranges and potatoes as well as farming livestock. The roots of his Celtic story began with his local team Hapoel Kfar Saba, who share an aesthetic connection in that both clubs play in green and white hoops. Though, as Benny suggests, they also have a similar fan culture: 'They [Hapoel] are like the team of the workers; they are socialist and pro-peace with the Palestinians.'

Social justice is something that remains important to Celtic supporters and that identity among generations has enriched the club over the last 125 years. Krieger's background and the well-known affiliations with the plight of the Palestinian people among many Celtic supporters immediately suggested to Benny yet another binding connection: 'The first time I saw it [the Palestinian flag] among Celtic fans I was a bit shocked. I was walking down the Gallowgate towards the city centre, I didn't recognise it at first; then I saw what it was. The supporters noticed me looking, maybe my expression wasn't very positive, they came over and apologised to me. But I didn't have a problem; I was just surprised to see it. To be honest I had more of a problem when I saw Israeli flags at an Old Firm game in the Rangers end. I felt really bad about that one because I know the occupation is wrong and what my government is doing to the Palestinians is wrong. With Celtic there is a sense of protecting the weak and the vulnerable, there is a sense of wanting to put the wrongs of the world right – the roots of the club are a beautiful thing. If you look at what Celtic is, historically the people that left Ireland, they had no choice, they didn't want to rule other nations or people; they were just trying to survive. Celtic supporters carry a sense of that today and it comes out in wanting to protect people, whether it's another culture or nation it doesn't matter, it's about protecting people from oppression, that's what it's about for me. I'm not a football fan; I support Celtic and my local team and that's it, beyond that I'm not interested.'

Not long after becoming a Celtic supporter politics had become part of the transaction for Benny. Not politics of a Scottish or Irish nature, but issues that affected Benny's life back in Israel. Not only that, he also had a historical link that punctuated the fact there was something missing from his life in Israel: 'My family is Jewish but my mum was born in England, her mother was an Irish protestant who left Ireland in the famine years. My mother worked as a volunteer on the boats in Israel with the kibbutz, which is a communal and social cultural movement and still ongoing. She was into saving the world and dug irrigation and canals for poor villages in Greece before she went to Israel where she met my father and had to convert.'

It was during a trip to Belfast that Benny first encountered a live broadcast of a Celtic v Rangers match. Beyond the River Lagan he met supporters who shared their passions, frustrations and stories around the table like ancient missionaries sharing the gospel. In 1997 Benny made his first visit to Glasgow to see another team in green and white hoops, a team he had heard a lot about: 'It was the stopping of the ten,' he recounts with a knowing smile on his face. Since that day he's become a regular at Celtic Park: 'I'm just glad that I got to be a Celtic supporter when Henrik Larsson was playing, because he is someone I will tell my children and grandchildren about; I don't think we will ever see a player like him again. It was something really special to live through. I got to go to a lot of games. Of course, a highlight is the 6–2 game. Someone loaned me the season ticket of a guy who was getting married that day; I hope the marriage lasted! Another memory is Seville, I took my nine-month-old son; he was confused because suddenly there were thousands of men who looked like me with cropped hair and the hoops. After all these years I've got friends in Glasgow who are like family to me now, it's like living a double life without a wife and kids. When Celtic played Hapoel Tel Aviv I took my father along, that was pretty special. We met some people we knew who were a bit confused when they saw we were supporting Celtic: to them it was just a team from Scotland.'

For a time Benny even opened his own Celtic pub in

Israel, Foggy Dew, where he set up satellite broadcasts, hung framed Celtic team portraits on the wall and imported Scottish beers and food to make an even more authentic experience: 'We had vacuum-packed bacon and sausages and we could get the eggs, beans, rolls and HP sauce. I sold my pub a few years ago, but there's another Babbity Bowster in Israel that does a similar thing. I still have cases of beer at my house, sometimes a keg. The food and drink is an important part of the whole experience. For me bacon is a bit like Celtic: it's the taste of freedom.'

Chapter One
The Croy Express

THERE'S AN ENDLESS flow of tea and chatter amid a group of elderly Celtic supporters gathered at Croy Miners' Welfare Charitable Society. Andy McGuire, a Parkhead season ticket holder from the East End of Glasgow, is talking about his first game, the Empire Exhibition Cup final against Everton in 1938. Tony Weldon of Croy, a dead ringer for Bill Shankly, recounts a leg-breaking tackle he executed playing against Walter Smith. Beside him, Hugh, an 'in-comer' from Coatbridge, is reeling off the Albion Rovers line-up that included Jock Stein back in the 1940s. Tommy Reynolds is reflecting on childhood memories featuring a cast of players that would become major names in Scotland and over the border. Anne Russell, a volunteer serving hot coffee, tea, sausage rolls and pieces is recounting the night of her honeymoon spent in the Black Isle watching Celtic win the European Cup. 'I can think of better things to do on honeymoon,' quips Weldon. Upstairs in the Croy Historical Society, Seamus Coleman is working in the heritage room; in front of me are glass cases packed full of various memorabilia including an antique football, which once had a former life at the centre of the action. The legendary Jimmy Quinn scored three against Rangers with the relic after Celtic went 2–0 down in the 1904 Scottish Cup final.

Football is one of the pillars on which Croy's male identity rests. The banter from these exchanges, both enlightening and entertaining, fills the room with an undeniable energy. The club was set up by the Regeneration Trust in 1999 and since its formation the associated society has worked towards preserving the area's local history going back to the Antonine Wall built by the Romans around AD 142. A major undertaking of the volunteers is unlocking Croy's Irish past, which also serves to help locals unstitch what are often complex and hidden narratives. Walking around 'Crowey Miners' as it's locally referred to and pronounced, I'm privy to the nerve centre of the community at full throttle. Many Scots were suspicious of the recent Tory ideological narrative, the Big Society, which seems to have rapidly expired. What I witness in Croy would appear to have the mechanics of a thriving and responsible society in place, yet they are exactly the kind of organisations that are struggling with cuts endorsed by the SNP and the Conservatives.

Both parties could do a lot worse than to look at the roots of Croy as an example of progression. It's a relatively new Scottish community built by a now elderly Irish-derived society who had escaped political, religious and economic turmoil in the early part of the 20th century. Surviving two world wars and the policies of the Thatcher Government in the 1980s, they were used to regrouping, reorganising and supporting each other collectively in the face of adversity and hard times. It's not difficult to understand why there is deep suspicion of the Tories in a politically aware and active area such as this. Fundamental to the community spirit is a strong work ethic, a profound Catholic Faith and a great love of Celtic Football Club.

The Croy Celtic Supporters' Club was formed in 1951. Life member John Cullen, born in 1930, is treasurer and minutes secretary for the miners' club. The former councillor is also a steadfast member of the Labour Party, Transport and General Workers Union and the National Union of Mineworkers. In 2005 Cullen received the Benemerenti medal from Pope Benedict XVI for his lifelong commitment to community work. In 1913 his parents moved from Ireland. It was the same year as the General Workers Strike in Dublin. Central to the organised protest was Edinburgh-born James Connolly and Liverpool Irishman James Larkin. Revolution was also rife in China, Mexico and Britain, where Emily Wilding Davison, the militant English suffragette became a martyr for the right of women by throwing herself in front of King George V's horse at the Epsom Derby. John Cullen's family joined the thousands of Irish sailing to various parts of the UK during this time of upheaval.

'My father came from Ireland to Scotland in 1913, he got married in Kilsyth, my mother came over with him and they moved from Twechar rows in East Dunbartonshire to the brick rows in Kilsyth and from there they went to Croy. The church and school were next door to each other at that time. What they were looking for was an education and a moral background; it paid off. I grew up hearing the Irish brogue; many spoke Irish as a first language – this whole area was Irish at the time. Housing was very poor. The Catholic Church stepped in because conditions were so bad and they got demolished. Croy village came into being around 1932; at that time the population would have been 1,600. It's dropped to something like 958 at the moment.

'In 1954 William Baird, the coal owners, split up the "miners' rows". Twechar was non-Catholic; Croy, Smithston and Auchinstarry were mainly Roman Catholic. We used to refer to Auchinstarry as "the Port" because that's where people from the village left for America. Those that couldn't afford to go stayed.'

The connection between Croy and Celtic is one that predates the football club. Its most famous son, Jimmy Quinn, remains Celtic's fifth highest goal scorer and memories of the enigmatic player travel round the table, passed on from the voices of family and friends who are now long departed. Born in 1878, the second generation Irishman secured eleven international caps for Scotland scoring seven goals, as well as scoring 217 goals in 331 games for Celtic. He eventually signed his name on a contract for Willie Maley (after previously knocking back Sunderland) on Hogmanay 1900. There are markedly few pictures from his playing days adding something of an allure to the coal miner and reluctant footballer who would become one of the most famous faces in the land during the Edwardian era. As one of Celtic's most complete centre forwards for the best part of 15 years he would have been discussed and debated by supporters, rival teams and the wider public taking until his retirement in 1915.

New media has gradually shifted the culture of the game today, but it hasn't altered the stature of Jimmy Quinn for the locals of Croy and other supporters who champion the unique nature of the club. Time and technology hasn't eroded the reverence in which the player continues to be held almost 100

3

years since his retirement. Like Kenny Dalglish in the 1970s and Henrik Larsson in the late 1990s and early part of the 21st century, such players leave a legacy that remains long after they have blazed a trail in front of the Parkhead faithful. John Cullen explains: 'We paid almost £18,000 for the ball from the 1904 Scottish Cup final, which gives you an idea of what he means to the community here. Growing up, Jimmy Quinn was a local hero; we wrote poems and articles about him, he was known by various nicknames like King James of Scotland, the Mighty Quinn and the Croy Express. In Croy we claim Celtic, we are part of the fabric of Celtic's history and really that came from this being an area of poverty and deprivation; that was the mining community.'

Quinn remained an important figure; his reputation went before him long after his retirement from playing. Successful Celtic teams of the day would have their picture taken with the player and he was used on a number of advertising products. His name and face continued to be associated with Celtic until his death in 1945. For the people of Croy his character was vital; Quinn was reserved and humble natured – despite exceptional talent he was initially reluctant to sign for Celtic. Cullen explains the story behind his breakthrough at the club: 'At Junior level he played for Smithston Albion, which was a miners' team. Celtic organised a charity game against them, but they didn't realise what they were coming up against. The story goes they were going to "show the yokels"; Willie Maley was said to have tore into them [Celtic] at half-time, even after that another four went in against them. They got beat 6–1. Ten of the team went senior and Jimmy Quinn signed for Celtic.'

Tommy Reynolds, born 18 January 1941, reflects on Quinn's status in the area: 'Jimmy Quinn was my grandmother's brother. One of my most vivid memories was when his brother Peter, who lived on the Constarry Road, took me to meet him. Peter would come home from the pit with his face black from mining, pour his tea on to a saucer and drink it. I was too young at the time to realise what was going on, but he took me up to see Jimmy Quinn on his deathbed. It wasn't until years later that I looked back at the dates and realised who it was, the significance of him taking me there and what he really meant to the community as the miner who became a legend in the true sense of the word; it's a moment that has stayed with me all my life.'

Significantly Quinn used his connections to recommend John (Jock) Morrison, another local star turn who would put in over 200 appearances for Celtic. Cullen reflects on another former great whose career was cut short by war: 'We used to say there was never a good Celtic team that didn't have a Croy boy about it. John Morrison was one of the top players of the time and was part of the team that won the Empire Exhibition Cup; he was another who might have easily just carried on as a miner without Jimmy Quinn's recommendation to Willie Maley. Morrison signed for Celtic in 1929 and played until 1940. He was a big powerful left back, but the war put an end to his career.

'During the war the normal league structure was abandoned. My first Celtic game was around that time, Christmas 1940. A few of us clubbed together with our Christmas money and went to see the Celtic; we beat Queen's Park 5–1. Johnny Crum scored two and Murphy scored one; I was ten years old. The next time I saw Celtic was after the war in 1946 against Hibs. Coming out of the army Rangers were able to keep a top team because of the jobs they held, Hearts nearly lost their whole team.

'Going to see Celtic had a huge impact on your life and it became part of your mentality and development as a person. We didn't believe in mediocrity. Sport, mainly football and boxing, taught you a discipline that was vital if you wanted to get on in life. Aside from the influence of my mother and father there was a boxer from Croy, Bill Clinton, who was a professional champion, he won forty out of fifty fights. Bill would take you into the ring and throw a few punches in your direction. Then he'd throw one at you and say: "Remember Cullen, you're a Croy boy, remember that." I'd leave the boxing guild and think: "that man must be off his rocker", but it worked for me and the many he trained and boxed with through the generations. It sunk in.'

Tony Weldon, now in his early seventies, explains the synchronicity between Croy and the roots of Celtic: 'We all have a connection to Jimmy Quinn in this town; the day of his funeral I was only about five years old and wondered what the big crowd was. I thought it was strange, the whole atmosphere of the place. I remember picking up a pebble in his garden the day of his funeral and I kept it as a souvenir. It was Quinn's story that made you proud to be a Croy boy, it was a mental attitude tied to Celtic, to the pit and to the village itself. I had a brother who passed away, when he was in hospital the doctor said: "I see you're a Celtic supporter" looking at his tattoo, my brother lifted up his sleeve and corrected him: "It's Croy Celtic son."'

A sense of the landscape and the environs to which they had to adapt became important to the Irish that finally put roots down in Croy where character, faith and a strong work ethic became central to the philosophy of the village. Whether it was football matches at Junior level, brass bands or boxing matches, the focus wasn't on the individual's skills or ability; it was the idea that they were collectively representing Croy. It didn't matter if the opposition team or opponent had a bigger parish, what religion they were, what team they supported or even how skilful they were. What mattered was to beat the opponent and win the competition. Tommy Reynolds explains how the mood of the village would change the night before a match: 'People would stop you in the street and say "you better win this tomorrow". Pride was fierce and it was made plain that if you lost you weren't just letting yourself down, you were letting down everyone in the village. It produced results and gave you that impetus to score and win games against other villages and teams that had a much bigger pool than Croy. That mentality was there before Celtic, we were all brought up in it; a sense of discipline and never giving in no matter what was drummed into us. It was very important.'

There is a rush of exhilarating optimism mixed with defiance around the Croy miners, their convincing shatterproof stance spliced with a certain chutzpah and wit springs from the very depths of their soul. Their story remains intertwined with the Irish that sailed over during days of famine and war but they've also fought their own battles in the pit and struggled in the aftermath of losing their livelihood while watching the world they inherited from their parents and grandparents change beyond recognition. The individualism of the Thatcher era and the virtual social world are alien concepts to the miners. Refreshingly, nobody in the room has the need for a digital fix: no one tweets, checks their smartphone, updates their status on Facebook or downloads any digital information while we talk. You can't help but observe the flow as the men trade stories like killer punches one after another. It's as though loose electricity is charging the lifeblood of others who join in or simply stand and listen.

What is especially contagious in this company is an unshakable ability to look forward, infused with a hunger to talk about what they believe in; passing their way of life on to the next generation. That world is built around the Celtic Supporters Club they formed in 1951. John Cullen explains: 'Going to see the Celtic was vital for us, it was always a tonic just travelling together on the train, but it also built up the community spirit. An enthusiasm for Celtic brought people close and got them away from the grind, it was something we could all rally around together. We chartered a bus to go to the Scottish Cup final against Motherwell in 1951 and beat them 1–0. That was our first major trophy since the war and we wanted to build on that enthusiasm so we decided to form a club as a result. After a meeting at Taggart's shed in the village we closed the book at sixty members, we were told it wouldn't last but we're still here. I'm still going today, although I'm the oldest member now.'

Significantly they are able to claim among their number another son of Croy who would leave further influence on Celtic Football Club, trading the community of miners for commerce and wealth. 'Fergus McCann joined the club as a laddie, he was only sixteen and he never stopped talking. The social convener said: "Why did you ask him?" "His father's got a phone," was my reply. Fergus had the last laugh because he very quickly turned the club into a functioning social organisation and started to run buses across the land. McCann put on first-class concerts, he was only sixteen, but he knew what people wanted and he was an excellent promoter. He certainly developed his mind, skills and ability here.'

Although the Croy mentality has reserve and humbleness among its cornerstones, it is not something as ineffective as sentimentality; its perspective is a compelling philosophy that summoned those charred by the struggle to feel invincible. Their outlook, a force to be reckoned with, evokes something of the showdown mindset which pervaded the character and managerial careers of Don Revie at Leeds, Alex Ferguson at Manchester United and Bill Shankly at Liverpool. These giants, still looming over the British game, transposed a way of life and thinking from their industrial or mining backgrounds that continue to provide inspiration that goes beyond sporting excellence. The underdog spirit along with a sense of being disliked outside of the inner sanctum of the club and its support are used to create a winning mentality. Undoubtedly, Manchester United, Leeds, Liverpool and Celtic have all used negative stories to their advantage, bolstering a sense of purpose in their teams.

In February 2011 there was an echo of this approach from then manager Neil Lennon who defined his own version of the tried and tested 'us and them' formula. He said: 'Everyone wants to beat us. Everyone wants to see us get beaten, apart from ourselves and our supporters.' It's often suggested that Neil Lennon's background as an Irish Catholic has made him a popular choice among Celtic supporters. For the Croy Celtic supporters the idea that Lennon was a more appropriate Celtic manager than Gordon Strachan because of his ethnic and religious background is not accepted. Yet for Weldon, like many Celtic supporters, Strachan remains an unpopular choice despite his success: 'I was regular at Celtic Park every week when O'Neill was there. It has to be said that Gordon Strachan did something I thought was impossible; he killed the atmosphere completely and I stopped going. Martin O'Neill's ambition was bigger than the club; if they had backed him I believe he would still be there, but there was no way he could take the club forward without money.' Hugh Quinn is also critical of key changes that were implemented during Strachan's reign: 'In Lennoxtown [which opened in 2008] the players are distant and isolated, each player has a diet sheet and a lot of science goes into their preparation, but can they kick a ball? We didn't win the league for a few seasons between 2008 and 2012.'

What made Neil Lennon an attractive option for Celtic fans is his attitude and the mental strength he shows under pressure. His arrival as manager was undoubtedly low-key compared to that of Tony Mowbray, but Lennon's ability to talk to Celtic fans through the media in a similar fashion to Martin O'Neill and Jock Stein while tapping into certain narratives returned to a mindset that had been lying dormant since O'Neill's departure. Regrettably he has was also a figure of hate among rival clubs.

John Cullen believes it's part of the Celtic mentality to turn prejudice and injustice into advantage: 'There's often opposition to Celtic, a good manager has to learn to cope with these things and use them to the club's benefit. The press have a lot of power and often use it negatively. As well as setting football precedence Jock Stein was a strong leader, he set the blueprint for dealing with the papers. One of the most controversial games was what's become known as the "Battle of the River Plate", which was the World Club Championship in 1967. It was organised after we won the European Cup the same year. Celtic won the home leg 1–0 and then we had to go over there. We got kicked stupid. Racing Club lost it, there's a film of Tommy Gemmell kicking a player's backside, and there was a hue and cry in the papers heralding it as a disgrace.

'The club's dinner and dance coincided with the aftermath, we received a call to ask if it would be OK if Jock Stein and Robert Kelly could come and address the fans at the supporters' dinner and dance, but that it was to be kept away from the press. There was always a buzz about the place for these nights and they attracted a big crowd so you can imagine when the curtain drew back and there was Jock Stein standing on the stage waiting to address the Celtic support after this game against Racing Club. It was obviously about putting the negative stories to rest that were circulating and it worked; the place went into a riot. Stein stated that discipline was very important at Celtic and that it was the club's prerogative to discipline the players, not the newspapers, commentators or anyone else when it came to Celtic's team. He talked about his own personal responsibility in picking a team that the fans could be proud of. The place went into raptures, he left you in no doubt that he was in charge and that it was a responsibility he took very seriously, nobody was going to take that power away from him; that was the size of the man.' Documents released in 2007 revealed that it was the events of this game that led to Mr Stein being denied a knighthood despite intense lobbying by Secretary of State for Scotland Willie Ross.

Among the men sitting here today there remains a tangible and intense respect for Jock Stein. For many the combination of his working-class mining background, his ability to diminish the negative power of the press and the strength of the authoritative personality he projected during his time as Celtic manager have made him an impossible act to follow. For Hugh Quinn, born in November 1930, this reverence pre-dated both his playing days and his managerial career at Celtic. As an Albion Rovers centre half Quinn remembers a confident and self-assured player who issued a verbal right-hander to whoever crossed him. He said: 'Coming from Coatbridge, aside from Celtic our local team was Albion Rovers. My first memory of Jock Stein was a Saturday afternoon at Cliftonhill, there was this piercing noise coming from the terracing behind the goal, suddenly all this ash cascaded off the roof and slithered onto the ground. I think the noise was that loud because there was hardly anyone at the game, behind the ash was Jock Stein, sliding off the roof after retrieving the ball. It wasn't long before he became a hero. There used to be some great battles between Bobby Flavell and Jock. Flavell spent a long period as a centre forward at Airdrie. He was significant at the time because he stuck two fingers up at convention. Those were the days when players would spend their whole careers at one club, but Bobby wasn't having that, in 1950 he went to Bogotá in Colombia to play for Millonarios alongside Di Stéfano. He was ahead of his time, when he came back he ended up playing for a number of clubs, but he was looked at as a bit of a rebel for that.'

Significantly Quinn also had an opportunity to meet Stein the same year he won the European Cup where he reminded him of his playing days at Clinftonhill: 'It wasn't long after Lisbon so he was signing various pieces of Celtic memorabilia for supporters, I went up to him and said "will you sign that?" I had written out the entire Albion Rovers team he played for in the 1940s and put it down in front of him. He looked up with a smile and said: "It wasn'ae like that every week."'

It was a strange aftershock from the 2010–11 season after letter bombs, bullets in the post and attacks on the Celtic manager that the blame should be left at the door of Catholic schools. John Lamont, the Tory spokesman for justice, caused widespread concern when he said that they were 'state-sponsored conditioning of sectarian attitudes'. Lamont's views aren't in isolation; in 2006 former education minister Sam Galbraith suggested that the schools were the root cause of sectarianism in Scotland. In the aftermath of the 2010–11 football season Edinburgh University hosted a seminar open to the public with the subject billed as: Sectarianism in Scotland: Myth or Reality? The responses from the audience proved to be captivating, particularly one retired schoolteacher who said: 'I spent my whole career in secondary education in both denominational and non-denominational schools. I have a very high regard for all the schools I've taught in. From my considerable experiences, by far the more coherent message given to children concerning love of neighbour, justice and peace, human rights, and that includes a message of anti-sectarianism, was in Catholic schools.' At the same event Dr John Kelly highlighted the absurd thought behind the theory. He said: 'If there's evidence that tells us that Catholic schools lead to ethno-religious prejudice, sending bombs to Neil Lennon and bullets to other Irish Catholic Celtic players, and indeed some people singing anti-Protestant songs and being anti-Protestant, perhaps if someone can show me that it is because of Catholic schools then let's have the debate, but it beggars belief for me that the solution to ethno-religious prejudice is to be prejudiced towards someone's religion.'

Since the events of 2011, when letter bombs were also sent to prominent Celtic fans, MP Trish Godman and lawyer Paul McBride (who sadly died suddenly in 2012), the wider media, politicians and even the law focused on the word 'sectarian'. Many Celtic supporters believe the intense rivalry with Rangers has little to do with a split over faith or indeed theological difference of opinion. For retired Catholic schoolteacher Hugh Quinn, the mainstream focus on social tensions between Celtic and Rangers supporters needs to shift beyond a perception of religious intolerance. In many ways the word sectarian, between rival fans at least, is redundant: 'For me it's really got nothing to do with a religious faith anymore. In most areas of Scotland today churches of different faith backgrounds are actually quite friendly and tend to work together, people from different denominations are married, work and live together; what the problem is really about is the partition of Ireland. The Union Jack and the Irish tricolour at Rangers and Celtic games clearly identify that. "The Soldier's Song" is not a religious song; it's political. In the past Catholic schools were referred to as republican schools, today the business of rivalry has much more to do with Ireland, its history and political culture than an actual religious faith.'

John Cullen agrees: 'In my work as a councillor there was no sense of separation in your job, you had a duty to respond to the needs of whoever needed help in the community, not what faith they had; that wasn't the way people went about things.' Despite going to separate schools and working in separate pits the Croy miners are clear that anti-Protestant feeling and sectarian attitudes were deplored by family, priests and the wider community.

Tony Weldon explains the rivalry with Rangers and the early separation from Protestant communities: 'Separation in the pit was a good thing for the time because the community was being built up and the separation was deliberate and it was right. The coal companies knew what they were doing; it got rid of a lot of bitterness and gave the Irish a chance to settle in. I'm a Celtic man but I'm not a bigot, my father wouldn't allow it. Anti-bigotry was drummed into us. It's taken lightly now; it rolls off the tongue this idea of playing for the jersey. But to me, the players I've seen, they played for the jersey and it had nothing to do with religion for the likes of Bobby Collins, Bobby Evans and Willie Fernie. It didn't make a difference to us what their religion was; that kind of ignorance wasn't tolerated. I couldn't sit in the company of a bigot. I remember playing against Walter Smith when he played for Ashfield. During his first spell as Rangers manager I was invited for a bite to eat at Ibrox with a wee pal of mine Tommy Traynor who had been Walter's teammate at Dundee United. When I got there [Ally] McCoist and [Ian] Durrant were there. I can even remember what I had – macaroni cheese. Walter comes over and says: "Are you enjoying your dinner boys?" So I said: "Aye Walter, but I've got to tell you something, I'm a Croy boy." Before I could go any further, he said: 'I know fuckin' fine who you are; you nearly broke both my fuckin' legs." The place went into hysterics. After that he sat down for a blether. That's the reality despite how the bigots or the papers paint it. For our generation it wasn't about if you supported or played for Celtic or Rangers or even whether you had any talent; it was about a person's character. Mentality, character and how you went about life was paramount for the generation I grew up in, these things were more important than anything else.'

Undoubtedly Catholic teaching has had a major positive influence on generations of Irish-derived Celtic supporters.

Celtic supporter and Scottish politician Jim Murphy has suggested the Catholic Church in Britain has been essential in shaping the nature of many immigrants coming into Britain from Ireland as well as the Caribbean and West Indies. More recently the Church has been essential in creating community and structure for many Eastern Europeans now living and working here. For many Celtic supporters, including John Cullen, the tenets of the faith became one of many essential guides in shaping the character of the immigrant Irish in Scotland: 'The priest gave you a sense of right and wrong, it was essential to the moral fibre of the village for us as individuals and as a group. You were taught to respect other faiths and groups, not to hate or discriminate. Father Sheridan was the centre of our community for nearly thirty years. He was the parish priest and he chaired the dinner dance for the Celtic Supporters Club; the whole thing was interlinked. He would also travel with us to the games; it was actually part of his pastoral duties and we would chip in to cover his costs.

'I remember a trip to Amsterdam; it was the quarterfinal of the European Cup, March 1971. The snow was belting down, it was Cruyff's Ajax and they tore us apart; they went on to win the cup. Before the bus left the priest would get on and give you a lecture; I mind one boy's teeth chattering while he spoke. Once he was asleep the young team would produce a half bottle. You had to have a bit of a sense of humour about the authority of priests, they had too much control, but now it's gone the other way.'

As Weldon suggests it was a love of football from early youth into adult life that brought what could be perceived as separate communities together. Junior football led to a number of significant encounters between the boys of Croy and Coatbridge and luminaries at rivals Rangers: 'We came from a Catholic community, but because of Junior football we were never really separate from Protestant guys once we started to play the game. Jim Storrie played for the great Leeds team in the 1960s under Don Revie. Jim married my cousin. My uncle [her dad] was Tony Weldon and he played for Everton and West Ham among a few other teams. Jim had to change his religion to Catholic. He was interviewed by the priest about the Catholic catechism; the first question was: "Who made you?" Instead of answering "God made me" he said "Don Revie". There was a temperament and a similar sense of humour in that generation which we all participated in, religion never came into it,' says Weldon.

'I remember meeting Bob McPhail, who would be considered one of the best players in Rangers history; he played alongside my uncle Tony at Airdrie. I met him at an *Evening Times* event, he was well into his nineties. The first thing he talked about was my uncle being a decent young lad. He said: "Tony Weldon was a gentleman and a grand wee player." The person's character always came first, talent and what kind of player was always second. Today it's the other way around.'

For young Catholics growing up in the early half of the 20th century the Protestant community still represented a feeling of otherness and fear of the unknown. Significantly it was playing against non-Catholics that eroded that sense of them and us: 'There's a particular occasion that stays with me,' says Quinn. 'My brother was selected for a reserve match playing for Airdrie against Rangers at Ibrox. During the game he picked up a cross with his chest on the wing and scored with a volley. Bang! Right into the back of the Rangers net like a lightning bolt, which I can still see even now. Ibrox was like the lion's den to us; here we were a couple of wee Tims from Coatbridge in the Rangers canteen. You can imagine how we felt. So we're sitting there with a couple of sausage rolls and in walks Bill Struth, who was like the Willie Maley figure for Rangers. Struth wasn't known for praising his players – if you did really well, you did "OK" kind of thing. He looks in our direction, picks up a tray and walks over to where we were sitting: "More sausage rolls boys?" "Thanks Mr Struth". He then walks away, but stops and turns on his heels and looks right at my brother: "That's the way to score them son."'

As members of what was once the most organised and advanced coal industry in the world – 180,000 workers at the start of the 1984 miners' strike compared to 6,000 today – the Croy men have had to confront the problems and worries of life head on after the Thatcher government created an economic structure that favoured city bankers and the service industry over manufacturing and industry. In doing so she tried to destroy hundreds of years of working-class progress, structure, identity and values while creating a new British culture of material greed, corporate arrogance and terminal selfishness.

John Cullen in particular is a man who doesn't appear to know when he's beat, almost single-handedly securing funds for the building we are sitting in today where brass bands, debt management, elderly support, bereavement counselling, a trip to Lourdes, youth unemployment and education, male voice choirs, religious processions, drug and alcohol support and co-op initiatives are all discussed, planned or debated. The locals also gather here to watch pay-per-view matches, each member makes a small contribution and the money is distributed to charities locally and around the globe. It's fair to say that in terms of jobs, security and the future nothing has ever replaced coal mining in the lives of these men but they have found a way to survive. Says Weldon: 'We've all supported Celtic together through hard times in our lives and in Celtic's history. Growing up we all played football at Junior level, if you didn't have a game on, you'd be on the Celtic bus. It was heaven on the bus, we all worked together in the pit and watched Celtic together on a Saturday, if anyone had a problem you'd sort it out together on a tea-break over a fag, nothing was carried on. That was the mining community; it still exists. Thatcher tried to break this, she could never do it; look around we're still here. The ethos is still here. I'm Croy till the day I die.'

Chapter Two
Five Years

*'The yellow kit with the green shorts was very strong and it
seemed to bring us decent luck at times, but any time we could
wear the proper hoops, we wanted to wear them, that is what
Celtic is about to me.'*
Martin O'Neill

TO ACHIEVE IN football as in life there often has to be a shift
in thinking, a shedding of the self and an understanding of
an individual's weakness along with a realisation of strength
and what should remain. In Celtic's illustrious narrative the
year 2000 will always remain an epic milestone. A new system
was implemented, seeing off an atmosphere of faded glamour
around the club. For most of the 1990s Celtic inhabited their
greatest rival's shadow across the city, it was an immensely
painful time for fans when Jock Stein's achievement of nine
successive Scottish league titles between 1966 and 1974
was equalled in 1997. In 1994 it was conceivable that Celtic
Football Club as we know it could've imploded had it not been
for a robust group of emotionally charged and determined
supporters putting their own lives on hold to form a pressure
group which ultimately brought down an antiquated board.
Without them it's unlikely the club in its present form would
be here today.

In the early 1990s mediocre managers such as Liam Brady
and Lou Macari were allowed to serve during a time now known
as 'the barren years'. John Barnes would leave an equally
dispiriting footnote at the end of the decade as the club's
second first-time manager in six years lasted only six months
in the job. There were moments of grace with the appointment
of Tommy Burns, who navigated the team through a choppy
stage as Celtic entered a more contemporary phase. His third
and final season in charge proved to be an exhilarating attempt
to wrestle the league title from Rangers. A talented cluster of

continental players heralded a fresh new era at Celtic, some of whom tapped the nerve centre of the support by displaying transcendent skill seamed with exotic flamboyance and folk-hero magnetism. These traits served as a lightning rod for fans' affections, but success eluded Celtic both domestically and on the European stage. Wim Jansen and Dr Jozef Venglos have become popular cult figures among Celtic fans for their singular seasons in charge. Jansen, in particular, will be forever remembered as the manager who halted Rangers' dominance with the 1997–98 title win, releasing Celtic fans from the crippling anxiety of ten-in-a-row and bringing Henrik Larsson to the club, but ultimately neither manager became anchored long enough to build a stable legacy.

An extraordinary transformation occurred with the arrival of Martin Hugh Michael O'Neill at Parkhead on 1 June 2000. The first Celtic manager of the new century posed for pictures in Paradise while telling fans he would do everything in his power to bring success to the club. The statement of intent proved to be true. The alchemy at work when Martin O'Neill was appointed was instantaneous, as if destiny had allotted him the position.

On meeting Martin O'Neill for the first of two face-to-face interviews for this book and before a number of follow-up telephone conversations, I remind him of the last time we met, at Led Zeppelin's one-off gig at London's 02 Arena back in December 2007. O'Neill had been listening to the band since the early 1970s. Significantly they had premiered 'Stairway to Heaven' at the Ulster Hall in Belfast in 1971 during their Back to the Clubs tour. Within months Zeppelin would rise from concert halls to board the Starship, conquer the world and become an insurmountable rock behemoth. That same year O'Neill was studying law at Queen's University in Belfast while plying his football trade at Distillery in the west of the city (they would later change their name to Lisburn Distillery). Conceivably the young Irishman could have been numbered among Celtic's Quality Street graduates and certainly would have had his father, a Celtic man through and through, had anything to do with it.

O'Neill casts his mind back to the early 1970s and explains the circumstances: 'I joined Distillery with something of a flourish, scoring a few goals and grabbing a few headlines.

Within a few months scouts and clubs in England were travelling across the water to watch me play, but disappointingly nothing immediately came of it. Celtic were among those clubs watching me in the Irish League. I recall some years later, when I had established myself as a player with Nottingham Forest, I met the legendary Jock Stein by chance one evening; he was gracious and polite in his conversation, straining to recall whether Celtic had indeed come to Grosvenor Park to run the rule over me. Anyway, it gave me the opportunity to say to him that my father would have been the proudest man in the world had his son worn the Celtic shirt at Parkhead. In a playing capacity my father said: "Son, if you ever get the chance to go to Celtic, walk there." Unfortunately he died before I ever became the manager of the club.'

The psychology behind Martin O'Neill's success both as a player and manager has been much deliberated. There have been many highlights of a world-beating mentality that has produced life-giving success of mythical proportions, whether it's scoring against Barcelona with Distillery during a Cup Winners' Cup match in 1971 or playing in a Nottingham Forest side that won back to back European Cups. But perhaps the most miraculous case of bumping the odds was as Celtic manager when he led the team to its first European final in 33 years. There's a mentality at work that has produced consistent success in situations that have been utterly compelling. It is said that your character is your destiny and without reservation O'Neill's father played an essential role in shaping his son's fledgling attitude.

Born in Kilrea, County Derry, O'Neill grew up in a typically Irish Catholic council house with a portrait of the Sacred Heart of Jesus alongside a small black and white framed picture of Padraig Pearse. O'Neill's father was also a founder member of Padraig Pearse's GAA Kilrea. In the traditions of the time soccer was often referred to in the pejorative as a 'foreign sport', Irish Catholics in the north expressed a love of athleticism primarily through Gaelic football and it was a social and cultural distinction to which O'Neill was profoundly affiliated. Despite the deep divisions between Catholic nationalists and Protestant unionists the aspiring sportsman was happy to embrace the contradictions of the culture. A picture of Manchester United hanging in his father's barber shop took pride of place: 'Yes, despite the fact he was a Catholic and co-founder of the local Gaelic club there was a large picture of the Busby Babes that hung in his shop for a very long time; he gave it to me and I'm hoping one day when I unpack all the bags from that time I'll find it again somewhere. I can still see the jaded red colour of the strip; it was fantastic. But he was a big Celtic fan. He told me that a few of the Celtic players used to go to Northern Ireland for their holidays, to places like Portstewart, and some of them visited my father's shop. One of the boys that came in was John McPhail.'

In Northern Ireland footballers and sportsmen in general have played a vital role in transforming cultures where there has been an ethnic, religious or political partition in place. George Best's status at Manchester United as a 'genius' player and pop culture icon celebrated as 'Georgie', 'the Belfast Boy' and the 'Fifth Beatle' is identified as an essential positive symbol, unifying both sides of the community as well as repositioning Belfast in the eyes of many in Britain who were being fed on a media diet of the Troubles and deprivation. Prior to Best's success the dichotomy at work within Celtic became an essential example of how the game could be used to break down destructive prejudices directed towards those of a different belief or cultural standing. Says O'Neill: 'In the 1950s, early 1960s a big player from Northern Ireland was Bertie Peacock. He was from Coleraine and relatively local, about fifteen miles down the way. The fact he was a Protestant playing for Celtic gave us a sense of pride. Celtic didn't seem concerned about a person's religion; they were more interested in ability. I was delighted that Bertie Peacock chose to play for Celtic. Bertie was a top-class footballer and came back home to manage Coleraine. I got to meet him a few times. Many of Celtic's best players were Protestants if you consider the likes of Kenny Dalglish and Danny McGrain to name a couple and, of course, Jock Stein; there is something uplifting about that.'

While at St Columb's College in Derry, O'Neill remained heavily involved in Gaelic football, but when the school united to watch Celtic take on Inter Milan in the European Cup final on 25 May 1967 the event had a profound impact. Within a few years he would have made the full-blown shift from Gaelic football to soccer. Other former alumni at St Columb's include two Nobel Prize winners: politician John Hume and poet Seamus Heaney. The institution's motto: 'Seek ye first the Kingdom of God', places a Catholic Christian ethos at the centre of the college's vision which aims to promote 'the dignity, self-esteem and full development of each person who is made in God's image and uniquely loved by God'. It's not tenuous to suggest a correlation between Brother Walfrid's intention for Celtic Football Club and the institution where O'Neill was educated. A football club with a heart for justice was formed to give hope to those that were struggling, under nourished and disenfranchised.

It would be disingenuous for the community that supports Celtic today to paper over this fundamental history, but the mainstream media remains hostile to Celtic's cultural past. *Daily Record* journalist Hugh Keevins suggested the club's Irish Catholic origins should be 'dumped'. While the journalist was ultimately referring to fans that celebrate the extremities of violent nationalism, he makes no effort or inclination to separate the two philosophies. O'Neill suggests the issues around Celtic's past should be addressed in a more considered manner: 'The soul of Celtic football club is inextricably linked with its origins. Brother Walfrid's philanthropic influence pervades Celtic Park, his deeds and concerns for the poor in Glasgow and the Irish itinerant workers moving into those areas are deeply rooted in Celtic's culture. In truth, that will never be erased. Asking Celtic to forget about its Irish roots and Brother Walfrid is like asking Barcelona to forget their Catalan roots.'

Rather than 'dump' its Irish past, Celtic Football Club can be proud that its formation has helped lessen various social divisions spread over a number of societies and cultures. Undoubtedly the Irish character of the club whetted the appetite for football in Ireland; it's one of the strange quirks of history that Celtic, with its lineage, could only have happened in Britain and arguably in Scotland where the Irish struggled most with hostility and resentment – though fortunately not enough to dissolve the club. With the demise of Belfast Celtic in 1949, the significance of the Glasgow club began to take more prominence in the north especially when it fielded Ulstermen with the character and flamboyance of Charlie Tully and Bertie Peacock. By 1967 such was the importance of Celtic's first European Cup final that O'Neill and fellow pupils at St Columb's were allowed to view the match in its entirety, leaving an everlasting impact on the budding sportsman. 'At St Columb's college we actually had half-day classes on Saturday, so as boarders we saw very little television. Perhaps the last half hour of the old sports programme *Grandstand* when the football results would be rolling in off the teleprinter, but when Celtic reached the final of the European Cup in 1967 all two hundred boarders were given permission by the dean of the college to watch the match that evening. I do remember we had some difficulty getting a proper picture on the TV. But just before kick-off a thump from someone's fist on the telly seemed to do the trick and we all sat down to watch what turned out to be one of the best European Cup finals ever played. It struck me as being a little strange that you could see trees in the background as if the game was being played in a rather large park. A few years ago I watched a documentary about Jimmy Johnstone [*Lord of the Wing*] when Jimmy revisited the stadium in Lisbon, it seemed to have changed very little in the intervening years. It's a park I would love to visit.'

Shortly after scoring for Distillery against Barcelona in 1971, O'Neill signed for Nottingham Forest where he was managed by a trio of Scots: Matt Gillies, Dave Mackay and Allan Brown, before Brian Clough was appointed in 1975. Lisbon Lion Tommy Gemmell played alongside O'Neill and John Robertson, who would later assist the Irishman at Celtic. O'Neill remembers a memorable first brush with 'Big Tam': 'Tommy signed for Nottingham Forest in late 1971, just a few months after I had joined the club as a nineteen-year-old from Distillery. I was somewhat awestruck by the whole essence of being a professional footballer in a major league and was probably in a state of flux when Tommy arrived at the City Ground. John [Robertson] and I in our first conversation with Tommy garbled on about the great goal he had scored in the European Cup final. Our obvious reference was to his equaliser against Inter Milan in 1967, Tommy quickly retorted with "which one son?" making us immediately aware that he had also scored a goal in the 1970 final against Feyenoord.

'A few seasons later the great Jimmy Johnstone, having left Celtic, found himself at Sheffield United. He was playing in some crotchety reserve game against Nottingham Forest at our ground and received an injury during the game. He was taken off to be seen by a doctor in the home treatment room. I came down from the stand where I was watching the game, just to peep in and have a look at him, actually I wasn't the only one who had the same idea, most of the Nottingham Forest first team had done the same thing, just to get a look at the little genius despite him being well past his prime at this stage.'

Celtic's immutable 1967 win earned the victorious players the nickname of the Lisbon Lions. The first British team to lift Europe's most prestigious trophy was made up entirely of players born within 30 miles of Glasgow. It is an unmatchable achievement. Soon after his appointment as manager of Celtic, O'Neill made something of a masterstroke by inviting the Lions out for a meal. It was a considerate gesture, and something that could have been overlooked by a less solicitous manager. It would also turn out to be one of the last complete gatherings of the team that triumphed that day, adding considerable gravity to the event. It was also bountiful on another level because it gave O'Neill the opportunity to draw upon the shared experiences, camaraderie and mentality that created Celtic's undisputed season of excellence, becoming the first club to claim five trophies in one football term.

Undeniably O'Neill thrived on the stories, spirit and humour and would endeavour to position the Lions as a model of consistency and unity for his own team. Speaking shortly before his passing in 2001, Bobby Murdoch suggested how much the occasion meant to him as he had felt a growing negligence around the legacy of Lisbon. He said: 'Most of the Lisbon Lions have felt for the past few years that the club had forgotten about the role we played in its history, but the first thing Martin did when he arrived was get us together for a meal.' When a club has hit a nadir long after reaching its zenith, when fans are subdued or discouraged and when European glory seems implausible, it's an astute progression to return to those origins of excellence. O'Neill had wanted to keep his meal with the Lions a private matter. But in a city like Glasgow knowledge on Celtic matters is impossible to obscure. The former Celtic manager is clear about his intentions that night: 'That was something I wanted to do from the moment I became manager at the club. Back in boarding school days I'd watched those very same players make Celtic the first team in Britain to win the European Cup. I'd arranged a dinner in recognition of their achievement, despite their own misgivings they were still revered by almost everyone connected with Celtic. I was there that evening as a listener, not a partaker, and when Bertie Auld is talking you have to listen anyway. It was quite a night. I did occasionally mention that I had twice won that very medal they were discussing with Nottingham Forest, but somehow it escaped their notice and no one minded one bit. I did not expect the dinner to get the public attention that it eventually received.

'I enjoyed that night immensely. To be with them for a meal all those years later really was a privilege, a lot of good-natured banter abounded that evening, especially when they ribbed each other about big games that might have proved costly if they had not bailed each other out, it really was fantastic.'

Significantly, O'Neill hosted the Lions two years running and pushed for their testimonial match against Feyenoord in January 2003, the sense of occasion was enhanced by O'Neill's return to the dugout as manager with a rolling contract was agreed after more than a fortnight of speculation about his future. Fortuitously for Celtic fans reported negotiations elsewhere never came to fruition.

When O'Neill arrived at Celtic the press told him that the winners of his first Glasgow derby on 27 August 2000 would win the league, so a loss at this stage would be fatal. 'I understood what the press were saying, but after one game against Rangers I thought those estimates were premature,' said the Irishman. The sun-dappled green grass of Paradise was swathed with anticipation prior to a fixture which has kept football fans around the world gripped since both Celtic and Rangers made their presence felt as European finalists in the 1960s and 1970s. With eleven of the previous twelve Scottish league titles going to Rangers, the event had huge connotations, as this was the start of O'Neill's revival. The match also saw the return of Henrik Larsson who had been absent from the previous four derbies after an alarming leg break. His return was marked by much conjecture over whether he would return as the same player.

Celtic fans watched in awe as a rejuvenated Bobby Petta ran rings around Fernando Ricksen, while Slovakian magician Lubo Moravčík set up the play for Sutton, Petrov and Lambert to make it 3–1 before half-time. Two Henrik Larsson goals in the second half and a 'last-minute Celtic' goal from six-million-pound signing Chris Sutton gifted a new generation of fans the most complete annihilation of Rangers in living memory. To top it off, the most significant rock 'n' roll star of the era, Noel Gallagher, was among the Parkhead faithful that day. After joining the manager post-match he left the stadium sporting a blue denim jacket with a green and white bar scarf, awestruck at Larsson's unforgettably brazen fifth goal; a superlative chip over the keeper's head. It was a symbolic affiliation that was hammered to the mast for all to see the day after Oasis played Glasgow Green with fellow Celtic supporters Primal Scream.

Said O'Neill: 'It was a magnificent game for Celtic, Rangers were very strong physically and very talented as they had proved the previous season, but we got off to an incredible start with three goals in the opening eleven minutes. Even then Rangers fought back strongly and despite a 3–1 lead I never felt they were out of the game. Chris Sutton scored with a few minutes left to make the score 6–2, that was the first time in the match that I breathed somewhat more easily than I had done in the previous ninety minutes.'

* * *

The model set up by Brian Clough and Peter Taylor at Derby, Brighton and Nottingham Forest also served O'Neill and John Robertson at Wycombe Wanderers, Leicester City, Celtic and Aston Villa. Writing in his 2002 autobiography *Cloughie: Walking On Water*, O'Neill's former boss observed: 'When you enter an unknown world, which management was to Martin O'Neill, irrespective of the club or the level, you take someone you know. You take a pal. Just like I took Peter Taylor, Martin O'Neill took his best mate.' As O'Neill explains the bond between his assistant John Robertson and coach Steve Walford was an essential ingredient at Celtic: 'John and I certainly went back a long way, starting with our playing days at Nottingham Forest. I also brought Steve Walford. I had played with Steve in my latter stages as a player at Norwich City and I brought him to Wycombe Wanderers where he coached the youth team and eventually to Norwich and then on to Leicester City. There was a strong bond between all of us and it was inevitable we would team up again at Celtic.

'John was from the outskirts of Glasgow and had not been home all that often apart from to see his parents in the summer time. He had left at fifteen to go to Nottingham Forest. Going back was a bit strange for him initially, he had been away from Scotland for all those years, but in many aspects he was glad to be close to the family and settled back in quickly. As did Steve, who brought his family up to live in Hamilton. What was important in all of this was that they also developed a strong bond with the team. The players had trust in Steve as a coach and John as an assistant manager. They knew that unless there were serious problems they weren't going to be reporting anything back to me, so the players had freedom in the dressing room and didn't have to worry about a misplaced word getting back to me. Everything was taken in good spirit and that spirit pervaded the whole club.'

Undoubtedly, the make-up of each individual player was the raw fabric he would reshape and remodel. Anyone set in their ways, no matter how skilled, wouldn't make it under the new manager. In addition to being able to provide a supportive arm around the shoulder, like his former manager Brian Clough, O'Neill would have to be able, as John Robertson puts it in his autobiography *Super Tramp*, to 'dish out bollockings'. He goes on to say: 'He did so when I was a player under him at Grantham and, at the other end of the football spectrum, there were times when he handed out criticism to a world-class talent like Henrik Larsson when we were at Celtic.' While Celtic supporters acknowledge the singular talents of Mark Viduka and Eyal Berkovic, they seemed to lack the application needed to be part of a winning Celtic side and significantly neither would become part of the O'Neill era.

As a player his clashes with Brian Clough were an essential factor in O'Neill's development, just as they were between the former Celtic manager and Neil Lennon. Clough had this to say about his former midfield player in 2002: 'There were many times when I clashed with him, usually when I left him out of the side, and I was forever hearing him moan, "I might as well go back to university."' While Clough didn't hold the same academic leanings, his worldly and sophisticated knowledge of players was more than enough to bring Old Big 'Ead a host of football's top honours. Today O'Neill reflects on his former boss: 'Brian Clough may be the most charismatic manager the game has known, he could be rude and charming in the same sentence. He could embrace and disregard you in a minute, but he made you want to play for him and that was the major strength of his man management.'

As well as securing the league title 15 points clear of Rangers, O'Neill's first season saw Celtic win both domestic cups, securing Celtic's first Treble since 1969. Domination over Rangers was completed as Larsson netted his 50th goal of the season in the dying minutes of another smooth 3–0 victory at Ibrox. The 3-5-2 formation O'Neill had deployed initially at Leicester brought much admiration from supporters. He brought in key players including one of Celtic's most intimidating and rapid central defenders Joos Valgaeren. The Belgian became something of a cult hero, as did Swedish hard man Johan Mjallby, known as Dolph because of his resemblance to action film actor Dolph Lundgren. He returned to Celtic Park as assistant and 'right-hand man' to Neil Lennon for four years between March 2010 and April 2014, Mjällby cemented his position as a popular figure with the Celtic support, and is remembered for his strength in the air as well as his robust performances against Rangers and in Europe. Celtic's unyielding defence would be completed in 2001 with the addition of Frenchman Bobo Baldé. The team was now more than equipped to deal with their old adversaries and a host of European opponents.

Reflecting on his Treble-winning season O'Neill said this: 'When I came to Celtic the club had finished the previous season behind Rangers and were well beaten in the league. I had great respect for that Rangers team, I remember Tom Boyd saying to me, "You're taking a lot on here, it's going to take an awful lot to turn things around. 'My immediate incentive was to get closer. The first big derby gave us a great lift although we were well beaten in the second game at Ibrox [5–1]. We had great belief along the way and we added a couple of decent players to strengthen the squad as the season went along. We won the CIS League Cup against Kilmarnock and the sense at that point was to keep going in the league. By March I thought we could actually do this, but we're going to need a bit of luck. We certainly had the capability. I was ecstatic to win it [the Treble]. It wasn't easy, but nothing had been easy for Jock Stein either.

'The 3–5–2 system suited us in the domestic game; we learned a lot more about European football later on. When we played Porto in the group stages of the Champions League (2001), they had one centre forward and two holding midfield players and this wasn't even under Mourinho, it was nearly two years before Seville in the UEFA Cup Final. But it made me think about adjustments for European football, I was learning all the time. But, going back to that first season, domestically we would be on the attack and more often than not the wing backs, Alan Thompson and Didier Agathe, were able to exploit some space and give Henrik more opportunities for scoring. Moravčík was a super player. He had a particularly memorable game against Rangers at the end of the first season. Perhaps I felt initially he was just a crowd pleaser but I soon realised that the player himself, although approaching his mid-thirties, still retained a hunger to win. People would say: "Why isn't he playing?" But I couldn't play him every week because he didn't have the energy. When he had the opportunity to turn it on and confidence was high he was a marvel to watch, he could do things that other players can only dream about.'

In O'Neill's second season, despite going eleven games without a goal, John Hartson made an impressive contribution. That and the human touch he brought to the team inevitably secured a firm place in the affections of the Celtic support. In true Celtic tradition Big Bad John became the fan on the pitch as he grafted and struggled with his weight while making typical front-page headlines such as 'Hartson's Late Night Booze Binge'. As a matter of fact the stories only strengthened a persona that evoked the nostalgia of days gone by. Although he didn't make the starting line-up for the UEFA Cup final, the buoyant Welshman played a crucial role in the charge towards Seville with a vital away goal in Galicia. He killed off the opposition a second time at Anfield with a sublime 25-yard shot which hurtled past Jerzy Dudek into the Liverpool net – a goal that continues to dazzle in the memory of the Parkhead faithful. It was subsequently revealed that Pope John Paul II had been earnestly following Liverpool in Europe that season, supporting his fellow Pole Dudek. Subsequently he presented the pontiff, an aspiring goalie in his youth, with Liverpool's No. 1 jersey. In conversation with Hartson shortly before an appearance at the Edinburgh International Book Festival he proudly displayed a Celtic FC tattoo while reflecting on his role in Martin O'Neill's side: 'My first season was very enjoyable. I scored a hat-trick against Dundee United and we beat Livingstone 5–0 to win the league at home, Henrik scored three and I scored two to clinch the title.' By the end of the campaign Celtic secured 103 points, 18 ahead of their Glasgow rivals. Says Hartson: 'My kids were on the pitch that day along with my mum and dad. We were walking round lapping it up; I wasn't used to those celebrations. We had a great side: with the exception of three or four players like Paul McStay, Mick McCarthy, Kenny Dalglish and Danny McGrain, we had the best side since the Lisbon Lions. Any of those players would have got in our team or the Lisbon team. I think the majority of Celtic fans would say we were the best team since Lisbon and we proved it by getting to a European final in Seville.

'In Europe we beat the best: Juventus, Barcelona, Liverpool, the list goes on. We beat a lot of big clubs at Celtic Park in Champions League football; we were a very strong side, our youngest player was Stan Petrov who was twenty two, but apart from him the average age of the team was about thirty. We were a team of men – Thompson, Mjallby, Sutton, Douglas, Larsson, Lennon, Agathe, Valgaeren and Balde. Martin often used to say "go and win"; that was all he used to say to us. The Liverpool goal was special because I grew up a Liverpool fan. The thing about that game was three days before I missed a penalty in the League Cup final against Rangers. In the warm-up at Anfield the fans were singing my name, they really got behind me. Chris Sutton didn't play that night so it was Henrik and me up front. Not many teams go to Anfield on a Thursday night and win as comfortably as we did. I played in a great side.'

Celtic's first run in the Champions League in 2001 had certainly whetted supporters' appetites for the competition. It's unlikely the most neutral observers, never mind die-hard partisans, would have predicted Celtic's premature exit the following year, going out in the third qualifying round against FC Basel, particularly with a 3–1 lead after the first leg at Parkhead. But a 2–0 defeat in Switzerland meant a loss on away goals. O'Neill was severely discouraged, particularly after such a convincing run the previous season. But a clarion call from the youngest member of his side proved that a dramatic shift in confidence and attitude had taken place among the players in Celtic's first eleven.

The former Celtic manager reflects on some vital matches that led to Celtic taking centre stage in European football for the first time in 33 years: 'Seville was a culmination of the whole run, but it started with the disappointment of Basel. I still remember Stiliyan Petrov, who was only a young kid at the time, said to me: "We'll just have to win the UEFA Cup." By goodness, that looked a long way off. We played Blackburn Rovers in the second round. Under Graeme Souness they were a pretty good team at that time, lying around sixth or seventh in the Premier League table. They were better than us in the first game at Celtic Park although we actually won the game. We got a late goal from Henrik Larsson, yet despite our victory "Men Against Boys" became the headline the following day in the newspapers, a comment picked up by the media that had emanated from the Blackburn Rovers dressing room and attributed to Graeme Souness when talking to his players just after the match. After that we were determined to make amends at Ewood Park in the second leg. And we did it with a tremendous 2–0 win.' Scottish football received a major boost from this victory as Blackburn Rovers were expected to knock Celtic out over the two legs.

'Beating Celta Vigo to take us into European football after Christmas was another big talking point. It was the first time in twenty three years that we had done that. You have to consider that a couple of years before we had to play a qualifying game against a Luxembourg side [Jeunesse Esch], it showed the sort of strides the team had made. We had another fantastic run against Stuttgart and Liverpool. That night in Liverpool is etched on my memory forever. The semi-final, away against Boavista, looked destined to be goalless; I would have hated going out on away goals at that stage and then Henrik scored in the eightieth minute and turned it around. Just earning the right to go to Seville was fantastic in itself.'

Undoubtedly, the positive origins of the club have given birth to a determination and sense of ethics known as 'the Celtic way', which is as much an attitudinal philosophy as a style of play. This by-now traditional attitude pervades the club and its supporters, rejecting pessimism like a soldier on leave. Predictably, rivals ridicule the idea, but the notion is essential to Celtic, offering a source of strength for supporters when things don't go to plan. It's these instincts and beliefs which are summoned in the upbeat rousing terrace favourite 'Willie Maley', a song that delights in the trophy cabinet as well as Celtic's archetypal players and technique. Celtic fans, fed on a sumptuous diet of attacking football during the club's early excursions throughout Europe in the late 1960s and 1970s, expect their teams to have flair even though historic matches – against Racing Club, Atlético Madrid and Rapid Vienna for example – introduced the rise of negative tactics and hollow victories. These games saw Celtic's opponents win by any means possible, be it violence, feigning injury or spitting, designed to stifle the philosophy of attack as much as the players' temperament. These actions brought a destructive end to some considerable European ambitions. Before the away leg against Atlético in 1974 Jock Stein told the *Herald*: 'Atlético offended me deeply. I like to think that football and sport are important, that being part of the game is an honourable occupation. What they [Atlético] did in Glasgow hurt me more than words can express. That's why I want to beat them here, fairly, on their own ground, in front of their own people.' Regretfully it wasn't to be due to further destructive behaviour in the second leg.

The methodology of Porto in the 2003 UEFA Cup final left a similarly bad taste in the mouth, particularly the behaviour of their goalkeeper Vitor Baía, whose contempt for the competition was clear from his self-humiliating time-wasting antics and goal celebrations that drained vital minutes. Like Stein, O'Neill was 'offended' by the opposition's tactics in Seville: 'I felt sadness, disappointment and anger in equal measure. The disappointment that we hadn't won the UEFA Cup was obvious. The anger at Porto's antics during the final was mirrored by the fact that they were booed onto the podium when they went to collect their winners' medals. They were a very talented team – as was proved when they won the Champions League the following year with a very talented manager in José Mourinho. But they resorted to every trick in the book, exploiting that old word "professionalism". In extra time the goalkeeper lay prostrate on the ground for three minutes not knowing which part of his anatomy he had supposedly hurt with three or four doctors looking on in attendance and nodding approvingly at his state of health.'

As the game drew to a close O'Neill considered the daunting prospect of penalties. He and a stadium full of Celtic supporters had the painful memory of a previous UEFA Cup exit at home against Valencia in December 2001 during which Celtic lost a shootout 4–5 after a 1–1 aggregate score. It was a tie from which many felt Celtic deserved more over the course of two memorable games, and the cruelly premature exit that night left a tangible sense of hurt. Regrettably, penalties that warm evening in Seville were not part of the script. In a heart-rending twist of fate Bobo Balde was sent off in the 96th minute, an act that changed the dynamic of the game and alerted supporters that the dream was coming to an end. A third Porto goal from Brazilian striker Derlei made it 3–2 in the 115th minute of the game.

It had been a somewhat unexpected but inspirational journey, with a clutch of enduring victories along the way. As O'Neill acknowledges, the era remains among the Celtic faithful's most cherished European memories. The UEFA Cup final was the culmination of two spectacular seasons during which Celtic regained the kind of European reputation they had enjoyed during Jock Stein's 13 groundbreaking years at the club. That shift began for Martin O'Neill in the Amsterdam Arena on 8 August 2001, where a now classic Celtic line-up was about to cement its place in the club's history by entering the group stages of the Champions League for the first time, as O'Neill explains: 'My view was that the winning of the game against Ajax was a very important breakthrough in our development as a side. Prior to the game there was a tremendous euphoria among the support, the team and the club that our name was in the hat. But I must admit there was a certain amount of anxiety because we had drawn a club with a fantastic European pedigree. They may have faded slightly from the teams that they had in the past, but it's fair to say that the Dutch league at that stage would have been considered a notch above the SPL. Here we were a year on from playing a qualifying game in the UEFA Cup and about to take on the might of Ajax. It's worth bearing in mind the kind of players they fielded at that time, such as Ibrahimovic, Mido, and Rafael van de Vaart. That night in the Amsterdam Arena was a magnificent victory, we played some exciting football with the wingers Petta and Agathe scoring in the first half and Chris Sutton scoring in the second. The whole team was outstanding. We had done a lot of the hard work by the time the second leg came around in Glasgow and were more than familiar with the idea that we could reach the Champions League group stage. This was an exciting prospect for us and for the support. You could feel the tension rumble around Celtic Park that evening, particularly when Ajax scored, putting us on the back foot. But we saw it through. The result that evening was everything, we had played brilliantly in the first game and that stood us in good stead later on. It's a significant point that we had to rely on away form during the UEFA Cup run the following season because our home results weren't always enough to see us through. We felt euphoric in the group stages of the Champions League and Celtic were now back in the big time. Little did we realise at this juncture that in less than two years' time we would be playing in a major European final.

'It's all history now unfortunately, but to go back to that evening in Seville, Henrik Larsson was superb and he got his reward with Barcelona a few years later when he came on as substitute to change the course of the Champions League final against Arsenal in Paris. I was absolutely thrilled for a great player to get what he deserved. I still feel some sadness for all those Celtic fans that travelled far and wide to support us in Seville. But it was an incredible experience for them and one that they will never forget.'

One of the most memorable moments of the whole experience was to hear the Celtic support jubilantly in song, for the ever affecting 'You'll Never Walk Alone' at the end of the game, offering scarves and handshakes to Porto fans who appeared bewildered by the positivity of their rivals in defeat. Many supporters cheered themselves up remembering the team that went out in the semi-final of the 1966 European Cup Winners' Cup only to achieve Europe's greatest prize the following year. Today, O'Neill suggests a wider shift had already taken place: 'I understand what fans were saying, that even though we got there we would continue to be pressing on. But I think a lot of things had changed in that time; there wasn't any money – Celtic and Rangers could have gone their own way in terms of TV revenue with league games and that might have earned them more. I know that suddenly there didn't seem to be any money in the SPL between 2003 and 2005 – we tried with the Wolves player Camara, we brought in Juninho but he was at the end of his career. In essence neither Celtic nor Rangers were spending: the days of big six-million pound signings like Chris Sutton and John Hartson had gone and it was all to do with TV revenue.' In August 2015 Juninho expressed some regret about his time at Celtic in *FourFourTwo* magazine saying: "things didn't really work out for me. I had this issue with Martin O'Neill and his tactics. I still can't understand why he wanted me at Celtic. He used to play with a 4-4-2 and he asked me to play out wide with defensive responsibilities, but this was never my style. It didn't suit me and he knew it. Maybe inside his head he was looking for the Juninho of the '90s, and maybe I'm to blame for that but a manger should know a player's style - you have to use them in the right way. It's a shame it didn't work out for me because Celtic is such a great club."

Around the time of a first meeting with O'Neill it was announced that Rangers had entered into administration as the result of a well-publicised tax case. The club had been deducted ten points in the SPL and current Celtic manager Neil Lennon queried the legitimacy of Rangers' titles won during the period as administrators voiced concerns over the handling of the club's finances. The then SNP leader Alex Salmond suggested: 'Celtic can't prosper unless Rangers are there.' The politician received criticism from the club for saying it, but O'Neill's attitude was similar. The prospect of Scottish football without Rangers was not a positive one: 'I must say at the outset that I am astonished even in these difficult financial days that a club as big as Rangers, with such a massive following, could find themselves going into administration. Actually, I would go as far as to say it was a shock in the footballing world. As for the strength of the SPL it is totally counterproductive. For Celtic to be strong; you need a strong Rangers and vice versa, but unfortunately in direct contrast with the Premiership in England, SPL clubs do not have the financial backing to flourish and if the league is weakened significantly, European results suffer and consequently a club will lose their coefficient ranking. Obviously qualification for the Champions league becomes more difficult each year.

'That's not to say that in time Celtic and Rangers might

have to ply their trade elsewhere. It nearly happened when I was manager and I was all for it. Celtic and Rangers would maybe have to start in a lower league, but in the scheme of things what's five or six years in the life of a football club? Celtic and Rangers would be strong, maybe not now at this moment, but they would after a few years building things up. Overnight Celtic would go from 60,000 to 85,000 supporters at home. Rangers would go from 50,000 to 70,000 without any serious problem; these are two unbelievably powerful teams. I can see why clubs wouldn't want them in the Premier League, but I have been an advocate for it and I believe they would do eventual justice, surpassing teams down here that are considered bigger in the sense of numbers coming through the door.'

At the end of the 2012–13 season his opinion hadn't changed, but he had this to say on the season that had just passed: 'Amazingly Celtic's results in Europe were incongruously brilliant last season. Neil Lennon might argue that he was able to concentrate more because not every result was absolutely vital in the league. In my day, the week before a European match we might have felt absolutely under pressure to get league points. We needed ninety-odd points and even then we weren't certain of winning. This season they won it with seventy-nine points. However, they had some tough European qualifying games, and these are difficult matches to be playing in the early part of the season. To then go on to the group stages of the Champions League and win in the way that they did against Spartak Moscow in Russia and Barcelona at home was really something fantastic. My own personal view of the game against Juventus at Parkhead is that Celtic were the better side. They attacked incessantly in what was a really spirited performance. Juventus must have got on the plane to Turin scratching their heads wondering how they won the thing 3–0.'

The subject of Celtic and Rangers being admitted into the Football League continues to dominate news headlines. In March 2013 the *Sunday People* published a story suggesting Prime Minister David Cameron was holding secret talks with both clubs with a mind to admit them into the league so he could 'catch votes' before the 2014 referendum on Scottish independence. The idea of introducing the Glasgow clubs to the Football League seems to be intertwined with fear and loathing in certain quarters of the media and many English fans remain anxious over pro-violent Irish republican and unionist songs as well as anti-Catholic or anti-British feeling. In an article published on the We Are Tottenham website Spurs fan Mike Hunt had this to say: 'Of course, there are obvious drawbacks to having Rangers and Celtic in the English Football League. Namely the Rangers fans' inability to travel to away games without rioting in the streets as well as the inevitable religious sectarian nonsense that goes hand in hand with the two clubs.'

In the aftermath of parcel bombs sent to Neil Lennon as well as incidents of some using social media to stir up the worse kind of violent feeling or posting actual death threats to the then Celtic manager, there is a palpable need to clean up Scottish football. The Offensive Behaviour at Football and Threatening Communications (Scotland Act), which was passed by the Scottish Parliament in March 2012, is said to criminalise behaviour which is 'threatening, hateful or otherwise offensive at a regulated football match including offensive singing or chanting.' Prior to the act Scottish pressure group Take a Liberty sent a statement to supporters of both clubs through a variety of blogs, websites, trusts and fanzines urging them to unite over opposition to the government's plans. The next chapter includes the thoughts of Celtic supporters in Belfast who believe there's been a shift in the north of Ireland since Lennon retired from international football as a result of a death threat. For many, a new tolerance and understanding of difference hasn't emasculated Northern Ireland's cultural, political and religious identifiers.

At present the singing of certain songs at Scottish football matches continues to be a contentious issue, but O'Neill is hopeful the nuances of Celtic and Rangers will remain intact despite much political hand wringing and posturing: 'Personally I feel it would be strange for me to go to Ibrox and not hear "Derry's Walls" or not feel a presence at Celtic Park with "Fields of Athenry" resounding from all four corners of the stadium. Anyway, I often ask myself what is right and wrong these days. I totally accept that no one wishes to take family or friends to football games and feel lives are under threat. Will viewpoints change massively or even at all in another 100 years, I really don't know the answer but I suspect not.'

Speaking in April 2015 Neil Lennon had this to say about the deeply controversial law: 'The bill punished the supporter more than anyone, it was a bit restrictive to the fans and in a nutshell I didn't think it worked. We lost a lot of supporters because of that and good supporters too. It's important that they correct it. '

In November 2004 one of Martin O'Neill's most impassioned acts was to stand beside Neil Lennon at Ibrox with his fist raised in the air as an act of defiance after rival supporters had hurled racist and sectarian abuse at the player for 90 minutes. The Celtic manager was questioned about his action in press conferences after the game. He was able to use these forums to draw attention to the abuse Lennon received that day and at other away grounds throughout Scotland. Today the former Celtic manager reflects on the notorious match: 'I felt that we were getting a rough deal that day. Løvenkrands had tricked the referee into believing that Thompson had head butted him and fell into a heap on the ground [the player later admitted that he had indeed feigned the head butt], but it seemed the referee didn't need much persuading to send him off, then Chris Sutton was sent to the dressing room early in the second half and we played the last half hour at Ibrox with nine players, losing 2–0. My actions at the end of the game provoked a media frenzy immediately afterwards, even spilling over an extra few days to the eve of the away tie at Barcelona with one member of the press in particular pursuing me to explain my actions.

'I felt it was all encapsulated in a moment or two where you felt Celtic were getting the thin edge of these decisions. That particular gesture at Ibrox was about appreciating the support we had from the Celtic fans at Ibrox that day. I think the referee was looking for any excuse to do it [the sending-offs]. We were beaten in the game with nine men. Neil Lennon had a pretty tough time of it, but he seems to have come through it all well. I first signed him from Crewe Alexandra and he performed magnificently for me on the big stage, so bringing him to Celtic presented no risk as far as I was concerned. He just picked up where he had left off at Leicester and was often instrumental in success at Celtic Park. He seldom wore the captain's armband during my time there, but he was in every way a leader. On the pitch his influence on the team was marked, although less flamboyant than others he often dictated the tempo of games and proved himself time and time again on the European stage.'

Two years after O'Neill left Celtic the club completed another reconstruction, moving their training ground from Barrowfield to Lennoxtown. Since launching the eight million-pound training complex in 2007 questions have been asked about the facility's suitability. Celtic is a football club where ghosts in the machine are not easily exorcised. In 2009, Lisbon Lion Bertie Auld criticised the new training complex in another way, stating that the move had built a chasm between the fans and players. In 2011, ahead of a league clash with Kilmarnock, Neil Lennon revealed concerns about the academy to the press: 'I'm not being funny, we're seriously looking at the pitches and asking whether they are a factor in what's happening [with injuries].' Today sports scientists and performance analysts film every kick of the ball at Lennoxtown. Undoubtedly there's value in these advances, but particularly with a club such as Celtic there needs to be consideration of balance. Neil Lennon once described Barrowfield as a 'throwback'. He understood the inescapable sense of history and romance that manifested around the facility which was a creative space for the Lisbon, Quality Street, Centenary and O'Neill eras. A complete move toward science creates a further shift from the maverick street talent and wealth of underdog spirit that characterised Lisbon.

In April 2010 *FourFourTwo* magazine included a sports science supplement with a feature on Lennoxtown that went some way to explain the division of opinion on the move. In an interview with one of the chefs at the new complex, he said: 'I work closely with our sports scientist who lets me know what the players should be eating. We've cut down on calories and salt; everything is grilled or steamed – and we generally avoid fat. It's pasta, poultry, fish, fruit making sure they get the right balance of protein and carbs.' The facilities on offer are also top of the range: an indoor hall, fitness centre, gym, medical facilities, sauna, steam room and hydrotherapy pool. Outside there are three top-quality pitches complete with under-soil heating. But have eight million pounds, superb facilities and an enhanced diet brought better results on the pitch? There will always be romantic associations with Barrowfield and as the quote from Neil Lennon indicated there were some teething troubles with the move but subsequent success in Europe revealed a Celtic side with a renewed strength of character and purpose suggesting a positive shift has now taken place.

O'Neill has his own thoughts on the matter: 'There's no doubt science has a part to play in the modern game, for instance the pre-match eating habits of the modern player contrasts starkly with those of players twenty five years ago and for the most part that should mean improvement in performances. But as my assistant manager John Robertson once said, if every team in Italy eats pasta for pre-match meals why do three teams get relegated at the end of the season? Science has its part to play, but it shouldn't take over – great players still win big matches. In my last season as Celtic manager I visited Lennoxtown when the club were thinking about moving from Barrowfield. I'm sure it is a very fine place now, but I loved Barrowfield. The 1967 team trained there with Jock Stein, Henrik Larsson and Chris Sutton – it was our home. We also had in John Hayes – given what little he had to work with – probably the best groundsman in Europe. He provided and prepared whatever we needed for big games and no one ever complained.'

It's notable that a number of players from O'Neill's first eleven have entered into British football management, among them Paul Lambert, who has bossed three of O'Neill's former clubs (Wycombe Wanderers, Norwich City and Aston Villa), Neil Lennon (Celtic, Bolton Wanderers) and Jackie McNamara (Partick Thistle, Dundee United). Said O'Neill: 'During Paul's final year as a player at Celtic he asked me if it would be all right to do coaching badges. He didn't have a regular place in the team at this point as age was catching up with him. He had been a terrific player for the club. He asked me if he could have some time off to study coaching in Germany, I said "absolutely". He'd had major success as a player at Dortmund, winning the Champions League, and had an opportunity to go back and pick up his German. He had some good friends over there and had always planned to go back at some point.

'I tried to give him a bit of help getting started, but he soon forged his own way ahead. I thought he did very well at Wycombe Wanderers and Colchester United, and he left a strong impression on Norwich City. He's done well in the big league too with Aston Villa. Jackie McNamara is also coming through and that's no surprise to me. As a player he had always been quiet in my company, but he was extremely popular with the lads in the team, maybe it took me a bit of time to realise what a very good player he was. I didn't always play him in the early stages, but he never complained, he wanted to play all the time. In my last couple of years at the club he became an automatic choice and one of the first names on the team sheet. Jackie's time at Partick Thistle was fantastic. He has now moved to Dundee United and under his guidance the men from Tanadise can be a force again. It's pleasing to see all these lads forging ahead in their own way; they all had a steely determination and the character to be successful.'

Since leaving Celtic at the end of the 2004–05 season to take care of his wife during a period of ill health, O'Neill returned to management, spending four seasons with Aston Villa between 2006 and 2010. In December 2011 he became manager of Sunderland for just over 15 months. It's fair to say Celtic supporters were shocked at his sacking, Neil Lennon in support of his former boss said: 'When you see a guy like that losing his job, you realise no one is safe.' Before taking the helm at the Stadium of Light, O'Neill made a brief return to Paradise. He has only returned to Celtic Park on exceptional occasions and rarely talks about his time there, largely out of respect to his successors, but his visits have been important as they were about honouring people he had worked with during his time as manager. 'I have only been back occasionally,' he explains. 'The first time was to attend a testimonial dinner for John Clark, one of the Lisbon Lions, with whom I got on very well. John was and still is the kit man at Celtic Park and I had great respect for him as a man as well as a player. I valued his opinion, only given quietly if asked, in the aftermath of matches.'

The second occasion saw O'Neill return to the dugout at Celtic Park for a charity match against Manchester United. The 'Legends' game comprised of former managers, players and well-known fans of both clubs in aid of Oxfam, and former Celtic player John Kennedy who handed his testimonial money over to the charity's East African appeal. O'Neill reflects on the event: 'John's career was just beginning to blossom. He gave towering performances against Rangers and Barcelona in the space of a few days before suffering a dreadful injury playing for Scotland in a friendly against Romania. It was one of the most horrendous tackles I've seen. When he asked me if I would come up to manage the Celtic team, I accepted without hesitation. I didn't know at that time he had also given up his share of the gate money to charity; that was an amazing gesture from someone who had not had time to earn any serious money in the game.

'It was rather surreal to walk into the dressing room at Celtic Park to see some familiar faces and some not so familiar and hold a semi-serious team talk to the assembled gathering, but as my old boss Brian Clough used to say, there's no such thing as a friendly game. When you walk outside and you see Celtic Park full to the rafters the old competitiveness kicks in and you just want to go and win the game; it turned out to be a very special occasion indeed.'

Two more of O'Neill's former players have also been on Celtic supporters' minds in recent years. John Hartson faced a long battle with testicular cancer after the disease had spread to his brain though he is now in good health. During the recovery process he publicly thanked Celtic fans for the prayers and support they offered at the same time discussing his own faith that has developed as a result of the experience. The club also organised a charity game to honour Stiliyan Petrov which saw O'Neill return to the dug-out for a third occasion in September 2013. Following his diagnosis with leukaemia, Celtic players wore shirts bearing his name and squad number (19) and banners at Celtic Park showed support for the popular player weeks and months after the event.

O'Neill reflected on both players' struggles after they left Celtic in 2006: 'When you are playing football for a living, you feel so healthy in your twenties – you feel indestructible. For a player to be diagnosed with a life-threatening illness at such an early age must be an unbelievable shock. Both John Hartson and Stiliyan Petrov have suffered such blows and both have fought incredible fights for life. They are two very different characters with an enormous will to stay alive. I will always be grateful to both for the huge roles they played at the club in those great years. John didn't like training, or at least running during the training, which I suppose constitutes the same thing. But he was brilliant in the opposition penalty box and no one will ever forget his goal at Anfield that glorious evening when we toppled Liverpool in the quarter-final of the UEFA Cup in 2003. Stan Petrov is a special person and player. He was already at the club when I arrived in 2000 and still a young man with a strong will to succeed at the top level. With movie star good looks, he didn't lack very much even then. He was great as an attacking midfielder for Celtic and he joined me at Villa Park a few years later, making an indelible mark before being diagnosed with leukaemia. He is continuing to fight that battle now and I've no doubt he will beat it.'

My final conversation with Martin O'Neill for this book was just a few hours before Celtic take on Cliftonville in the second leg of a Champion's League qualifier. Significantly he had just finished a lunch time meeting with Dermot Desmond, a figure he continues to hold in high regard, particularly as it was Celtic's majority shareholder who brought him to Glasgow all those years ago, changing the course of the club's history. Since then of course O'Neill made a fourth appearance at Celtic Park as manager of the Republic of Ireland. He likely wasn't bowled over by sentiment after getting beat by Scotland in November of 2014.

Celtic's revival in 2000 started with a tower of imagined possibilities and an indomitable sense of will. O'Neill raised consciousness among the support, the club and himself over what Celtic had achieved in its history and immediately transferred dominance from Rangers who previously looked implacable. It began with that complete and indispensable 6–2 destruction. During this time Celtic would create new records in the positive after the aforementioned European conquest against Boavista they became habitual victors against their Ibrox rivals, winning seven encounters between the sides in a row. They would also create a British record of 25 consecutive league wins in the 2003–04 season. No doubt the journey to the 2003 UEFA Cup final gave the fans new grounds for faith in a hungry and authoritative side that looked self-assured in every match they played. O'Neill replanted firm foundations on which Gordon Strachan and Neil Lennon were able to build while reawakening the dreams and aspirations of thousands who would permanently dash the romantic Roman, Renaissance and Gothic architecture of Seville with splashes of green, white and gold, in the reminiscence of many at least. The Irishman's bond with the Celtic support is unlikely to diminish with the measure of time; beyond the success, he struck up an emotional chemistry that led him to fight their corner on issues beyond the concerns of an ordinary football manager.

Before the end of our interview O'Neill explains the affection he continues to feel for Celtic and the Dear Green Place: 'I loved Celtic Park and I loved Glasgow regardless of the weather; it's a football and cultural city. Going back to those years in Scotland, my wife and I spent our first year in Edinburgh, a really fine city. My daughter went to school there, both the school and house being a fairly lengthy stone's throw from Murrayfield. I suppose I felt that in Edinburgh I might want to escape from the fever surrounding Celtic and Rangers. There was soon a realisation that actually I wanted to be in the midst of it all so we bought a house in the west end of Glasgow where we had a wonderful time aside from the neighbours telling us to cut to the front lawn a little more often. Glasgow is a truly wonderful city. If the sun ever came out there for two consecutive days in July then it would rival any city in the world for just about anything.

'I could count the number of times on one hand that I was verbally abused on the streets of Glasgow, although that didn't apply at visiting grounds when Celtic were the opposition. Aberdeen could be particularly difficult, and on occasion I might have had a tête-à-tête with one or two of Aberdeen's establishment. Naturally I would love to change the results in Seville and against Motherwell in 2005 when we lost the league on the final day, although we should have won the game by three or four goals. Their goalkeeper made two saves he didn't know anything about, one from John Hartson at point blank. But we did win the Scottish Cup a week later. It was a genuine privilege to be in charge of the club for even a part of its great history, to be able to turn fortunes around was very special – they were really great days. For us to change things was great, as were those European nights – the first twenty minutes listening to the fans sing when we were playing Liverpool at home and the Rangers games will live on with me forever. You really would have to go some to get anything like it anywhere else in the world.'

Chapter Three
Cliftonville Skyline

'I had a text the night before the draw from one of our supporters, it said: "I went to the Clonard Monastery in Falls Road last night to pray that we get Celtic tomorrow; good luck." I was in Nyon at the draw thinking "we've got a one in seventeen chance". It then gets down to one in six, then one in three; I just couldn't look, I was shaking. I then heard Warsaw got New Saints and Cliftonville have drawn Glasgow Celtic. Our community is often in the news for the wrong reasons, but this gave people something to be proud of. We've had a long relationship with Celtic but to get them in the Champions League coming to Solitude was our wildest dream coming true.'
Gerard Lawlor, Chairman of Cliftonville F.C.

'We have strong links with Ireland even now, we generate a large support from there, it's remarkable. We are a Scottish club but with Irish roots, we know that we take stick for flying more Irish flags than saltires but a lot of us are second, third, fourth and fifth generation Irish, that's where we've come from … are we embarrassed or ashamed of that? Absolutely not; we embrace that. I understand on the political side it's something we've come a long way on. But Ireland as a country has moved on too. We are proud to get the support that we do from Ireland.'
Michael McDonald, Director At Celtic Football Club

A FORTHCOMING FEATURE film chronicling Celtic's triumph in Lisbon is certain to have no shortage of supporters involved in its production; as chapter ten illustrates there's an abundance of Scottish talent who could potentially direct, act in, write and produce a record of Celtic's greatest adventure. Already forums are awash with speculation about the film; undoubtedly the treatment of the story and who is involved are things the producers have to deliver on. For many of us around the globe our own life story shares a deep connection with the oscillations of Celtic and many of those accounts would be just as worthy of the silver screen. A quote from Willie Maley: 'This club has been my life and without it my life would have been empty indeed' graced a particularly striking banner seen among the Green Brigade's masses at the 2009 League Cup final against Rangers. The phrase united every Celtic supporter in the ground by making an instant appeal to the essence and spirit of Celtic Football Club. Fans' shoulders drew back with pride amid delighted faces when Maley's words took centre stage before kick-off in a final that saw Celtic 2–0 victors. The Green Brigade has managed, at times, to express the values we all share in as Celtic supporters.

As a number of fans from Belfast illustrate in this chapter, these are values that don't come from mainstream newsprint, political spin or television. Neither are they parochial or inward looking. I am heading for Solitude, the home of Cliftonville, in the company of a Celtic-supporting Belfast taxi driver who was celebrating the recent form of both Celtic and Cliftonville. The 2012–13 season proved to be one of the most significant in the local club's history. 2013 saw them secure the Irn-Bru League Cup defeating rivals Crusaders 4–0 in late February 2013. They built on that success with a league championship the following April after winning against old rivals Linfield securing a historic Double. Over the course of the next 24 hours I have arranged to meet with Celtic fans whose support of the club provided an essential focus during the north of Ireland's years of bloody conflict.

My journey in the city begins in a suburb of north Belfast at the home of Ireland's oldest football club. Cliftonville was formed in 1879 by local Protestant businessman John McAlery. Like many of the versatile pioneers who fashioned football organisations in the Victorian era his two-pronged approach was as much to build community as business for the area. McAlery was on honeymoon in Scotland when he found inspiration within the unique character and development of its football, falling in love with the game so deeply as to want to bring it home with him. Advertisements for players placed on 20th September that year caught the imagination of like-minded locals and nine days later Cliftonville played their first match at the home of the local cricket club. As well as fulfilling the role of secretary McAlery captained the club while playing at right back.

The team first played Celtic in a friendly over Easter on 19th April 1897. Two weeks prior to that event the Glasgow club had appointed their first secretary and manager shortly after becoming a limited company. That manager's name was Willie Maley.

Fulfilling a similarly versatile role at Cliftonville today is Gerard Lawlor. The current chairman is not unlike Maley or McAlery in that he lives and breathes the affairs of his club with a tangible sense of pride. Much like the custodians of Celtic throughout history, his dealings concern a succession of issues that don't impact on more ordinary clubs. After our interview, he tells me, he has a disciplinary hearing concerning a fan that recently ran on the pitch and 'chinned an opposition player'. For Lawlor, asserting Cliftonville's identity can be demanding. The character of the club's support was cemented when many Catholic/nationalist families were relocated to north Belfast in the 1970s. Following the Reds brought a much-needed cohesion to the community and a healthy distraction from the daily tragedies associated with their city's political struggles. By the time they won the Irish Cup in 1979 Cliftonville had pulled in an invigorated Catholic support from across the city.

Born in May 1975 Gerard Lawlor was one of those supporters growing up in what was formally known as the Unity Flats in Belfast. But Cliftonville wasn't his first love, if anything his connection to Celtic was even deeper rooted: 'Celtic was unique in that I didn't have any affinity with Belfast Celtic in the way that previous generations would have as that was all over by 1949 [when the club was disbanded], so that didn't hold any interest for me. My grandfather would also tell us stories about him being chased out of Solitude for being a Catholic. The Catholic support for Cliftonville only took off around the 1970s. Some of the social clubs around there would still have been playing "God Save the Queen" up until the early 1980s. Like most boys from the nationalist community growing up during the height of the Troubles I was a Celtic supporter and so was my father and my grandfather; the affiliation and affection for Celtic is part of an Irish tradition. It was an important part of who you were and what you did. All my friends would have been Celtic supporters; it was everything.

'The other important thing I associated with Celtic was

the journey itself. In those days it was a holiday for men, an excuse to get away from what was going on here in Belfast. We didn't have the luxury of cheap flights, city breaks or foreign holidays; going to see Celtic was our getaway. I started going in the 1985–86 season with an older cousin.

There was a real nervous apprehension the first time I went to Glasgow, what hit you was the pride people in the East End felt, the guys with the stalls selling Celtic gear outside Barrowlands. I could sense straight away how they felt.

'Outside of the community, the first question people would ask is "are you a terrorist?", but that didn't happen in Glasgow, you felt no different and there were certainly similarities and things you could relate to. I would say we shared the idea that Celtic was a city thing; we were both from industrial towns. The other bond was that both places mirrored two separate communities; you would also have had similar sectarian problems, which was the biggest uniting bond of it all. At that time I had this philosophy that my life was all about where I lived in the Unity Flats and what I identified with. As an altar boy I would run out of one o'clock mass to go to a game against Linfield because when you're a small boy these rivalries are exciting. After the game you'd be running to make six o'clock mass and there you'd be telling the other boys about your experiences which would be along the lines of: "I saw police, I saw a riot and I even saw Protestants." I was about sixteen or seventeen before I knew or interacted with a Protestant; unfortunately, that was life in Belfast at the time.'

Celtic's visit to Solitude for a friendly on August 14th 1984 has gone down in history, but not because of the football. Pictures from the era show supporters climbing on the ground's roof. Some, dressed in the period's replica green and white V-neck shirts, are waving the tricolour, others are in tune with typical urban fashions with white socks and black slip-on leather shoes. A photo of a moustached John Colquhoun reveals Celtic players playing fast and loose with the defining trends of the 1980s. The player, who went on to characterise his career with Hearts, scored for Celtic within minutes of the game kicking off. Full back Graeme Sinclair also scored twice in the 73rd and 75th minutes of the game to make it 4–0; after his second a full-blown riot ensued.

Celtic had brought a strong first-team squad that day,

including a number of key players who would define the era, among them Frank McGarvey (also on the scoresheet), Pat Bonner, Danny McGrain, Murdo MacLeod, Peter Grant and Roy Aitken. Also playing was Willie McStay, he said: 'There had been a carnival atmosphere leading up to the game, it was the first time I saw fans not being segregated. The big thing that stood out was seeing supporters in green, red and white together, everything was intertwined between Celtic and Cliftonville, that was the atmosphere the game started in. During the first half we heard a roar behind the terracing; it was a strange noise. Trouble had taken place outside and spilled into the stadium so that was a factor in the disturbance. At half-time we were told if things didn't change the whistle would go to end the game and we would run for the tunnel, and that's what happened. Something was alight at one stage in the corner of the stand; the whole game was marred by things going on around it. Something happened in the city the day before which caused a little bit of concern. Heading towards the stadium there was a heavy presence of police.

'Whatever happened the hostilities weren't between the supporters, there was no threat to the bus or aggro towards the players, we stayed in the stadium for a while until things calmed down and then we left. It was a weird situation, in years gone by we had seen skirmishes between Celtic and Rangers fans such as the 1980 Scottish Cup final, but this was something ongoing through the match which had nothing to do with the game itself.'

Lawlor remembers the day vividly as news of the game and ensuing trouble made its way around Belfast: 'As soon as I became involved at board level with Cliftonville one of my aims was to bring Celtic back here. I remember the day they came here in 1984. I had been on holiday with my family in the Glens of Antrim when word got out that there was a riot going on at Solitude. From there on I remember bedlam breaking out on the beach between Catholics and Protestants; even holiday camps would have been segregated in those days. The problem wasn't between Celtic and Cliftonville fans; there had been a lot of tension in the city. A young Catholic man had been shot dead in the lead-up to the game. In the ground there had been further trouble with the RUC coming into the crowd heavy handed using batons and plastic bullets after some trouble outside. In the commotion a policeman had his gun stolen, after Celtic scored their fourth that's when the riot broke and the match was abandoned.'

A competent fan at board level is a considerable asset for a football club, away from the game Lawlor is also House Manager at Belfast's Grand Opera House. After becoming chairman in 2010, at the age of 35, as well as on-field success his three main aims were to build community in the area, to clear the club's debts and bring Celtic back to Solitude. Cliftonville were Irish League Champions in 1998, but a few years later the club nearly buckled under the weight of a crippling tax bill. His first task was to deal with this, something he succeeded in doing in 2011, paving the way for unprecedented success in the 2012–13 and 2013-14 seasons. Gerard has built up a strong reputation for the club and is undoubtedly a man worth listening to. In terms of community Lawlor has used Celtic as a model in dealing with the obvious sectarian tensions associated with life in Belfast. Perhaps the hardest task he faced was in breaking a previous Celtic chairman's vow never to return to Belfast after the events of 1984. For Lawlor there was a ghost in the walls of Cliftonville that needed exorcising. The club had previously celebrated Cliftonville's 75th birthday when Jimmy McGrory brought a team over in 1954, then came the riot of 1984. For the chairman the desire to see Celtic return to Solitude after a 25-year absence in 2009 to celebrate the club's 130th anniversary was a major requirement in creating change.

'I managed to get a meeting with Peter Lawwell,' explains Lawlor, 'and I went across to Scotland to be honest with him. I had to sell him the game a bit and explain that there was a massive fan base here in north Belfast, but I told him the relationship had become one way. I felt the attitude from Celtic was: "You come on over here and buy our shirts and season tickets and we'll not do anything in return." There was a growing apathy among people; they had wanted Celtic to come back for a very long time. Life had changed and moved on here beyond recognition and it was time.

'The big question then was "Why do people support Celtic here?" The truth is that Celtic and Cliftonville are very similar, and unfortunately we have some people who go to football grounds to abuse another section of the community. We are not trying to create a fake Celtic with a team running out in green and white hoops, other teams have recently tried that and it doesn't work. You have to have a bit of a psychology driving what you are doing. At one time the attitude would have been "he sang a song throw him out". No, you have to embrace people and create an open forum for fans to discuss the reasons why they are behaving in a certain way. Our view is that it's not acceptable and to tell them, yes, we are proud of who we are, but certain attitudes and songs have to go. The songs I'm talking about would be "The Roll of Honour" and "The Boys of the Old Brigade", songs about the IRA and hunger strikers. I wouldn't sit here and lie to you, these are songs that I would've grown up with because they were around the community and I would also be lying if I said to you that I never threw stones at the police too . . . but society has moved on. Ultimately, I would add that some of those people don't give a shit about Cliftonville, Celtic, the club or their fellow supporters. They are not supporters because they are costing us money, they are harming the club's reputation; they are ultimately hurting the club. I don't think that sectarianism is the ultimate goal for young people. My attitude is bring them in and have a debate and educate. For too many years we've been ashamed of our support, but the board did nothing about it, they took no action to address it. We are trying to appeal to them and I think that's the kind of debate Celtic is having with its fans too.'

The popularity of both Martin O'Neill and Neil Lennon as well as Paddy McCourt have all given a fresh context to supporters in the north of Ireland since the Good Friday Agreement. In recent years Neil Lennon was particularly vocal in urging Celtic supporters not to sing songs and chants that glorify terror groups, particularly when the club was penalised financially by UEFA. Lawlor suggests there is some confusion about what Celtic represents to a new generation of football supporters in Ireland. For some they are just another football team, for others they represent an association with the dark days of the past: 'Celtic has a difficult balance to strike in terms of the brand. I think the true identity is in danger of being lost. On the one hand Celtic are trying to build a successful product and business, in recent years their pre-season tours have been in locations such as America and Australia, but at the same time they have to keep those original values which Brother Walfrid invested into the club, and in that way the brand is under threat. My son hasn't taken up Celtic as his club; he supports Man United. Many boys today here are supporting Liverpool, Manchester United, Chelsea and now, of course, Manchester City have a very strong brand. The tradition of supporting Celtic here is not being carried on the way it was. I told my son "I'm taking you to see Celtic in the cup final" and he gave me a very flat response. I think one problem for a few years was that potential new fans didn't have a clear understanding of what Celtic was really about. Martin O'Neill and Neil Lennon have been very good for Celtic because in their own way they have been enigmatic characters that the support can identify with; Celtic is in their hearts and in their blood. Paddy McCourt is very popular here too. He has carried a certain idealism on the pitch because he's a Derry boy who has done well. For my generation Paul McStay was the Catholic boy who had come good, not only good, but a world talent. Paddy McCourt is the Jinky [Jimmy Johnstone] type of player, he's someone that your older Celtic fan could buy into; he's a throwback to another time. Paddy wasn't a million pound player or a big-money buy. He played for Derry City and Shamrock Rovers and now he's pulled on the hoops of Glasgow Celtic. There's a great romance in that story, you need younger people to be able to tune into these narratives.'

Perhaps Celtic's initial hesitation in returning to north Belfast was understandable, but as Lawlor pointed out new heroes and mavericks from the north of Ireland had played a vital role in revivifying Celtic's fortunes in the modern era. After phone calls, letters and meetings the days turned into weeks, the weeks into months and Lawlor began to wonder if his plea to Celtic had been unrealistic: 'It had been a journey trying to get Celtic, I had written four letters. In fairness to them, it took a while, but they always came back to me. I missed a call one afternoon in midweek and it was a private number, but they had left a voicemail. It said: "Neil Lennon here from Celtic Football Club, Peter Lawwell asked me to give you a call, we'd like to bring a team over to Solitude." I was literally trembling; that for me was the biggest moment of it all. So much work goes into a moment like that; I let out a roar in the street, I was grinning from ear to ear, I just wanted to tell the whole world: "CELTIC ARE COMING!" In that moment I felt a tremendous relief; there was a sense of "We've finally cracked this at last" because twenty-five years is a long time especially after what happened. When I called a meeting with the board that night I think they thought I was going to announce that the lights were going out at the club with the troubles that we had. I'll never forget the feeling in the room when I told them and what it meant, the energy and the glow rising off people was beyond words.'

Significantly Cliftonville won the match 3–0, scalping a Celtic B-team with Barry Robson appearing as the only first-team regular, but more important than the result, the match had healed a wound and re-established a connection that dated back to the late 19th century. Lawlor reflects on Celtic's return to north Belfast that autumnal October evening in 2009: 'Solitude was packed to the rafters that night and we opened the new part of the ground. I remember going to pick Tony Mowbray up at the airport, again going back to the idealism, in my mind I'm thinking "I'm on my way to pick up the manager of Glasgow Celtic here." I called Tony who was in Birmingham and in all honesty I would have understood if he'd just wanted to get up the road home to Glasgow. I always had respect for him as a person and that night even more so for coming to Belfast. Neil Lennon couldn't have been more helpful, he spent time with the fans and answered questions; he really got into the spirit of the thing and had time for people. I said to him: "If there's anything we can do for you just let us know." After that I had a call from Celtic's trainer Hugh McGovern, he said: "Gerard I need a favour. I need to go to mass can you find me somewhere on Saturday?" I came off the phone smiling; it was straight back to that ethos of what it's really all about.'

* * *

There's more than a hint of melancholy that travels beyond nostalgia when considering the history of Belfast Celtic Football Club. Inspired by Celtic, the club formed at 88 Falls Road in 1891 and entered the Irish League in 1899 winning 14 league titles and four Irish Cups. While having a strong Catholic and nationalist identity the club not only shared its strip with Celtic but also its anti-sectarian ethos while providing a vital social outlet for people living in poverty and tension in west Belfast. The club's fate was sealed on Boxing Day 1948 during a hard-fought encounter with city rivals Linfield, who were traditionally supported by the Protestant community's industrial workers. That day the ancient tensions spilled on to the pitch when Belfast Celtic's centre forward, 19-year-old Jimmy Jones, was attacked by an unenlightened gaggle of Linfield supporters who broke the player's leg during a pitch riot. Jones, a bold, exciting player, had notched up 33 goals that season and 63 the previous year. Unfortunately, his success had made him a prime target.

When you consider the history of Belfast Celtic and its ground, also known as Paradise, it's deeply lamentable that the land now houses the Park Shopping Centre after spending a number of years as a dog-track. Journalist, author and playwright Padraig Coyle is chair of the Belfast Celtic Society, which was set up as a charity in 2004 aiming to preserve the rich cultural history and story of Belfast Celtic while drawing on the ethos and positive values around the team. A historical trail and a museum, both set up by the charity, are working to mark the history in west Belfast. The museum, marking the site of the old ground, includes murals of the stadium and ex-players like Jimmy Jones, Charlie Tully and Paddy Bonnar. Undoubtedly there is still a crackle in the air and a sense of the team and fan culture that once existed. Coyle, who documented the history in his excellent memoir of the club *Paradise Lost and Found*, suggests Belfast's green and white could have continued saying: 'The violence was reprehensible, but supporters were never given an official reason for Belfast Celtic's demise. It left a massive void in their lives.'

While the violence that day was a factor, leading to their withdrawal from the league that season, it's also true that the club was struggling with economic problems and internal fighting which may have been the real reason for Belfast Celtic's permanent departure after a final friendly with Coleraine in 1960. The sense of loss was palpable within the community for many years, particularly among fans who declined to take up support of another club. While the stories of life during the Troubles have often remained embedded or hidden in the communities, Coyle has also written plays to stimulate discussion and acknowledgment among football fans in the north of Ireland. His ambition is to weaken the tribal pressures while encouraging the idea that their past should now be talked about openly with respect and consideration. Through extensive research his body of work has chronicled something of the compelling story and mystique of Belfast Celtic as well as looking at the political nuances of both sides in productions such as *Home Rule?*, which brought to life the hidden story of Winston Churchill appearing at Belfast's Celtic Park in 1912. He's also written a one-man play *I Left My Heart*, which celebrates the colourful life and character of Celtic and Belfast Celtic legend Charlie Tully. Another of his plays, *Lish and Gerry at the Shrine*, in particular, has helped supporters reflect on that famous final clash with Linfield in 1948. Said Coyle: 'I interviewed a number of supporters and one of them summed up how people felt about this club when he said: "When we had nothing, we had Belfast Celtic. Then we had everything." I think it's time to discuss these things with maturity; what happened is not the fault of anyone who is alive now. For the supporters it's important because they never took up another team. There was nothing to look forward to on a Saturday, and it left a dark cloud in the lives of the support. I wrote the play, which was supported by the Irish FA and a community group called Healing Through Remembering, with a focus on Elisha Scott, who was Belfast Celtic's Protestant manager, and Linfield's Catholic trainer, Gerry Morgan. Afterwards we would have supporters of both teams discuss the game sharing memories and talking about the events that affected them. Rather than keeping their feelings buried, it's been a healthy endeavour to get how they feel out in the open and keep the memory of the club alive.'

By the late 1960s, during the re-emergence of the Troubles, a new generation of football supporters would take up support of Glasgow Celtic. It was an era when Catholics in Belfast wanted to increase their position in wider society by harnessing the non-violent philosophy of Martin Luther King and the American Civil Rights Movement. The organised peaceful protests and marches were intended to highlight the discrimination Catholics were suffering in matters of education, housing and employment. The symbols of Celtic Football Club have become one particular expression of Catholic and nationalist life in Belfast, and while that link is often viewed with suspicion due to an association with violent republicanism, the reality in Belfast is more varied and complex. I travelled to the Falls Road in the company of Peter

Finn, the principle of St Mary's University College, who wanted to explain the significance of Celtic's relationship to Northern Irish life and culture. Whether it was Victorian Glasgow or Belfast in the 1960s and 1970s, the club's supporters discovered a very real sense of empowerment when little or none could be found. While some communities might feel their employer, government or even church didn't have their best interests at heart, they did find solidarity with Celtic Football Club when it was needed most. Finn explains: 'Whether they set out to do it or not, the reality is that Celtic developed on a values basis. This football club was born in challenging and extreme economic and social conditions, it was born in a time when there was very little money and what little supporters had they made the decision to invest in going to watch the team when to pay and watch football was a luxury. These economic models were built on people making an individual decision to put their pennies into an emerging football club, from that transpires values that are very deep. In my context I work in higher Catholic education and my institution is rooted in gospel faith, peace and love, but those things exist outside of formal religion – religion is not the preserve of values, far from it.

'When Celtic came into being, like many other organisations at the latter end of the nineteenth century, there were very few sources of empowerment for the working classes. Jobs and lives were entirely controlled by the industrial model; people got up and worked in a mill or a factory owned by someone else, their empowerment was virtually nil. There's an argument that suggests the arrival of organised sport and particularly football enabled people to have a sense of who they were and what they were outside of a controlled industrial environment. They could affiliate to a sense of purpose, a sense of life, identity and a reason for being. We have no idea what it must have been like to be an industrial worker in those days, to be totally under the control of the system. But this is an idea about democracy and about a human right to make a comment that didn't exist. Suddenly along came Celtic Football Club and they offer people something different.

'Empowerment is a powerful tool in one's armoury, if you can get it. You will find a lot of people in this part of the world who support Celtic outright; they are Celtic supporters through and through and that is how they see it. But now there is also a broader, more informal and less affiliated mould who have an affiliation to one club such as Manchester United, but who will also hang on to Celtic as a second team. It's an interesting question: why would a whole class of kids today affiliate to Celtic now? To answer that you need to go back to people like myself growing up in the 1960s and 1970s; I don't think you can walk away from the reality that in this part of the island of Ireland there was a strong sense of injustice. You were labelled second class growing up here and I certainly had difficulty affiliating to the country in which I was born, Northern Ireland, because as much as I was aware of the prejudice that was going on, you are seeking to overcome it in a positive way, and that's where support of Celtic comes in.

'They were wearing green and white hoops, there's a big Irish connection in the name and the history so the connection was natural. As you sought to find some way out of the mess we were in, and it was a dreadful mess let's not deny that, at that time it was not good to be Irish and living in Northern Ireland. But to look across to Scotland and see Celtic being successful and powerful was massively important to the community here because we didn't have anything big and powerful, we didn't have political representatives or businesses that were big and powerful, we didn't have anything. So you looked outside of your life and said: "Where can I find something that gives me a sense of my own strength" and you looked across and my goodness there was Glasgow Celtic being managed by Jock Stein and winning the European Cup.

'There may well have been people who were attracted to Celtic for sectarian reasons, no doubt, but there was also that broader appeal with Celtic, there were nuances that were representative of the society you wanted to live in. You could say: "It's not working here, but look at Scotland and particularly look at Celtic being managed by Jock Stein." We all knew who Jock Stein was and you looked at Celtic as a model of how things could be. At the same time you don't have to throw away your Irishness or your religion, you don't have to throw away anything because you can mix these things together and out of it comes something very positive – a team that are the best in European football. I do believe that what really made it click over here were the forays into Europe; this was romantic stuff beyond belief. Now we talk about clubs in Europe like it's going down to the local shops, but back then people were only starting to become conscious of life in Europe and a European community and a union, all of a sudden Celtic were playing the best teams in the world and winning, let's not underestimate the example and power of winners.'

While Padraig Coyle's passion has played an essential role in remembering Belfast's version of the hoops, he's not from the city and wasn't even born when the team played their last competitive match. But it wasn't long after he moved from Dublin that Coyle began exorcising ghosts. He explains: 'I grew up on the south side of Dublin not far from the Milltown area where Shamrock Rovers played, and I followed them as a kid and, from afar, Sheffield Wednesday. I fell upon the story after moving north to work in journalism, at that time I wasn't really aware that there had been a club with that kind of stature. In their heyday Belfast Celtic and Glasgow Celtic were equivalents; that's how they saw themselves. The story has massive importance here in Belfast and it was one I became very passionate about. The club began with a ten-pound gift from Glasgow Celtic who helped them get started. The area itself was very depressed, and there was a lot of disease and unemployment. Out of all those social problems people had the football club, which turned out to be very successful. The club gave people an identity and a reason to exist. The one thing they had after that was pride in the club; if Celtic won, they had won. It began as a team designed to raise the community spirit and gradually it began to generate a lot of money and the middle classes became involved: publicans, merchants and solicitors. It was similar to Celtic in that it was anti-sectarian; as long as you wore the hoops with pride you could play for Belfast Celtic.'

It was while living in Belfast that Padraig connected with his Celtic-supporting family living in Glasgow after a family bereavement, forming a lifelong support from across the sea. It's a connection he has passed on to his own sons in Belfast: 'I had a cousin living in Greater Glasgow called Frank Coyle. He was a primary school teacher and he did a bit of talent spotting for Celtic, Lou Macari was a player whose talent he recognised early on. Frank was a pal of Bertie Peacock; they had shared digs when he was a student. I had a number of Glasgow cousins and my grandfather's brother owned a pub on London Road called the Benburb Bar, which was named after a town in Ireland on the border of Tyrone and Armagh. My father died very suddenly in 1971 and Frank was over at the time of the funeral, we had become close and he took me over to see Celtic. It was against Motherwell in 1971 on a Monday night, Celtic won 3–0. I remember Jimmy Johnstone and Willie Wallace both scored. It was one of the most marvellous and exciting things I had ever seen, it was that special period and I immediately fell in love.

'In those days the chance to take a trip somewhere wasn't really there so it was a big deal to visit Glasgow. Opportunities to travel in those days were far fewer than now so for me the radio became very important. I still think very little compares to the quality of the broadcasts you would get from Scotland, even today in terms of the passion that is generated, if you couldn't get to a game it became part of your life on a cold winter night during the week or a Saturday afternoon. Over the airwaves and over the sea you were transported to this world of excitement and passion at Celtic Park, Ibrox or Easter Road. To me the radio broadcasts epitomised what Scottish football is about, you were as much part of the drama of the game as the supporters in the stadium. I would be sitting in Belfast with the hairs standing up on the back of my neck. Often the radio gave you a different perspective from the people that were at the game, it really brought to life the drama of the Old Firm. Today I prefer to watch the games, but the radio was an important part of my relationship with Celtic.'

As the Belfast Troubles reached their peak Coyle remained in the city working as a sports journalist where events would often be marred by the threat of a bomb or a riot: 'Living here you had to learn the rules, there was a lot of tension, you had to be careful. It was the days before mobile phones or social media so you had to let someone know where you were going and you tried to avoid difficult areas. I was covering a story once and my car was blown up at a car park in Armagh. You just had to operate and exist the best you could.'

Despite its dark past there is something undeniably spellbinding about Belfast. If you enter the city via the Broadway Roundabout you can see the RISE sculpture, a gigantic steel sun in the sky. Visible for miles, the sculpture inspires or infuriates the restless imaginations that shape this society. Recent protests at the removal of the union flag from

City Hall, which began shortly after the flag was withdrawn in December 2012, have created a visible anxiety in the city. There is concern that the culture is reversing back to the dark days of the Troubles. The late Nobel Prize for Literature winner Seamus Heaney, one of the few voices that managed to provide hope and positive ideals to both communities throughout his life, urged people to understand and tolerate both sides of the argument. Referring to the protests shortly before his death he said that the loyalists 'perceive themselves as almost deserted. And right enough. I think Sinn Féin could have taken it easy. No hurry on flags. What does it matter? But – it matters utterly to them. And now there's no way they're going to go back on it, of course. As someone who knows something of prejudice, from early on, I can understand the loyalists.'

The people of Belfast could never be accused of apathy. Take the RISE sculpture as an example, some will argue vehemently that the money could have gone towards more deserving causes, others suggest that it points to a new European mentality and are spirited away when the award-winning steel dome lights up the Belfast sky at night. Here Scotland's 'Big Two' continue to mean something beyond football and the evidence is everywhere. The city's peace walls stretch out over a haunting wasteland that runs for 13 miles, dividing the loyalist Shankhill and nationalist Falls Road. Although built in 1969 as a short-term solution, the walls remain in operation today. Once through the gates I arrive at the Falls Road Garden of Remembrance. The first houses we arrive at are bomb proofed; outside a back-garden trampoline suggests the inhabitants' determination to lead normal lives in spite of the past. The Hoops Barber on Falls Road would be a welcome addition on Glasgow's Gallowgate now that Bairds Bar – similarly decorated in eye-catching memorabilia – has departed.

While there's indifference about church and government around modern Britain, there is a political sharpness and strong philosophical belief that remains here. The majority don't want to return to the days of terror and bloodshed, but they are devoted to holding on to their identity, which as Peter Finn explains remains rooted in a political and ethno-religious culture: 'The future here lies in accepting difference. Things have moved on out of necessity and the model in the political arrangement is based on the sharing of power and give and take principles that are about accepting each other's identity; in other words it's about living together. No one says there is one way. Broadly speaking there are two versions of reality over here and we have to learn to cope, live and get on with it. It's not in any sense about throwing the baby out with the bathwater. That's not happening because what you find is people are still holding on to their basic traditions and values while respecting the other side and saying, "That may not be for me, but I have to respect the right of the other community or individual". And that's been happening politically, explicitly with people like Martin McGuinness going to Windsor Park and Peter Robinson attending his first Gaelic football match. It doesn't mean to say we abandon everything we hold dear or affiliate to; it's about accepting diversity and difference and learning to live with it.'

As Finn explains the one-size-fits-all Orwellian mindset espoused by politicians and the media which drifts towards a rootless and meaningless secularism, whether Catholic or Protestant, is an idea that far from dividing communities unites them in the understanding that they are both absolutely tied up with a history, faith and social context. Recent initiatives in Northern Ireland look at the positive associations gained from a religious background, community and education.

More significantly there is an understanding and respect of the other's identity that disconnects from violence and returns to original values and traditions. The idea that they should give these up doesn't convince either side. Says Finn: 'We're not into blandness over here. There still are two large community groups: one is politically and ethnically British and the other is Irish. Any political blanding that suggests a sense of togetherness is having little or no success, that kind of thing is seen as artificial and emasculating. The parties that are having success are not about that. There is a sense here that we are proud of what we are, there is a greater acceptance of Catholicism and we've thrown off the shackles of this idea that Catholicism was somehow an evil religion. There is a much better understanding of the Catholic side. The Celtic phenomenon falls into that, more people here are respectful of what the club stands for, it's history and what they are trying to achieve, there's less negativity from certain sections of the community here than there was in the past. The [sectarian] issue is not as alive as it used to be. There is also a greater understanding among the different denominations within the Protestant faith and the contributions that both religions have made to society, schooling, education, social life and everything else.'

We live in an age when a supporter's identity and values are questioned; in Britain Tottenham Hotspur and their Jewish association has been the subject of much debate. The identity grew out of many families and communities from Jewish backgrounds supporting the club from various locations in London, but a number of commentators would like to see it go. In 2010 the club's fans were asked not to bring the Star of David into a match against Inter Milan at the San Siro. Supporter Benjamin Davis said: 'It's great that two of my greatest passions, religion and football, converge so closely. But in a foreign country which may not understand Tottenham's Jewish cultural links, it is probably not necessary to bring attention to it.' A Spurs spokesman added: 'It is common policy at football grounds in the UK and elsewhere in Europe that flags of an overtly religious and political nature will not be permitted.'

It's deeply deplorable that travelling Spurs supporters were attacked because of their religious identity when playing Lazio in November 2012 and Lyon in February 2013. Fans of the club have also suffered anti-Semitic abuse from supporters in the UK. This kind of abuse has led to commentators asking the support to drop the use of the terms 'Yid' and 'Yid Army', a word the club's fans use to self-identify as Jewish. In November 2012 the Society of Black Lawyers said if the fans continued to use these words they would ask for a prosecution of racism; the club then found itself in the position of defending its supporters' use of the term. When Jewish comedian and football fan David Baddiel backed a campaign to stop its use, a number of Spurs fans felt that the comedian had ignored or misunderstood the context. Lawyer Robert Samuelson writing on the Harry Hotspur website contributed this: 'Let me be clear. On its own, out of context and away from the stadium, calling someone a "Yid" is insulting and offensive. Spurs fans refer to each other by the use of this term not to offend others, but out of a sense of uniqueness through togetherness. It is a complex concept, merging together a small religion's sense of persecution into a large societal movement, acknowledging our isolation by letting a larger association take on our struggle with us. This is not about shouting the word "Yid" randomly on the street. It is about understanding why Spurs fans use the term, where it comes from and what it means. When you go to the trouble of learning the situation's nuance, intricacy and history it puts the onus back on David Baddiel to refocus his efforts more appropriately to the situation.'

Supporters and the club are locked into a fight against both the far right and dogmatic political correctionists who fail to understand the Jewish history and meaning for supporters of the club. Asserting the message of what Celtic as a club stands for, particularly in an era where the human condition is defined by a new digital expression and an ever-changing current message of the moment, also presents a challenge for the club and its supporters. Celtic, like other clubs, will always grapple with the dichotomy of the community that it represents and the need to remain a club of sporting excellence. But in the year of its 125th anniversary it successfully transmitted and rebooted that message with a mass served at St Mary's in the Calton area of Glasgow in celebration of the formal constitution of the club in its church hall on 6 November 1887. The mass was attended by supporters from around the globe, as well as majority shareholder Dermot Desmond and then manager Neil Lennon, along with representatives from F.C Barcelona prior to the clubs' encounter in the Champions League the following evening. While the mass had nothing to do with football it had everything to do with community, tradition and a renewed solidarity with everything that matters about Celtic beyond the game.

While many deride the game as a replacement for faith, with Celtic there has always been a relationship with a much broader framework. Says Finn: 'Celtic are not unique in that it is a football club that deals in values. Barcelona is another example where there is an identity relating to a culture, language and way of life. There is also a club that plays in Cyprus, Anorthosis Famagusta. They are in exile as a result of the [Turkish] invasion of Larnaca in 1974; there is a lot of Greek philosophy and influences from the Orthodox Church around the team. In 2005 they played Rangers in Europe, I went to see them. But the night that really impressed me was when they were playing a Turkish team, Trabzonspor. I've never seen anything like it, how they used flags, statements and the singing of songs that have nothing to do with football to create an incredible atmosphere. With these clubs history is not based on something superficial. Football stadiums are the modern cathedrals and I say that not to take away from church or religious beliefs, but to say that this is where people are interacting at a human level in the twenty-first century. They are not conducting their lives through non-human interaction, which is how I would describe a Facebook or Twitter relationship, which has no depth in humanity whatsoever. People are going to stadiums in their thousands for matches and meeting before and after and having the emotional ups and downs of crying, laughing and singing that go with being there. That's the real human passion that is left in us; this is humanity. The great modern example with Celtic was Seville, that event in the club's history wasn't about the winning but the sheer amount of people that showed up, that was the biggest mass movement of people in modern times, it was a colossal achievement to do it in the spirit in which they did.'

While Celtic welcome those of all faiths and none, the club's roots and culture don't need to be forfeited in the process to fleeting ideologies or dogmatic politicians. Many Celtic supporters mark the Irish famine on its memorial day to honour ancestors who struggled to make a life in Scotland. That is why the year 1845 is as significant as 1888, 1967 or 2003 in the minds of supporters because it gives us a context today while retaining a bond with previous generations. If we aspire for Celtic to mean something to our children and grandchildren we have to continue not just to know our history but also to protect it. Our community survived by being a community in the face of war, famine, bigotry and intolerance, the challenges we meet today have a different face but remain just as potent. The question in essence is: are our values, traditions and history worth holding on to? There will always be competing ideologies, ideas, identities and dogmas, but in the face of that Celtic is a club that offers absolutes, which point to charity, ethnicity, faith and self-worth as well as the worth of others. This was a football club created for the poor. These beliefs haven't been watered down for 128 years. While there will be detractors in the media, other clubs, wider society and even government, these values have the same appeal that they did on 6 November 1887 because ultimately they are life-enhancing and unifying, they work to strengthen Celtic and the supporters. Between those two entities there is also a continuing balance to be settled and it's the toing and froing between them that protects the institution. The commonly shared values set boundaries for the club, team, support and wider community; they give everyone involved something to aim towards that isn't necessarily tied to other mainstream institutions.

Celtic's history stands for something bigger than the football club and more important than the ideas of the age. As Peter Finn explains: 'Some football clubs and their supports have represented the most negative aspects of human thinking, but these clubs fail to remain healthy. In Rome you have two main football clubs: Roma and Lazio. One represents a very nasty political ideology with wrong values. Those values simply don't last. Football clubs like any institution can take on the current flavour of the month, but bad values are never enduring, they don't deliver on anything positive. If you take fascism as an example of a political ideology, it's had its day. Good values will endure because they have an appeal from generation to generation; bad values don't deliver on anything positive and human beings are not impressed by fascism or those who attach themselves to it. Just now we have a final throw of a culture that is dying; nobody wants to be associated with a football club that is continually associated with negativity.'

The positive values and sense of self that was offered to industrial workers in 1887, people growing up in Belfast who felt like second-class citizens in the 1960s or new supporters in 2015 are fundamentally the same despite the dictates of government, the game, commerce and the challenges of the day. It is something to be thankful for that those Celtic supporters have opposed becoming estranged from the ideas, values and faith on which the club was built.

Chapter Four
Streams of Whiskey

'I grew up thinking the great mottos of Scottish culture
happened to be written on whisky bottles. They seemed to speak
directly to our experience of what it was like to be born and live
in Scotland. The best was the one for Bell's Whisky. It said very
simply, almost Zen-like: "Afore ye go". Afore ye go where exactly?
I thought it was worthy of Samuel Beckett. Afore you go out for
the night? Afore you go to bed? Afore ye go into a meeting? Afore
ye take your last breath? Take this drink, afore you go to the
place you always meant to go, a place you never knew the name
of, but you knew it was there. There used to be a neon sign for
Bell's Whisky above Glasgow Central Station – right next to the
one for 'yer other national drink', Irn-Bru – and in the dark
nights of the 1970s when I was just a boy, the legend appeared to
burn through the dark as we came down Renfield Street. "Afore
ye go." It didn't just seem like an advertisement, it seemed like
an invocation to something all of us knew already. It appealed
to an idea that is more common to Scotland than to most places,
I believe – a part of our nature.'
Andrew O'Hagan

PARKHEAD, SATURDAY 6 April 2002. Celtic are about to lift
the SPL trophy for the second year in a row under Martin
O'Neill after thrashing Livingston 5–0. In Glasgow's pre-
match hyperactivity a rumour is circulating, which will appear
in *The Scotsman* the following Monday suggesting Shane
MacGowan, Bruce Springsteen and Noel Gallagher were going
to appear on Paradise's green lawn at half-time in support of
the Lisbon Lions, who were appearing alongside the Celtic
Chorus to perform 'The Best Days of Our Lives'. Perhaps that
idea was wishful thinking on the part of Glasgow song-smith
John McLaughlin, who had hit upon the idea of writing a
charity single in celebration of Celtic's European Cup-winning
team at a time when the club seemed to let the anniversary

of its greatest achievement drift by like cherry blossom in spring. McLaughlin also had a high-pressure deadline to meet in writing and recording the B-side in 24 hours to make the single's pressing. It turned into a particularly memorable experience for the songwriter when, against the odds, one of those luminaries emerged on the championship-winning weekend to co-write with him into the wee small hours of the morning.

Undoubtedly Springsteen would have made a worthy contribution, his paternal grandmother, Martha O'Hagan, was only two generations away from ancestors that had left Westmeath on a coffin ship during the Irish famine, settling in the singer's eventual hometown of Freehold, New Jersey. Springsteen himself admits his Catholic background has had a profound impact on his work, relating to one interviewer the well-worn adage: 'Once a Catholic; always a Catholic'. As a songwriter he's carried that sensibility forward by raising awareness towards life's struggling, invisible and excluded. One of his most successful attempts was the story of a man suffering with HIV on the 'Streets of Philadelphia', sound-tracking the film of the same name. The less familiar 'Sinaloa Cowboys' focused on illegal Mexican immigrant brothers trying to cut across the American border in a bid to transcend the social, political and economic structures that condemn them to a hopeless existence. In 2006 Springsteen released his version of the Irish folk song 'Mrs McGrath' on the album *We Shall Overcome: The Seeger Sessions*. More recently he's successfully managed to strike the intricate balance of Irish folk and rock 'n' roll on the likes of 'American Land' and the penny whistle-fronted Pogue-like 'Death to My Hometown'. Perhaps the shared territory of Woody Guthrie's 'This Land is Your Land', with the revised Scottish/Irish perspective sung by Celtic supporters would undoubtedly have made a rousing terrace chant. Springsteen's cultural allegiance to Ireland evokes Carl Jung's theory of a 'collected unconsciousness' where the memory of his Irishness and its associated experiences of famine, Catholic faith and sense of a struggle continue to exist.

Closer to home, Noel Gallagher may have seemed like a better bet to appear on the pitch at half-time, having worn the colours of Glasgow's green and white while watching Celtic at home. In the aftermath of the Celtic v Rangers league cup derby in February 2015 he told me: 'The Old Firm game a couple of weeks ago was a bit tricky. [His wife Sara is a Rangers fan]. 'It was a bit of an anti-climax in the end because it was kind of over in fifteen minutes but you know what Rangers fans are like, if it's not going their way they just leave the room! Then they claim the moral victory because it was only 2-0! My mates who are Scottish want them to go completely out of business, it's difficult for me to get into the politics of it all, if it was Manchester United I'd be loving it but if I could stand back and be as neutral as possible for a minute if that was my club- I would be devastated because it's not any old club, it's not Brentford this is a big institution. The people at the top have mismanaged and cheated their way to nine fucking league titles in a row so I feel for people like my father-in-law who are proper Rangers – he is disgusted with it all. 'But really we're all sniggering a bit', he says with a glint. 'They've [Rangers] been trying to have a meeting down here but the hotels have been getting death threats, my stage manager is a Rangers fan, he called me and was like: it's fucking you [making the death threats] isn't it!' When asked to chose between England and the Republic of Ireland there's not a hint of hesitation for the second generation Irishman: 'Oh Republic of Ireland; I don't consider myself to be English at all.'

Beneath the bluster it's Gallagher's most unworldly songs that have lasted the pace and cemented his lasting popularity. Although now lost to technology and the download culture, Oasis fit into a long line of great British bands who recorded B-sides that could not only rival but better their hits. For every 'Cigarettes & Alcohol' or 'Roll With It' there was also a 'Listen Up' or 'Rockin' Chair', which showed the second generation Irish Catholic at his most contemplative, vulnerable and emotionally free. Although a spokesman for the Catholic Church in Scotland once described him as a 'clown' for aping John Lennon's 'bigger than Jesus' line, the truth is that Gallagher's music, at least, continues on an exceptionally Catholic journey. He himself admits: 'I don't know what I am; if I was an atheist I'd just write songs about not believing in God.' With his High Flying Birds in 2012 he offered the live debut of another B-side 'Let the Lord Shine a Light on Me' to a fervent audience in São Paulo; part gospel rival anthem and part hymn, it was once again and not for the last time Gallagher asking spiritual questions.

While Bruce Springsteen and Noel Gallagher are worthy contenders, it's hard to imagine anyone taking up the Celtic story more than Shane MacGowan who did actually turn up on the pitch at Celtic Park that day. The Pogues singer's favourite spot in Glasgow is the run of bars around Central Station where he could often be found revelling among a multitude of Celtic supporters. While Shane MacGowan might not have a seat for life inside Parkhead, there's no other world-class songwriter who has been as close to the heartbeat and lives of the support. Over the last decade there have been substantial fallouts, hell-raising adventures and even a scrap at Celtic Park. But most importantly Celtic supporters have been left with an exhilarating trilogy of songs: 'Tomorrow Belongs to Me' (2002), 'Road to Paradise' (2004) and 'The Celtic Song' (2011).

Shane MacGowan had all but retired from songwriting when he completed *The Crock of Gold* album with The Popes in 1997, stating that he preferred touring to working in the studio. Since then he's made the odd guest appearance and charity record, most notably turning up on a reworked version of Lou Reed's song 'Perfect Day' for the BBC's Children In Need in 1997 with the likes of Bono and David Bowie. In another charity appeal he organised the recording of Screamin' Jay Hawkins's song 'I Put a Spell on You' with fellow Celtic supporter Bobby Gillespie and Nick Cave. Writing about Glasgow and Celtic was an attractive proposition for MacGowan when he first put pen to paper on the subject just over a decade ago. The proposal of a complete album was perhaps ambitious, but his ideas at the time concentrated on the light and shade of Glasgow's vast social history, among them songs about the 'Bible John' murders, the Irish who came to Glasgow during the famine and a lament to the River Clyde, which all greatly enthused MacGowan's inner circle who believed, as a writer at least, he was the most motivated he had been in years.

The singer has visited Glasgow for over thirty years and each time he's submerged himself in the social world and culture of the city's Irish population. Within the community you would be hard pushed to find a more popular figure outside football so universally loved and revered by the vast majority of Celtic supporters. The English-born Irish iconoclast who shares his birthday with Christ, the punk Brendan Behan who won a literature scholarship into Westminster School, the singer and co-writer of 'Fairytale of New York', the greatest Christmas song of the last thirty years, arguably of all time; it could only be one person. MacGowan's mammy knew her son was gifted; the local priest even described him as a 'genius' while he was still in nappies. Few have travelled MacGowan's path or have his elucidating way with words. Like a troubadour from another age he nomadically shifts from one Irish diaspora to another where he remains a semi-fabled folk anti-hero outside the normal confines of mainstream society. In an age where the public and media have become obsessed with proving 'authenticity', Shane MacGowan remains free from accusations of deception or edifice. In his dirty black suit with wild overgrown rockabilly hair and trademark missing teeth, his way is the antithesis of modern celebrity. *Is Shane MacGowan Still Alive?* was Tim Bradford's irreverent homage to Ireland, the title reflecting the number of times he heard the topic being raised in the 1990s when MacGowan's drink and drugs intake had reached mythical proportions.

MacGowan cuts more of a settled country-boy figure when in his family home of Nenagh in north Tipperary. I once interviewed him there as he sat with his cousin, the photographer Sean Fay, underneath a framed illustration of Jock Stein in a bar where he was free from the anxiety of touring commitments. With its strong Irish subculture, Glasgow is a place where MacGowan feels similarly at ease and his time writing and recording in the city remains a compelling episode. Songwriter John McLaughlin explains that it was the singer's familiarity and observations which encouraged him to record a song for Celtic: 'For me Shane was at the dead centre of what we wanted to write about, he was living that life. Not only is he one of the world's greatest poets, Shane also has a great love for Glasgow and for Celtic. As a songwriter it doesn't get any better, he's up there with the likes of Tom Waits, Bob Dylan and Bruce Springsteen, for him to write a song about Celtic was a big deal. He arrived in Glasgow to sing 'The Best Days of Our Lives' on the pitch at Parkhead. Before he met the officials at Celtic I had to buy him a new suit! In the tunnel my heart was bursting out of my chest trying to get the lines in order, all the while Shane is tugging at my shoulder: "When do I get to meet Jimmy Johnstone?" I was like: "Shane; I need to concentrate;

you might not need to but I'm rubbish and I'm shitting myself." Out on the pitch he took a swing at Hoopy the Huddle Hound live on Sky TV. I looked around and there he was, rolling about on the pitch with Celtic's mascot. Over the course of the fifteen minutes I had both the proudest and most hilarious moments of my life.

'The important thing was that it wasn't a one-way street. I could see it was something Shane really wanted to do and he hadn't been in the studio for a long time. I know for a fact that the songs he has written and recorded about Celtic and Glasgow mean a lot to him. He's all or nothing and especially nowadays; he only does what he wants to do. In terms of writing about the city; he's done the tours of duty from his time with The Pogues. He knew parts of Glasgow that I didn't even know like Easterhouse and Ruchazie and I'm from the Milton. He was able to draw upon a lot of sources: ex-girlfriends, books he'd read on the gang fights etc. We talked about the Tongs, the Possil Fleeto, the guys on the corner selling the *Evening Times* – he wanted to get right into that very working-class world of which Celtic is an essential part. When he started with those first couple of lines about the Clyde, we knew we were off.'

'Tomorrow Belongs to Me' is an irresistibly warm shuffling folk hymn to the Dear Green Place. At the time MacGowan enthused over a number of Scottish influences, from Robert Burns to Jimmy Shand. Free from the restrictive boundaries of a typical football song, it's perhaps true that a club such as Celtic with its stirring urban history and unavoidable romance could warrant such a lament. As MacGowan himself revealed over a pint on Hope Street: 'I can't just churn them out. We wrote it here in the pub in Paul McGinn's place. Paul is a great guy to know. Whether he ran a bar or not I'd still be drinking with him, he's got some great records. While I was here he put on a lot of Matt McGinn stuff from his own private collection. He's got Matt singing "Kevin Barry" but to the tune of "The Sash". There was one night I was in and a guy came into the bar, he was obviously not a Celtic supporter and Paul put that track on. He announces: "That's my song" kind of thing, but halfway through the guy clicked it was "Kevin Barry". He didn't find it very funny, in fact he walked out without finishing his drink.'

MacGowan fills the room with a familiar devilish hiss before picking up the story: 'My idea was to do a few records in

Glasgow. With "Tomorrow Belongs to Me" I was thinking about old traditional Scottish anthems like "I Belong To Glasgow", that kind of thing. I'm Irish so I thought about the Liffey in Dublin and the river running though it, it starts with that line: "My mind wanders back to that old winding river carrying the bodies to the sea. Big black stinking manky old river, the stench still smells beautiful to me". Every river has a history, bodies in suitcases and so on. We sat down in here and wrote the words on beer mats and went to the studio to record it.'

Paul McGinn is the owner of the Two Heided Man, formerly called McGinn's, a thriving tribute to his uncle Matt located on Glasgow's Hope Street next to the lower level of Glasgow's Central Station. It's a well-known Celtic pub and pit stop for Pogues fans and tourists keen to sample Glasgow at its most undiluted. Today the philosophical Glasgow barman reflects on the first of his many encounters with Shane MacGowan: 'He took up residence here to write "Tomorrow Belongs to Me". On the Saturday it was the game against Livingston when Celtic won the league. We had to borrow, beg and buy some suits for some of the boys going on the pitch at half-time. John McLaughlin bought a smart black suit for Shane. He was bursting to meet Jinky and wanted to look the part. Phil Ferns was one of the co-writers. I borrowed a brand new suit from a tailor on the promise he got the suit back in the same condition. Phil actually ended up a bit blooded and battered after falling down a manhole, so he had to pay full whack for the suit. If you see a guy with one trouser leg walking about Glasgow, that's him.

'On the Sunday it was a free bar in here for Shane and Charlie and the Bhoys. Shane was keen to write and the drink flowed from midday till midnight while he got to work. I think he was recovering from rolling about the pitch after his square go with the Celtic mascot. Shane organised three bin bags full of drink: one of whisky and two of beer. He turned round to the band and said: "Do any of you want anything?" It got a bit surreal when we got word that Shane had got lost on the way to the recording studio in Lenzie. Someone had instructed his taxi driver to follow the motor with Charlie and the Bhoys in it. But they never gave the driver or Shane the address, and the next thing we knew Shane was circling round in a taxi during the early hours of the morning not having a clue where he was.'

A year later McGinn picked up the relationship with MacGowan again, booking him and The Popes for a late night gig at the Barrowlands, which was scheduled to take place after a big-screen showing of Celtic's UEFA Cup final against Porto. He explained that the gig was a 'verbal promise' while reliving the tension of the evening: 'I had a call from Shane's manager to say he was still at Dublin airport when he was due to be in Glasgow. At that point it was the second half and Celtic had gone 2–1 down. Thankfully he did actually arrive about 10.15 and was on stage by 11pm.'

While in Glasgow MacGowan and Ferns discussed further writing and recording, this time the project, another charity single for Celtic, would be in support of Jimmy Johnstone who was suffering from motor neurone disease. MacGowan's enthusiasm for the player was clear; he didn't need to be asked twice, telling me in 2004: 'I walked on the pitch with Jimmy Johnstone. A few others were present, we had to present a cheque to this young girl who won the draw, it was a lot of bread, a lot by her standards anyway. The minute I walked on the pitch they went barmy, and then Jimmy came out and they went even barmier obviously. I heard about Jimmy's illness and I know it can be cured with money. The reason for doing this record is to raise money and prolong Jimmy's life, which is as good a reason as any. Put it this way: I hope to be having a drink with Jimmy in a few years' time.'

'Road to Paradise' was released on the same disc as Simple Minds and Jimmy's version of 'Dirty Old Town', a song previously popularised by The Pogues. Prior to writing Ferns flew to Dublin to meet MacGowan. At that point the singer was a long-term resident of the luxury Deer Park Hotel in Howth. I arrived a few days later to interview MacGowan for *Scotland On Sunday*, as he had recently been the subject of a documentary film *If I Should Fall From Grace*. Persuading MacGowan to produce new material in recent years has been no easy feat and it once again proved difficult. Ferns initially found Shane discontented and unreceptive; his enthusiasm to write had diminished since their previous conversation. When McLaughlin and Ferns had presented MacGowan with a fresh muse in Glasgow and Celtic, the possibilities seemed endless, but Ferns remembers the second song had a much more complicated birth. He says: 'The first single had done really well, in the first week of release it shifted 32,000 copies, it was outselling Oasis. For a soccer single we hit big sales. But working with Shane is not so much a song-writing process, more song-writing chaos. Shane had said that he wanted to write something more anthemic for the second record, the first song was a beautiful folk ballad. His first aim was to write an ode to Glasgow. Some people perceive Glasgow as ugly, Shane's take was to portray the city as beautiful and that beauty came from the people. It was really Shane's song with a bit of input from John and me; it was a track he was really proud of. The second record was a different experience completely. I arrived at the hotel in Dublin that Shane was staying in and his first words to me were: "What the fuck are you doing here?" We didn't write for three days. Suddenly he had these streams of freeform words and consciousness – his hotel bed was like a junk shop covered in literature, poetry books, comics, videos, an acoustic guitar and a banjo, just a random selection of things to call upon. Eventually they [the words] came. He tends to work fast after that and tightens everything up.'

The weekend of the recording MacGowan returned to Glasgow for a slot with The Popes at the city's Celtic Connections winter music festival. The following night he joined Primal Scream on stage for 'Loaded' and a version of Johnny Thunders's 'Born to Lose'. After spending a night in the company of the band, MacGowan was physically and mentally exhausted by the time he entered the studio on Sunday. He looked the worse for wear but persevered again with a tight deadline. Reflecting on the weekend, he said: 'It's a bit like being held in a Colombian jail with electrons being attached to your balls and every time you wake up you get another zap [working with Ferns], but that's how we get the records done. The idea for "Road to Paradise" was a team that came from hell: hell being Ireland in the famine years and after, Paradise being Celtic Park. I must say that Glasgow was paradise compared to Ireland, it's quite widely used as a description and I know they call it other things, but that's how it worked. We pulled in some girls at Paul's bar, some luscious blondes that worked in the pub to do the backing, there was quite a lot of strange puritanical aggression directed towards them, "What are you doing on the record?" kind of thing. My attitude was c'mon you want Dusty Springfield and Tamla Motown, they were really good singers and really good looking.' Musically 'Road to Paradise' has a passing resemblance to 'Yeah, Yeah, Yeah, Yeah, Yeah', his previous American hit with The Pogues. Likewise it's not a particularly Irish sounding track, reflecting MacGowan's inner-city love for Northern Soul and the accompanying movement that came to pollinate British working-class subculture in the 1960s and 1970s. Ferns even drafted in a brass section whose CV included the Rolling Stones and Primal Scream. Once again MacGowan's enthusiasm was flourishing; he promised a return visit to Glasgow to film an accompanying promo that would hopefully give the record a maximum chance of denting the charts. While the sound was more mod than folk, the lyrics focused completely on MacGowan's knowledge and experience of Celtic. Once in the studio he was precise about every detail of the recording and the lyrics.

Ferns recalls: 'The track took two or three hours to record and three to produce it, Shane actually likes to get into the technical process and is clear about the sound he wants. He's gifted in that he can do both [write and produce], a lot of modern-day writers can't do that. The first idea I had for the song came from a picture in Paul's pub; it was of Celtic supporters walking to Seville along the Green Mile. I suggested the name "The Green Mile", but Shane didn't like it. He took it in a better direction; all the Northern Soul inspiration came from him. He also liked the fact that Celtic Park was right next to a graveyard and correlated that with the famine and the Irish coming to Glasgow, but he turned it into a pop song. There are a lot of levels to how he puts it together. We then brought in the Kick Horns who were the Stones' horn section for a time, they also worked on *Screamadelica,* after that the record was complete.'

On 8 April 2004 MacGowan arrived in the East End of Glasgow, joining supporters along the Green Mile as they made their way to watch Celtic take on Villarreal in Europe. Fans poured out of afternoon boozers to join the singer performing in front of the camera outside Bairds and The Brazen Head. A few hours later Henrik Larsson would revive Celtic's chances in Europe once again against a vigorous Spanish side by scoring another essential European goal as MacGowan cheered from the Gallowgate. Even in the digital age the film has become impossible to locate, although a number of photographs exist as proof of the shoot. MacGowan's trip to Glasgow was nearly the last public outing of 'Road To Paradise', aside from a handful of performances with The Popes. Unfortunately for a number of reasons the song didn't generate the attention expected, and MacGowan was largely unable to take on promotional work due to being hospitalised following an unprovoked attack while in London. Despite being a charity single, witless record stores in England refused to stock it on the grounds it was specialist interest and national DJs were equally unmoved to play it. Without explanation the song was withdrawn from The Bhoys From Paradise charity single. Significantly it was Simple Minds and Jimmy Johnstone's version of 'Dirty Old Town', which gained notoriety among Celtic supporters, it continues to be played at Parkhead to this day.

'I think they had a bit of a fallout,' says John McLaughlin of MacGowan and Ferns. 'I was in London at the time. Something happened, I don't know what, but yeah the track list did change. Shane's a mysterious figure, I remember at the time when they were doing the record I provided some musicians. My original idea was for Shane to record "Lord of the Wing", but it was a time thing. Jimmy Johnstone heard the demo and asked to keep my vocal, so that clinched it. But I thought the track "Road to Paradise" was great, it should've been a hit.'

The operetta *Pirates of Penzance* is said to be at least one influence behind 'The Celtic Song', the definitive version performed by the Scottish music-hall entertainer and shipyard worker Glen Daly. On first hearing Shane MacGowan's version I was reminded of a previous review: 'Backstage with MacGowan is like being on board a seventeenth century pirate ship with Glaswegian, Irish and Cockney shipmates.' For the fiftieth anniversary of the song MacGowan summoned the same energy on his recorded version in the winter of 2011; it seemed between Shane and Celtic there was some unfinished business. Since 'The Best Days of Our Lives', John McLaughlin had retained a connection with the club and was asked to put together a single: 'There was talk of Shane doing a Glasgow trilogy; I suppose you could say that's complete now. Celtic talked to me about the reissue of the original and suggested Shane as he seemed like the person most Celtic supporters would want. When I asked him he was honoured to do it. Again it's not something MacGowan needed to do, but he wanted to sing it. We recorded in Dublin, I told him "Do it your way; put your stamp on it". Once Shane got a handle on the song he decided it should be much more aggressive; he brought a much harder punk edge to the track and made it even more up-tempo. Some of the lyrics changed, the language was of the time, so while paying homage to the original we wanted something that brought the song into the modern era. Many of Shane's songs have been played at Celtic Park. For him it's a two-way thing: Glasgow's been good to him and he doesn't forget that.'

Of the many excuses you're likely to hear from a Celtic supporter for missing Seville, Paul McGinn the Glasgow barman who MacGowan befriended while recording in the city arguably has the best. 'I was actually in hospital,' says McGinn with a smile that neuters the negativity of the statement. 'When Shane came here he often missed a number of flights back to Ireland, there was one time he pulled out a CD cover as ID at passport control, needless to say he never got on the plane. When he went back to his hotel he'd forget that he'd checked out. He started thrashing the door of his room wondering who was in it. When the woman inside started screaming for security we nearly got arrested. It took a number of phone calls to Mr Ryan of Ryan Air to get him on another flight. When you are with Shane people are lining up to buy him a drink, the only piece of advice I would give is don't try to compete with him; the man is an athlete. He's got four kidneys and three livers. I made that mistake and believe me it was a mistake, that's why I missed Seville.

'Being a Celtic supporter is an emotional life; that period with Shane was just another chapter. My hope is that one day there'll be a blue plaque on Hope Street outside the pub commemorating one of the best songwriters of our times who wrote a song here. We managed to get a glimpse of his talent.'

Shane MacGowan has a reputation for tardiness – missed flights and cancelled appearances are part of the legend. But his timing was faultless when The Pogues' expression of Irishness found international acclaim in the 1980s, a decade in which to self-identify as Hibernian was met with contempt following IRA bombing campaigns on mainland Britain. It was a time when the diaspora expression was associated with those atrocities, and racism was widespread across British society. As a result The Pogues and their brand of Irish folk punk possessed a cultural power and influence that was nothing short of spellbinding, particularly during their live shows where the audience could celebrate that identity openly and without fear. Their emergence was a vital part of the process that halted invisibility among a new generation of Britain's Irish diaspora, and nowhere was their energy more apparent than in Glasgow at the riotous Barrowlands gigs. Their appearances coincided with events such as a cathartic performance played in the aftermath of Jock Stein's tragic death and a particularly memorable day out on St Patrick's Day 1991 when Celtic beat Rangers 2–0 in the quarter-final of the Scottish Cup.

Before his sad passing after a long illness in October of 2013 Pogues guitarist and songwriter Philip Chevron reflected on those events while offering his insight into the band's associations with Celtic, the supporters and the Irish diaspora in Glasgow. The game, known among the support as the 'St Patrick's Day Massacre', was followed by a Pogues concert at the Barrowland which created much carnival merriment along the length and breadth of the Gallowgate: 'I remember it well,' says Chevron, 'I was there, poncing it up in the directors' box with my friend Billy [yes!], while some of the others were in various parts of the stands. Earlier that day our manager Frank Murray and his wife Fearga were having one of their children baptised and we went to that too. Then we had the Celtic win and The Pogues' show that evening. 'I met Paul McStay, not backstage after the show, but at a Parkhead reception earlier. I liked him and Packie Bonner very much. To be honest, I'm not sure if it wasn't all a tad too much, this orgy of cultural Irishness and Catholicism, the very combination I had spent half my life railing against! At the beginning, our connections with Glasgow were real and heartfelt and tacit. By 1991 I was afraid we were in danger of becoming a bit of a cliché.'

Going back further to September 1985, Cait O'Riordan's dedication to Jock Stein the day after his death remains a particularly memorable moment from the band's early shows in Glasgow. Says Chevron: 'I remember it as an extraordinarily emotional moment and its recollection still makes me emotional. Cait O'Riordan's number, "I'm A Man You Don't Meet Every Day" was the best possible way to mark it. She changed the lyric "Jock Stewart" to "Jock Stein". There's nothing else or more you can do in a situation like that.'

Irish journalist Eamonn McCann attended The Pogues' Christmas gig at the Barrowlands in 1988. He wrote: 'I've never been at a gig like The Pogues in Glasgow where the mood and the music and all the expectations and underlying assumptions seemed so exactly in tune, never been part of an audience that felt so uplifted and validated by being there. I've heard arguments and banter occasionally as to whether The Pogues are most accurately described as an Irish band or an English band or an Anglo-Irish band or whatever. They are none of these things. The Pogues are a Glasgow band.' Undoubtedly this mythical gang in black suits (described by MacGowan as 'paddy chic', like people who had been out all night drinking and dancing and lost their ties) had a unique currency in Glasgow, where audiences immediately claimed the band as their own. Despite the fact that venues such as the Barrowlands were heavily populated by Celtic supporters, fans of the band who also supported Rangers weren't afraid to show their colours among the throng, perhaps suggesting how much The Pogues resonated with other facets of Glasgow life.

Chevron casts his mind back to the city in the aftermath of punk rock: 'It was almost an entirely new experience for me. Although I had played in Glasgow before with The Radiators From Space in 1977, my abiding memory is of the cantilevered balcony at the old Glasgow Apollo literally bouncing up and down! So I knew Glaswegians knew how to have a good time, but I never particularly associated that with The Radiators' Irishness or Thin Lizzy's Irishness or whatever. I knew all the old variety comedians' jokes about dying on a Monday night in Glasgow and considered we must have just passed *that* test. And still with The Pogues, eight years later, I was uniquely deaf and blind at first to the cultural significance The Pogues brought to the table, but I very quickly caught on and fell in love with that connection.

'It wasn't actually Eamonn McCann who first said: "The Pogues are not an Irish band, they're a Glasgow band", it was me. I hoped it was both self-evident *and* pregnant with meaning when I said it. But I was less inclined than, say, Spider Stacy or Shane MacGowan, to wear the Celtic paraphernalia and Irish nationalist stuff that got thrown up on stage to us. In fact, I always made a point of noticing and appreciating the few stray and possibly brave souls in the crowd wearing blue Rangers shirts because, one, if The Pogues were celebrating anything, we were celebrating outsiderdom. I had to assume that nobody seen at the Barrowlands in a Rangers shirt was likely to be offering a few bars of "The Sash" on his flute; and I loathed and despised working-class sectarianism as a destructive and alienating divide-and-conquer trick of Empire and could not find it in my heart to play that game. So I found other, quieter ways of signalling my understanding that Catholic sectarianism was not quite the opposite of its Protestant equivalent. Mainly, I did that by identifying as a Celtic supporter. But note, and I'm willing to be corrected on this if necessary, I don't recall a single incident of sectarian aggression at a Pogues show in Glasgow.'

Second-generation Irish guitarist Johnny Marr has suggested that many of Britain's Irish offspring formed new subcultural and social identities around punk gigs and on the football terraces where there was an evident socialist ideology of which Celtic became associated not just in Glasgow but throughout Britain. 'It is definitely a factor in football culture where most big cities in Europe with two major teams are perceived to have a "right" team and a "wrong" one, and usually these are defined by whichever club most represents socialist or left-wing or working-class or liberal ideas of nobility. So for all sorts of reasons, Celtic would be the acceptable face of Glasgow football to people who had no actual interest in religious traditions or nationalism. It all seems a bit ludicrous now when football is one of the most venal strands of aggressive modern capitalism, but that's certainly how it was up to the 1980s. The punk-football thing Johnny Marr mentions was definitely a factor too. The people producing the better footie fanzines were the same kind of people – erudite, smart, on the case – who started the punk ones.'

While you might not find Philip Chevron draped in a Celtic scarf on stage, he has indeed found more subtle ways to show his support, particularly when the identification with Celtic has a meaningful resonance. Significantly it was multi-instrumentalist Chevron who wore the Celtic supporters' Famine Memorial Day pin badge in one of the band's recent Glasgow shows, a move profoundly appropriate in relation to Celtic and the diaspora story: 'The Great Hunger, to me, is such a raw and unresolved tribal memory for Irish people everywhere in the world, that I welcome every opportunity to mark it, not resolve it – I think that is now beyond all our powers – but there can be no doubting it fucked us up and still does. It shattered our morale and our sense of self-sufficiency. And we don't talk about it because what would we say? We know so little about how it actually affected our own ancestors, like the First World War soldier who, if he lives, never speaks of it again throughout his life and no one ever asks because they feel it must be too terrible a secret to divulge. One of the more potent pieces of useful psychobabble you hear in addiction treatment centres and rehabs is, Secrets Keep You Sick. And they do, they really do. In parts of Ireland, even as comparatively recently as when I was a boy, you could still see old women peeling potatoes so closely they only just lost their skins. It was an act of prudence they themselves had learned at their grandmother's knee.'

During the 1980s, an era associated with banal synthesiser pop, The Pogues, while breathing new life into traditional music and Irish drinking songs, reminded the world of the country's rich lyrical tradition, poetry and culture when it was being obscured by the pessimism, sorrow and distress of the Troubles. As well as writing about folk myths and Celtic warriors, The Pogues chronicled the restless spirit, the wistful yearning for another way of life; that place which exists inside every imagination where the notion of belonging is somewhere else. It was Philip Chevron's live favourite 'Thousands Are Sailing' that raised further 'raw and unresolved' questions for a new generation of those from Irish origin in Britain. The song suggests an atmosphere of being left behind while evoking the 'coffin ship' horrors that were inflicted on the many whose ambition was to reach the promised land, in this case America. Certainly the song gives a voice to those who didn't survive or didn't reach their destination, summoning that in-between state.

There is also the question of how the Irish and its diaspora in Scotland or England feel towards Irish–American culture. Chevron explains: 'The migrant world tends to be divided into two groups – those who made it to the New World and those who didn't. Though my own family migration history is more connected to the Huguenots taking refuge in Dublin than to transatlantic voyages, I've always felt the Irish and those of Irish origin have a great ambivalence about America. It's a country we helped build, not just physically, but in terms of political systems and the black economy and of course the culture. So we have an enormous stake in it which, I think, we jealously guard even if we are now powerless to greatly influence its direction. The "Yank" in Irish culture is an acutely complex figure, as we see from John B. Keane to John Ford, and the Returned Yank, as in "Don't come the Returned Yank with me, boyo", was a figure of deep suspicion for many years. So any "genetic memory" expressed in "Thousands Are Sailing" – and yes, I believe it to be there – is one of great melancholy. And what I've never quite been able to decide is whether the melancholy reaches out to those who made it to America or to those who made it only as far as Glasgow! A little of both, I suspect, and that's almost certainly the source of the ambivalence.'

Another area of discord has been that the culture of the diaspora is seen as tawdry or low by the native Irish and by a new aspirational middle-class expatriate culture wishing to distance itself from the more popular working-class aspects of entertainment and leisure be it Celtic F.C, The Pogues or activities such as Irish dancing. In a sense The Pogues seemed to embody all the high and low distinctions of Irish culture and the diaspora experience from showbands to language and literature while adding the essential punk-rock snarl of MacGowan and the band's shared reverence of 1950s rock 'n' roll sensibilities. Philip Chevron considers The Pogues contribution to the culture while examining his own journey as a first-generation Dubliner journeying the seas of diaspora life and experience: 'What I think of as "*Irish Post*" Irishness, what I would recognise as diaspora self-consciousness in which the children of immigrants were in ringletted Irish dancing troupes or amateur Gaelic sports teams or in which there may have been a direct identification with one or other "county associations", is so far removed from Irishness as practised in the homeland as to be almost alien to someone like me who grew up on the island of Ireland. In the 1970s and early 1980s we'd have run a mile from such an overt and visible association with so reactionary an Ireland.

'It took me quite a while to figure out that there were solid reasons why diaspora-Irishness had its own distinct cultural markers and connections. Shane MacGowan, for instance, who largely grew up in London, was always more connected to those emigrant pulses than I was, and was a great deal more tolerant of Foster and Allen and Brendan Shine, etc. than I could ever bring myself to be. When I moved to London in 1977 with The Radiators, just about the last thing I would have thought about was searching out the Irish ghettoes of Kilburn or Cricklewood although, as the Irish were quite well represented in the punk-music scene – Stiff Records, Chiswick Records, etc. – maybe I had no need to anyway. But what I'm getting at is the sense that to me Irishness in palatable form was Horslips, not Big Tom or Ann Breen. That said, I did quite quickly recognise and become interested in the phenomenon – there's a song called "Johnny Jukebox" on The Radiators' second album *Ghostown* that locates part of the album's narrative in an Irish pub in Camden, which is where we hung out because that's where Chiswick Records was back then.

'It took a trip to America with The Pogues in 1986 and exposure to still another form of Irishness to realise that being Irish as I understood it as a native Dubliner was likely to have been a minority experience. The hard fact is that being born *in* Ireland is by no means the principal condition for Irishness. Irish-identified folks from New York or Chicago or Glasgow or Birmingham have at least an equal claim, as did their cultural expression, whether through Eugene O'Neill or Denis Leary or Notre Dame [Fighting Irish] or Liverpool F.C or Andrew O'Hagan. Even Foster and Allen. It came as a shock but, once I had processed it, I came to embrace the versatility of it. In a sense, when an Irish theatre company, like Druid, tours the world now with the works of Synge or Tom Murphy, they are in a very powerful way attempting and succeeding to represent that wider community too by focusing on the lingering unfinished emotional aftermath of the Great Hunger. And I think that's what The Pogues did in the 1980s. By refusing to accept the host country's belittling stereotypes, in part by repossessing them and burlesquing them, we found a voice for a whole generation in Britain who had grown up through the Irish racism linked to Irish republican activity as their parents had suffered the "No Blacks, No Irish, No Dogs" notices.

'The change The Pogues helped bring to Irish communities in England and Scotland, the defiance we inspired is, I believe, one of the great untold modern stories. Of course, none of it would have meant a damn if there hadn't been the beauty and poetry of the songs to sustain it, so that when the "bunch of drunken Paddies" thing got wearisome, there was always a "Fairytale of New York" or a "Rainy Night in Soho" or a "Thousands are Sailing" to better explain The Pogues and ensure longevity, a body of work that would transcend its life as a mere cultural signifier.'

Since The Pogues reformed in 2001 for a series of Christmas dates, whether in Paris where they celebrated a thirtieth anniversary gig in 2012 or in New York where they performed at the Roseland Ballroom on St Patrick's Day 2007, the green and white hoops have become as evident as Guinness, crucifixes and Claddagh rings. Says Chevron: 'Today, interestingly, that "Celtic green" you see at Pogues shows around the world is a universal marker not just of Catholic Irishness, but of Irishness in general, though I suppose there is an underlying presumption of republicanism (in the sense of the opposite of the hereditary monarchism) in the wearer. You won't like the analogy – I know I don't – but wearing a Manchester United shirt in Tokyo does not subject you to the same package of cultural assumptions and derision as it would in north London. Something similar has happened, I think, though on nothing like the same commercial scale, with the Celtic colours. Our own show merchandising people even do a Pogues top like that from time to time. People like the association it forms which, on balance, is almost certainly a positive thing.'

Chapter Five
Sparkle in the Rain

*'For me Tommy (Burns) was a friend always; he was like one
of the players and he loved to join in and play with the team
during practice sessions, he would take part in the five asides.
The way Tommy handled a situation and people was different
from other managers, you know sometimes people in the game
are stubborn; it's their way or nothing. But Tommy wasn't
like that; he could see past that kind of thing, he was open. I
had come from a country where people think a lot and they
sometimes think too much, everybody is pushing an idea and
an opinion in Holland. I could speak easily with Tommy, he
was sociable, he had a sense of humour and he'd use that to
change things. I had so many other managers in my career but
not like him, I would always pick Tommy; he stood up when he
needed to. He was the father of our team. Before the Old Firm
game I had guys like Tommy, Paul McStay, Billy Stark and
Peter Grant telling me about this match, these guys hammered
the importance of it; they would tell me; you can't make a
bad season good but you can go out there today and give the
supporters back some pride.'*
Pierre Van Hooijdonk

*'What the Tories are doing is placing the chav myth at the
heart of British politics, so as to entrench the idea that there
are entire communities around Britain crawling with feckless,
delinquent, violent and sexually debauched no-hopers. Middle
England on the one hand and chavs on the other.'*
Owen Jones

OWEN JONES'S BOOK *Chavs – The Demonization of the Working
Class* made a compelling argument for the stereotyping of a
social group struggling to get a foothold in modern society.
The left-wing commentator suggests that those at the bottom
of life's social ladder have become hate figures for a new

generation of politicians, entertainers and writers where television grotesques have often replaced more favourable representations such as *The Likely Lads*. The BBC comedy set in the north-east of England presented an enduring snapshot of two everyman football fans who worked in a factory just as 1960s guitar pop and its associated ideas repositioned British youth culture irreversibly. The fact that they were part of a struggling working class didn't stop them from being impressive characters or having valid opinions and ideas often presented in typical pub conversations, particularly in the 1973–74 follow-up series *Whatever Happened to the Likely Lads*?

Since then positive slice-of-life mainstream examples of the working class and a struggling underclass have been in decline – Frank Gallagher from *Shameless* or *Little Britain*'s Vicky Pollard have become the standard. Channel 4's *The Secret Millionaire* is one recent example of a more vivid representation of struggling communities where more charitable characters throw all their energy and resources into helping the less fortunate, the troubled and the disabled. At the same time, the series doesn't always reflect a rose-tinted utopia of perpetual goodwill. In one disconcerting programme an unstable teenager in Croydon threatened to set the incognito millionaire on fire. Undoubtedly wealth does allow room for a more philosophical approach to life and in the episode's climax the entrepreneur, Bobby Dudani, is compelled to lend a game-changing hand to the serial offender whose life has become hopeless and barren. Though it can be compelling and emotive television, unsurprisingly, like any reality series, it has no shortage of critics. In a *Guardian* article, journalist John Crace suggests the programme is manipulative, saying: 'I'm all for the well-off giving some of their wealth away, but I'd rather they did it off camera.'

But perhaps Crace is throwing his champagne out with the cork. Undoubtedly *The Secret Millionaire* could be a bit hit and miss, but when the undercover protagonist sparked up a genuine chemistry with the community it was television that makes the spirit soar unlike the deluge of *Benefits Street*-style documentaries that function to demonise and sensationalise. At least two Celtic fans took part in the programme, most recently Gordon McAlpine, a software entrepreneur who assisted the GalGael Trust in Glasgow's Govan area. The episode centred on a charity that has revived the dying local art of shipbuilding in an effort to re-energise the culture and lives of those left vulnerable to alcoholism and drug addiction with no sense of community or purpose. The programme ended with McAlpine walking into Parkhead and joining the green and white throng on an overcast match day. Walking towards the ground while soaking up the pre-match atmosphere is a spine-tingling moment for any Celtic supporter but having watched the businessman build community while tapping into the roots of what Celtic are all about made the journey all the more emotive. McAlpine's journey honoured a number of Glasgow's mavericks who, against the odds, had managed to 'overachieve' in their ambition to rebuild lives.

The other Celtic supporter to feature in the programme is Tony Banks. A veteran of the Falklands War, ex-Para Banks greets me in the aftermath of a heated business exchange at the well-heeled Blythswood Square hotel in Glasgow where he urged some fellow executives 'to get their gripes out on the table like men'. Banks is a straight-talking and congenial personality, emboldened by a clarity and honesty in his approach that typifies the customary working-class values with which he was raised during a somewhat nomadic childhood in the 1960s. He earned millions during a period of economic stability in the 1990s, establishing a reputable firm that specialised in private care for the elderly.

By his own admission Banks doesn't exhibit the typical identifiers or traits of the average Celtic supporter. In fact he opened a recent business talk inside Celtic Park by admitting as much, saying: 'I'm probably the most unlikely Celtic fan you could get. I was born in England, my father supported Dundee and I joined the 2nd Battalion Parachute Regiment, the most hated regiment in Ireland. I'm also a Scottish nationalist. I come from a Catholic family, but not overtly religious. My mum was a Protestant but became a Catholic when she married my dad. I was made to go to chapel every Sunday even though my parents never went. The house was immaculate, like a surgery. I think it was more obsessive-compulsive disorder than anything else, and that's what I inherited about Celtic. My two older brothers and sister were all born in Scotland, but my mother was too ill to fly back for my birth. I'm as passionate a Scot as you can get so I hate to admit that I was born in England.' Banks says this with a relaxed smile that confirms his desire is charged with typical folk romance rather than anti-Englishness.

With a parent in the armed services, Celtic initially provided an unfamiliar channel of consistency and structure when starting a new life in Scotland. Although his parents insisted on attending mass, football wasn't necessarily on the agenda, as Banks explains: 'I had been living in Canada with no connection to Celtic whatsoever, the European Cup win hadn't even registered with me. I started to follow Celtic at primary school around 1968, but it was nothing to do with Lisbon or being Catholic. In Scotland you must have a team, as my new classmates told me, and so there it began. Most of them were Dundee or United fans, but I randomly opened the paper and Celtic were top of the league so I thought: "That'll be my team." After that I could tell you everything about Celtic, I'd reel off scores from cup finals, players from previous eras or how many times we'd won a competition. In the late 1960s live football on television was a rarity, if the game was at night I'd take a wireless the size of a small loaf to my bed where there was as much crackle as commentary. If they got beat, especially in Europe, my mother would come in to find me in tears. She'd never experienced that before because my two older brothers weren't into it and my dad never let on he was a Dundee fan until years later.'

One notable cause for tears for Banks along with every other Celtic supporter glued to a wireless or a black and white television set in May 1970 was when John 'Yogi' Hughes hit the post during extra time in the European Cup final against Feyenoord. Hughes remains one of Celtic's most understated and stylish talents of the era; his emergence as a cult hero alongside the likes of George Connelly has not gone unnoticed. Yogi, said to be named after the Hanna-Barbera character, was a versatile talent but, much like Georgios Samaras in the modern era, would split opinion among the Celtic support during his eleven eventful years at Parkhead (1960–71). He once suggested that his miss on that rain-sodden night in Milan's San Siro stadium was the reason for his exit from the club soon after. As one of Kelly's Kids, Hughes has lived in the shadows of the Lisbon Lions and the more eminent members of the Quality Street Gang ever since. Although a mercurial talent he was undoubtedly an essential part of a Celtic side that could be raw and impulsive, but always compelling against more disciplined and dour Scottish clubs. Hughes formed a convincing partnership with Jimmy Johnstone that particularly shined against an imposing Vojvodina at Parkhead in the second round of the European Cup in 1967. He also played in the side that faced Zurich and Dukla Prague, which secured him a European Cup medal despite not being picked for the final.

The mere mention of Hughes breathes life into Tony Banks as he reflects on his formative years watching the player's every move: 'Big Yogi was my first Celtic hero; he still is one of my heroes. Any great team has to have unsung talent and for me it was him. Aside from being a prolific goalscorer, what I liked about him was the fear he created in the opposition; players were visibly frightened of him because of his sheer presence and size. He was also one of the most versatile players I've seen, Jock Stein moved him from centre forward to the left wing which was an inspired move, he could also play in a supportive role with Jimmy Johnstone. All great teams need players like that in the way we needed Neil Lennon breaking up the play for Larsson to score. Hughes scored a number of significant goals for Celtic, but the most memorable was against Leeds in 1970. After beating them we had reached another European Cup final within three years; those players set a benchmark that still stands.'

Banks's first game evokes the kind of Celtic performance that exhilarated the club's supporters during the late 1960s and early 1970s: 'I lived near Dundee's ground and on Saturday I would watch and listen to the supporters walking to the ground. Home games for me were when Celtic played Dundee or United. My first Celtic game was in January 1971 against Dundee. It was a murky, grey winter's day; I remember it clearly because Celtic thrashed Dundee 8–1. It was a surprising result because Dundee had a strong pedigree at that time. In Europe they'd reached the semi-finals of the European Cup in the 1960s and played in the Inter-Cities Fairs Cup. My dad never let on they were his team, so it must have been hard for him to stand and take it while they got humped 8–1. Jinky, Willie Wallace and Harry Hood scored two apiece. You were watching the remnants of the Lions, the men who had won the European

Cup, still putting away goals along with talents that would define Celtic in the early 1970s: Harry Hood, Jim Brogan and Tommy Callaghan who were all celebrated players at the time.'

Significantly, it was his unquenchable passion for football that convinced producers on *The Secret Millionaire* to send the Celtic supporter to Anfield in Liverpool. Tellingly, it wasn't long before he tapped into the beating heart of a community pulsating with life. After navigating his way through some feral and hazardous inner-city life, including an arson attack on his temporary home, Banks formed a number of emotive connections, among them a war veteran, who like himself, since serving in the Falklands, was struggling with post-traumatic stress. There was also an elderly disabled pensioner without family and widowed since 1966 and a blind man working voluntarily as a sports organiser for disabled and able-bodied youngsters. Banks explains: 'They knew I was a mad Celtic fan and that football was a big passion in my life, they knew I could assimilate into a city full of football fans, they understood that I had that mindset. But the producer got very pissed off at me because I wasn't really shocked by Anfield. I'd been brought up in a Dundee slum with no bath or toilet. Their point to me was that I was no longer living that life and in fairness they were right. I didn't live in this kind of dog-eat-dog society where people need money every day for the immersion heater, I made the mistake of leaving it on all day and burning away my budget. Then it sunk in that I had lost touch.

'All money does is give you more choices: a better car, a bigger house, nicer holidays and maybe a £100 shirt over a £20 one. But that's all it gives you; it doesn't make you a better person and I think that is one of the ideas associated with Celtic. At Celtic Park as one of the 60,000 it doesn't matter if you are a brain surgeon or a scaffy; you are part of a family, that's the foundation Celtic is built on and not every club has that. My other-half is Polish, her mum was visiting and I took her to Celtic Park. I stretched my arms out and said: "Welcome to my cathedral; this is my church and these are my people."

'If a neutral was at the stadium on the last game of the season when we did the huddle [2010–11] you'd think we'd won the league. The fans were celebrating and still supporting the team and Neil Lennon; I don't think you would see that anywhere else. The feeling that day is what Celtic is all about to me.

'In secondary school my French teacher ran a bus to Celtic Park. At about the age of 12 I was going to every home game. I remember going to a Cup final at Hampden against Rangers and the bus getting bricked. At that point I had no concept of the sectarian divide or the rivalry between fans. It was then I also became aware of this idea of the Celtic family. What it automatically meant in school was if you were getting bullied or hassled the top boys from the bus would step in and look after you. When my time came I did the same for the boys in the first year. To this day I still get texts from those lads on the bus.'

By his own admission the Parachute Regiment and their association with the Troubles in Northern Ireland, particularly the events of Bloody Sunday on 30 January 1972, don't endear them to your average Celtic supporter. Significantly Banks's own family were against him joining the forces: 'My older brother was a lawyer, my father was in the RAF and was an educationalist, he was from a working-class background and turned down a place at a grammar school because he wanted to be with his mates. It was something he deeply regretted so he was quite heavy on the education side with us. He talked me into studying accountancy; it was that very working-class idea of bettering yourself. My dad was very proud to have one son a lawyer and another an accountant. At that point I lost Celtic and I went to do my degree. I was still only seventeen when I saw an advert about earning money parachuting. I didn't realise it was the Territorial Army. If someone told me what it was really about I wouldn't have went. Like most working-class guys a couple years before I was a punk, I was a Celtic fan. Joining the army was the last thing on my mind, but that's what happened. I was a young guy full of raw energy, but I didn't expect to find myself in the middle of a war zone. I knew we wouldn't be going to Ireland because the regiment had lost men there just before I joined. Before I knew it, I was in Argentina. I knew nothing about the place apart from the fact that Scotland had played there in the World Cup.'

Banks returned to Scotland in the late 1980s with his spirit in decline at the end of what had been a relentlessly harsh decade. He had witnessed countless horrors and lost comrades during the Falklands War. But his homecoming provided an opportunity to rekindle his love affair with Celtic after some years in exile: 'I had been disengaged with Celtic in the 1980s because of my army career; we didn't have satellite broadcasts in those days so football was low on the agenda. When I came back I started travelling on the Brechin and Montrose bus. So much had changed, it wasn't Celtic winning nine-in-a-row anymore, it was Rangers and the days of Gascoigne and Laudrup. You'd have a drink and stop for a pish and a fish supper in Auchterarder on the way home after a game. We weren't winning much, but I still loved everything about Celtic, there was still that underdog spirit but most of all it was that feeling of a family.

'Growing up the club had always been a broad church, I'd lived through less tolerant times when the public face of Celtic was seen to embrace culture, race and colour no problem. There's a sense of fairness in the roots of the club and I like to think I've carried those ideals on in business. You have to be true to yourself in life. I don't do backhanders and I don't double-deal; you have to have integrity because as soon as you compromise that you've sold your soul to the devil. I think there is something of that in Celtic. I've always been a team player and that's what I love about being part of the family and what it stands for. Once you get in the ground it doesn't matter if you're in a shell-suit or a suit. I think that attitude comes from the Irish roots because generations of people had to find their place by sticking together. Unity is important and negativity isn't tolerated, it's important to remember that, but it cuts two ways because Catholics are now in powerful positions. Any true Celtic supporter should respect and understand the roots while not accepting any kind of bigoted viewpoint about others.

'The feeling I have for Celtic is the same as the Paras: when you lose a comrade in battle it really is like losing a member of your family. The night before we played AC Milan in the Champions League I saw an accident involving a Celtic supporter who tragically died while crossing the road. I'll never forget how it felt. All I could think about the next day was that one of our guys had been killed supporting the team; he was one of us.'

Banks's point about Catholics now being in positions of power is worth a moment's reflection. Recent history seems to place Celtic as an advert for meritocracy in that a number of Celtic 'punters' have become some of the most powerful people on the planet. But, as Banks suggests, to take pride in the club's business pioneers is somewhat inordinate and it's also rare for the fans to be monolithic in their support for the men who wield power inside Parkhead's gates. However, he is positive about some of those who have steered the ship in recent years: 'I think we've had some very powerful and sophisticated people running our football club who have got there on their own steam. Brian Quinn was vice president with the Bank of England. Fergus McCann is another figure who is very important in the history of Celtic, if you look at what he did on paper it's a no-brainer, but at the time there was no one else willing to step up. I remember him getting booed at Celtic Park. I hope those people now have the intelligence to look in the mirror and be disgusted with themselves because there wouldn't be a Celtic if it wasn't for that wee man. All around the stadium there was terrible deprivation and when you first saw the new Celtic Park it was like a phoenix rising from the ashes. He was clear from the outset: he gave us a five-year plan and one of the best stadiums in Britain at the time. He did exactly what he said he would, which is all you can ask from somebody. John Reid is another much talked about figure, he's intelligent and actually quite a warm person on a personal level even though he's the minister that took us to war. In terms of politics I'm a Scottish nationalist and I support the SNP. I know a lot of Labour politicians and Glasgow council members support Celtic, but there is a nepotism there that I don't like. I'm not a unionist because I think it's every country's right to self-determination. We've always retained that punter element with the likes of Jim Kerr and Rod Stewart who have succeeded under their own steam. These guys come from ordinary working-class backgrounds, but they identify with Celtic because they understand the values and history around the football club, I think that's really important. It's because of that we are much more than a club. I don't believe in the old boys' network and I'm not a royalist, I believe if you are talented you should get a job, and ultimately, these are Celtic's values.'

Celtic director Michael McDonald's perspective would certainly support Tony Banks's beliefs that the concept of a family with certain values is what the Celtic 'brand' is all about. He said: 'Celtic is first and foremost a football club but we have values that go with that, our view is that we are much more than a football club, the charitable aspect and the relationship with supporters is part of that. I've been to Celtic games in America and the stadium is sold out, playing a team like Manchester United in a friendly there was 60% Celtic fans in the ground. In Las Vegas there was something like 3,000 Celtic supporters going to a convention, someone said to me; "where's the game?" I said: "there's no game, this is about the ethos of the club, they see themselves as a family" and that family brand reaches far and wide be it America, Australia or other parts of Europe.'

Among a certain vintage of Celtic supporter Baron Haughey, better known as Willie, is a familiar name. Like Woody Allen's Leonard Zelig, Haughey is often in or around major events in Celtic's or even world history. As well as having direct involvement in the running of the club he has retained a close friendship with a variety of its most popular ex-players and managers. A vital board member during the Fergus McCann era, he appeared on BBC's *The One Show* in November 2012 discussing his business initiative to encourage some of the UK's richest private companies to take on new apprentices as youth unemployment hit almost one million. A segment focusing on the philanthropist's work spoke to one of his new apprentices, Liam Boyle. Just months before Boyle had left school at 15 with no qualifications. He was without a job and a home when he discovered his girlfriend was pregnant. By his own admission Liam's future was hopeless. The entropy of life in Glasgow was pulling him down until he was thrown a lifeline. He said: 'There should be more people like Willie Haughey in the world; he's changed my attitude to life.'

Haughey's thriving business centre, Caledonia House, is situated on the old Gorbals where he grew up, just a stone's throw from Celtic Park and St Mary's, Calton, in whose church hall Celtic FC was founded. He exudes a sense that his destiny was always in his own hands saying: 'If you look at Africa, how can I ever say I was poor in the Gorbals? I didn't realise what poverty was because I was just as rich as everybody else.' There's an evocation of optimism when Haughey discusses the Glasgow he grew up in. Undoubtedly the pattern of his life suggests there was an uncompromising state of mind at work from an early age, taking on a milk round at the age of eight before becoming a telegram boy. After completing an apprenticeship Haughey had the skills that would take him to the United Arab Emirates where he would make the connections and develop business plans for over two years. In 1985 he returned home to Glasgow and set up his own company, City Refrigeration. The company won contracts with Scotland's major brewers including Tennent's, and later also moved into facilities management. Today, Haughey has lucrative contracts with Asda, Waterstones, House of Fraser and Ladbrokes as well as continuing to provide work for Walmart-Asda. One of Scotland's top business minds, he is a regular donor to the Labour Party and his charity work throughout Scotland has won him a number of plaudits and accolades.

Despite Haughey's positive slant, 1950s Gorbals was associated with intense poverty and degradation. Through players like Tommy Docherty and Pat Crerand, Celtic brought some much-needed pride to the area. Sitting down with Haughey in his office, he's philosophically contemplating a question his Rangers-supporting hairdresser has just posed him: 'Why there were no figures similar to himself, Matt McGlone or Fergus McCann, who became involved with that club's plight?' Matt McGlone will offer his undiluted view of the period in a later chapter, but our conversation begins when Haughey suggests, I presume jokingly, that he and McGlone might write a book about their behind-the-scenes experiences at Celtic. While it's often pointed out nobody came to the rescue of Rangers in the way that figures such as Haughey and Fergus McCann did at Parkhead, history could have turned out very differently. Haughey explains: 'This is an exclusive, I was actually in the Rangers end when they beat Celtic 3–0 in 1963; I can remember it vividly and I was only about seven years old. I was taken to the game by my uncle, who wasn't really a football man. Another uncle who was a Celtic supporter caught wind of this and thought "we're not having that. " My first Celtic game was a year later under floodlights one night during the week for a League Cup quarter-final against East Fife. Celtic won 6–0.'

Footage of the game still exists and shows centre forward Stevie Chalmers offering something of a masterclass – his fourth goal of five led enraptured Celtic supporters to invade the pitch. Impressive enough as that was, it was Willie's second game that cemented him as a Celtic supporter and one that distinguished Celtic as a new force in the Scottish game. 'I got a bus from the Gorbals with my uncle for the Scottish Cup final when we beat Dunfermline,' he recalls. 'That match is looked back on as the beginning of the Stein era, it was his first trophy and one that meant a lot to guys of my generation, Dunfermline were a good side. I think it was that game where I first noticed Bertie Auld: he scored two goals [with Billy McNeill scoring the winner in a 3–2 win]. In those days he was like the bandleader when Bobby (Murdoch) and Bertie were playing they made the game easy for Jimmy, Bobby (Lennox) and Stevie; they were our Xavi and Iniesta. They were true footballers and the activity and movement they created is still amazing to think about now.

'Something that stands out for me about it was after that game the streets of the Gorbals were lined with supporters. Jock Stein brought the team, but the bus couldn't get through. Stein did come to my school with the Scottish Cup and I remember him talking about a young player called Tony McBride. Unfortunately Tony went the wrong way, he had a few problems.'

A telephone call takes Haughey's attention for a moment but, after arranging a meeting, he picks up the story without missing a beat: 'But when Jock Stein stood up and said something he meant it. He knew that Tony had what it took to make it. Tony was a Gorbals boy and there was great hope for him. Ex-Celtic players like Paddy Crerand and Tommy Docherty were local heroes, Tony could have been one too, Jock wanted to give these guys a chance in life.'

The roots and the associated ideas of the club continue to be radical, not because they relate to left-wing politics or Irish ethnicity, but because the club can change lives for the better. Celtic's reputation for openness is one that even religious institutions would struggle to match as would a number of other Scottish organisations. As a former board member Haughey believes it is essential for the club to continue to be a symbol for these values and to offer a sense of community to those throughout Scotland whose daily interests relate to the club. Says Haughey: 'I think there is a difference between being a world-class football club and having a world-class reputation.

But, because money has had such an impact on the game, it will be very difficult. Take one of the most successful European clubs ever, Liverpool. Until the American financiers came along they were struggling and they have struggled to compete in Europe in recent years. But you can't feed in millions without a return. It's very difficult now to be a world-class football club, but it is always possible to have a world-class reputation.

'I was interviewed by the *Celtic View* a few years ago, I only gave the interview on the condition that they printed everything I said. One of the things I wanted them to print, which they did, was that in my eyes we would be the most successful football club if we gave a million to charity every year, I wouldn't care what we won. I still feel that today. Football in general has perhaps led us to forget what we are all about – a football club set up to help the poor. We are also an outlet for the working class.

'During that era in which I was growing up, in 1960s Glasgow, the pride that people got watching the Lions lifted people, it made them into something. It was like having an accreditation. It wasn't a degree, but it gave you a glow and the mentality of "I'm a Celtic supporter, this is how it's done". I read something last week, where a professor said something about environment not affecting your mood, I'd love to meet him, where is he getting his data? It's true that people who supported Celtic didn't have a lot, but there's no doubt when people came together to support the team they became enriched by it, it changed their daily lives. I still see people getting that from Celtic today.'

The Labour peer became a Celtic non-executive director in 1994 after former club writer Matt McGlone introduced him to Fergus McCann. His exit from the club involved an alleged disagreement with McCann over the sacking of Tommy Burns. The era remains one of the most written about, discussed and debated periods in Celtic's history. To this day fans are divided over who saved Celtic. Whatever the truth, there remain palpable bones of contention between McCann and some non-executive members of the board. Said Haughey: 'Fergus thought I was in the Tommy Burns fan club, but when I stuck up for Tommy it was to protect the board. Fergus wanted to do some things the fans didn't want. The fact is that Fergus had one view and I had another, he thought he could bring his shares into the boardroom, but there were seven of us and we all had a vote. I think everybody during that era got what they deserved, the credit and the barracking.

'Fergus and I parted company. People would expect me to pour scorn on him, but I wouldn't do that. I fell out with Fergus about a few things, but most of the things he did were right and he should get the credit for that. For me, and this is not to take anything away from Fergus, and I do mean this, Dermot Desmond should get all the credit in the world because we'd done the first part in taking the debt away, but it was actually the floating of the company that put us where we are now. That's what made Fergus's business plan work. Dermot Desmond didn't come along and say: "I'm going to put four million pounds in and I'm only going to do it if you match it." The big business was done when Dermot took Fergus out. My only disappointment with Fergus was that he didn't leave some money to build an academy or something. He said he'd be happy if he got ten per cent on his money. I don't know how much he got, but concentrating on Dermot, he must have ploughed about £40 million into Celtic easily.'

In the summer of 1995 while Haughey was on the board at Celtic, it seemed for a time that former French internationalist David Ginola, then aged 28, was heading to the west of Scotland, trading the red, white and blue of Paris St Germain for Glasgow's green and white. It's fair to say that Celtic supporters felt let down when he opted for Tyneside at the last moment. But he was only one of many players associated with the club during a frustrating time in the shadow of rivals Rangers. Haughey reflects on the incident: 'One of my worst moments with the board was when Tommy convinced David Ginola to come to Celtic and Fergus said: "Yeah, but you need to wait to find out whether he can play on a cold wet rainy night in Falkirk." Tommy kicked me under the table. The story goes that Ginola then went away and phoned Basile Boli after agreeing to come. Boli had just fallen out with Rangers and said: "Nah, you don't want to go there." After that he signed for Newcastle. Can you imagine David Ginola as a Celtic player during that time?'

As Haughey suggests here Tommy Burns's struggle with the board at Celtic was nothing new. Billy McNeill's well-documented reason for leaving the club in 1983 was due to his exasperation with the damaging mentality of the Celtic directorate who refused to provide him with a budget fitting of a club such as Celtic, they were also selling on developing players without his consent; a case in point was Charlie Nicholas's transfer to Arsenal. Celtic in the 1980s were in the throes of the 'biscuit tin' era that would take the club into the abyss. Despite his frustrations and a mostly difficult time in England managing Manchester City and Aston Villa, McNeill returned for another stint as Celtic manager in 1987. A loss to Borussia Dortmund 3–2 on aggregate had frustrated the die-hard fan as much as the professional player in Burns: 'Years before that [boardroom scene with Fergus McCann] I was sitting with Tommy when he was a player. We had just got beat in Europe, he was so disappointed that the board hadn't given money to Billy McNeill. He would say to me: "Look at McStay in his prime and we're bringing nobody in to help him. We're burning players out, we've got the nucleus here of a good team, a bit of experience, good kids and we're bringing nobody in to help them." He was so disappointed; I always remembered that moment with Tommy. The same thing happened to him as a manager; he didn't get any support.'

Every so often a player or a manager arrives at Celtic Park that changes the landscape while elevating the lives of the support not by introducing radical or revolutionary new methods or ideas, but by tapping into the meanings and values that have stood to serve the lives of the support and the community around Celtic. Tommy Burns was one such person. A word that continues to be associated with him is strength. The word appeared countless times amid the overwhelming sorrow and many poignant eulogies he received after his passing in 2008. Pundit and former Celtic player Charlie Nicholas had this to say: 'Tommy captured the imagination of the young Celtic support. He truly was Mr Celtic and he has become such a focal point for what Celtic means to young people now. It's something from which Tommy's family and all of his friends have taken incredible strength. I've been at Tommy's house over the past few days and the strength that the family has taken from the tributes at the ground, particularly from the Celtic support, has been extraordinary. It's been an absolutely incredible tribute. There are lots of other fans involved too, but as we know Tommy has become an icon of Celtic. He himself was one of the most recognised Celtic fans.'

As well as being a successful player, manager and coach at Celtic, Tommy Burns didn't shy away from tackling the difficult aspects of Scottish football and life. His faith was a test and measure of everything. In the aftermath of his death many thousands of supporters lined the streets of Glasgow's East End to pay tribute. Among Tommy's friends and Celtic team-mates were Rangers luminaries Walter Smith and Ally McCoist who also carried the casket at his memorial service, an act which encouraged the many positive tributes left by fans of Celtic's greatest rivals on websites and forums. Tommy Burns was a man who managed to transcend the bigotry so often associated with life in Glasgow by walking humbly. He exemplified that it takes great strength to be positive, compassionate and kind when faced with the more negative aspects of human nature. For many Celtic supporters the words of Tommy Burns provided a sparkle in the rain when it was needed most.

Contributing to the *Celtic Minded* series of books, he offered a thought-provoking chapter about his palpable Christian Faith. He said: 'Faith helps make me a less self-centred person, it makes me appreciate that I can't do it all myself. Faith is good, it's focused and it's true. It also helps us deal with people who might be hostile towards us, like maybe football teams with a history against us. We can see beyond that and see them as human first and foremost – and just as important in God's eyes. That's always the number one ingredient before we think of them as supporters of "the other" team. We should not allow ourselves to hate just because someone hates us or belongs to something different from us.' Significantly, Burns also used the opportunity to highlight others who exemplified the Celtic values he held so close: 'Paul [McStay] recognised the example people like him had to give as Celtic people. He stayed here during some very tough times. He knew the importance of Celtic and tried to set a good example. It's important that the people at this club can pass on what has been and what remains valuable from our past.'

Haughey suggests that Burns's greatest legacy is how he lived his life: 'I was close to wee Jimmy (Johnstone), he was my hero; I idolised Kenny Dalglish, I called my son after him. But Tommy Burns is somebody who epitomised everything Celtic stood for and I don't think I could say that about anybody else.' While Haughey believes Burns is in a league of his own as representative of traditionally what Celtic values stand for, he retains similar respect for another player he was close to during some of Celtic's darkest days. 'Paul McStay was different class as a man and as a player. Paul and Tommy were very close, they loved each other like brothers. Paul McStay carried with him his family's involvement with the club over decades and that was a badge he wore with pride. Other people brought up in the tradition, like Peter Grant, also knew what it meant to play for Celtic.

It's also fair to say that a number of foreign players under Tommy Burns came to recognise what it really meant to play for Celtic, in some instances that feeling grew stronger only after they left. Pierre van Hooijdonk is a player many supporters still hold in high regard and his winning Scottish Cup goal in 1995 granted him a significant place in the club's history. Here he reflects on the period: 'The best thing about my time at Celtic was witnessing what it all meant to the fans that day, that moment when I realised we had won the Scottish Cup final. It was then I realised what the club was all about. After the agony of those six years of winning nothing, the people that support Celtic were hurting so much, when we brought success that day, we lifted the supporters up; we gave them back some pride. I didn't know a lot about Scottish football before, of course I knew the name Celtic but I didn't realise how much this club meant to people. When I was there the club was going through changes; I was part of a new kind of Celtic team with players like Di Canio, Cadette, Thom and others. The club transformed very fast and the wages eventually moved up; it's part of the game. They soon had the opportunity to sign even better players with the likes of Larsson and some other big names. But I'm glad I was there in the time that I got and that I played my part in rebuilding the team and bringing it back where it belongs. Sometimes when you are away, you get a better picture of what a club is about because when you are playing the weeks move so fast. When I look at the European final in Seville or the win over Barcelona you see just how massive the support is; people all over the world support Celtic and it means a lot. I'm proud to have played for this club.' For many that Scottish Cup win of 1995 over Airdrie was something of a re-birth, the feeling of victory that day was all the more potent having suffered a League Cup defeat six months earlier. To taste such a bitter loss only encouraged an even greater sense of unity and desire for change. After six years of struggle and endurance it remains a vital turning point in the club's history, here Lord Haughey reflects on the time:

'When we lost the League Cup final against Raith Rovers in 1994 it was one of the hardest days in our history. I remember getting back to Celtic Park, we were still there at two o'clock in the morning and there were players breaking their hearts. It was like the closing scene of the *Long Good Friday* where the Bob Hoskins character is kidnapped and you see him going through all the emotions of his darkest moment. But it was a stepping-stone for many of them. McStay could have gone anywhere, but players like him stayed through loyalty. I can honestly say all they wanted was what was best for Celtic. Paul loved Celtic so much that when he was offered a new contract, which he could have signed and collected wages for another two years, he didn't because he knew his leg was knackered. Jock Stein summed it up when he said: 'These shirts don't shrink to fit inferior players'. This is a big club and if you come to play here everything is expected of you, first and foremost as a person and then we will look at your skills. In the modern era we have lost that a bit and perhaps we put up with things that we wouldn't have before, but I still think character is everything at Celtic. Which other club had the same manager for fifty-odd years or four managers in a hundred years.

'Brother Walfrid was the original torch-bearer and he quite literally handed the torch to Willie Maley when he went to his house in 1897. Walfrid had originally gone to the house to ask his brother Tom to help out. It's almost as if fate decreed that he would be absent leaving Willie to take on the role. But I don't think Celtic fans have always been conscious of Brother Walfrid, certainly not my father's generation, I don't think he would have known about him. People get credited at different times and it wasn't until the 1960s that there became an awareness of Walfrid's influence. After his involvement the club went limited and became a business [in 1897] laying the foundation stones of Celtic, but Maley carried that torch for fifty-odd years and cemented what Celtic were about right down to the way the team played. I think we can become overwhelmed by the present and I don't think Maley gets the credit he deserves.' ?

[It's worth noting that Willie Maley was manager for 43 years. Maley, Jimmy McStay, Jimmy McGrory and Jock Stein cover an 81 year period between 1897-1978.]

Lord Haughey's name continues to be associated with a takeover at Celtic. As one of the wealthiest fans of the club with a number of positive associations many supporters would like to see his involvement again. However, for the time being, that seems unlikely. Says Haughey: 'I would have to be honest and say I'm very happy with the present custodians of the club. I was involved in the Fergus McCann takeover and with getting Dermot Desmond on board. I'm one of the founder directors of Celtic PLC, I got involved with that because the club was going bust and that is the only reason I would get involved again. At the minute Celtic is being run well; Peter Lawwell is doing a good job. I'm Celtic through and through in my heart, but I understand the economics of running a football club. When you see what's happened across the road we should be very thankful that we have been prudent and in that time we have had a bit of success as well. We've had so many owners and business minds from the sublime to the ridiculous. Going right back to John Glass and John McLaughlin, a number of individuals have played an important role in the club's history, but the people who have kept this club what it is are the generations of fans. They are like missionaries for the history and the positive values; they are the real custodians of Celtic Football Club.'

Chapter Six
Keep the Faith

*'If you look at the history, Hibs were the only club that was
exclusively Catholic. Celtic weren't, they were for everyone. If
it was a discriminatory Catholic club or it excluded people I
wouldn't support them because I think that sends out a message
of supremacy and I don't believe in discrimination; I lived
through that in South Africa.'*
Jim Murphy

*Sent To Me From Heaven Glasgow Celtic You
Are My World*
Green Brigade Banner

THE TERM 'OLD FIRM' has blighted the landscape of what it
means to be a Celtic fan for a generation of supporters who feel
the expression conveys nothing about the distinctive way of
life, attitude and traditions of the support. Bill Murray writes
in his book *The Old Firm* that the business association with
Rangers F.C 'has been a great financial boom to both sides,
and the early games between them were as much influenced
by financial factors as any other.' The book refers to a *Scottish
Referee* cartoon from 1904, which appears to be the first
reference to the much maligned term. Murray adds that the
illustration was 'just one variation of a common theme of the
time.' Both clubs' interest in maximising profit and the initial
cordial relations between the institutions explain the root of
the expression, but its common use now by the media and
by followers of rival Scottish clubs is to suggest that Celtic
and Rangers supporters are an equal blight on society with
sectarian attitudes and repugnant political associations which
stem from both clubs' social and historical links with Ireland
and in particular the north of the country.

More recently the 'Old Firm' has become associated
with domestic abuse after Strathclyde Police claimed a rise in

recorded cases in the aftermath of the Glasgow derby. In regard to Celtic supporters, the Scottish media's secular agenda often dismisses the faith aspect of the club's history. While the club rightly stresses that it was formed to aid a community made up of both Catholics and Protestants, Celtic shouldn't be uncomfortable about making it clear that the club's Marist founder, Brother Walfrid, was from a Catholic tradition or that his motives were driven by his Christian faith, particularly in the club's mission statement.

The reputation of the Celtic v Rangers derby is high among football fans around the world who are fascinated by the complex relationship between the rival fans with their polarised ideas on ethnicity, religion and politics. Recently swapping her home town of Glasgow for Boston, Massachusetts, Carole McQueen, a lifelong Celtic fan and season ticket holder rarely missed a home game for over forty years. For that reason, among others, she had a unique perspective on these high-octane encounters. Her Scots-Irish-Lithuanian background suggests something of Glasgow's cross-cultural stew. The city has the largest Lithuanian community in the UK with Celtic's Billy McNeill and Manchester United luminary Sir Matt Busby both hailing from the diaspora. Coming from both Jewish and Catholic traditions, chapels were given a boost by the latter community who had much in common with the immigrant Irish population: Said Carole: 'My family was both Irish and Lithuanian, on the Lithuanian side the big difference was the food you would eat on feast days, my Lithuanian granny would paint eggs with us and put them in a basket at Easter time. My mother was from County Cavan in Ireland, she was illegitimate bless her, the result of my granny and a boatman. My granny lived in the shadows of Celtic Park just off Springfield Road. I used to say I was going to see her and would go to the game instead. Sometimes I would go with an uncle and other times I would go on my own. My first game was against Dunfermline, I was about thirteen and from that point on I had a deep love of Celtic. Whenever I went to see my gran I could feel the ground drawing me in, especially if the game was at night. With the floodlights on, it was magical. My parents lived in Clydebank and my dad was very much a believer that you should support your local team and encouraged me to watch Clyde before that, which was OK, but it wasn't Celtic. This was around the mid-

1960s and I didn't know any other women that went. I stood in the old paddock at Celtic Park with my scarf and tammy close to the running track because that was the only way I could see. The supporters looked after me. If I couldn't see they'd offer me empty beer cans to stand on to get a bit of extra height. I'd loved football since I was a wee girl and I could kick a ball, I couldn't understand why there was no facility for me to play as there is today. I hate prejudice of any kind and I think it stems from that. After the Dunfermline game I saw every game Celtic played, but I couldn't go to Lisbon, my mother wouldn't allow it. I wept buckets, but I have the programme and my scarf was there at least. I saw all the home rounds: Zurich, Nantes, Vojvodina and Dukla Prague.'

Though Celtic would eventually topple back-to-back winners of the 1964 and 1965 European Cup, Inter Milan, who were widely regarded as the greatest European side of the day, among the team, including captain Billy McNeill, it was felt that Vojvodina Novi Sad was the greatest challenge the Lions faced during that campaign. Significantly they were the only side to record a win against Celtic in the competition, which happened in the first tie away from home. The second leg of the quarter-final at Parkhead remains one of the greatest encounters in the club's history, as Carole remembers: 'The game against Vojvodina was the best game of football that I remember in well over forty years as a supporter. They were a confident side; their passing was spot-on. My favourite player at the time was John Hughes, I remember him and Jinky attacking the defence, they were relentless. My memory is that they had slowed the game right down and everything boiled down to the last few moments. It was almost like slow motion watching Charlie Gallagher's cross which Billy McNeill sent sailing into the net after ninety minutes. I'll never forget the sheer adrenalin of seventy thousand Celtic fans going mental at that moment. I almost died of excitement and I don't think I've ever experienced the same intensity as that particular game because we knew they were a great side, but we also knew we could beat them.'

Carole's love of Celtic didn't diminish in adult life despite marrying a diehard Rangers fan and coming from what was perceived as the other side of the cultural, social and religious divide that existed (and to some extent still does exist) in

Glasgow. Similarly, joining Strathclyde Police would not have been a typical choice or experience for a Catholic woman in 1970s Glasgow. Carole explains: 'You could say I had the triple whammy. I was a Celtic supporter, a Christian and a woman. I think people were accepting of who I was; I didn't try to hide it. Glasgow is a tough city and every cop is different, but often if someone was struggling to cope they would ask to pray with me or they'd want to talk something through. When you are dealing with life at its darkest you sometimes need to look to something beyond your immediate world to get you through.

'Football and Celtic remained an important part of my life and who I was. One of the cases I worked on was the tragic death of Mark Scott who was killed outside a pub on London Road. He was on his way home from a game and killed in an unprovoked attack because he was wearing Celtic colours. The killer tried to say in his defence that he was linked with the UDA so he could serve his time elsewhere – that is the mindset you were dealing with. While there was no actual terrorism in Glasgow there was a very strong association with it in the 1980s. It was absolutely there and there was a strong hatred of opposing sides linked to it. I worked for intelligence and on specific match days you'd be looking for certain individuals or groups in particular locations, plain-clothes officers would often be dispersed among the supporters, but that's not so prevalent now. There were a few scary things going on linked to sectarian violence that didn't make the papers, there was often a question over how much the public should know. For me as a Celtic supporter I would get quite angry on a personal level at Celtic being linked to the IRA by some fans. I didn't want my club associated with the atrocities that were going on.

'Another perception in the media is that sectarianism is a west of Scotland problem or a Glasgow problem. I don't think that's true. In reality what you have are tiny groups or gangs of people warring against each other. It's a kind of mini-culture. I think a lot of the government legalisation recently linked to Celtic and Rangers is nonsense. It sets boundaries, but it won't solve anything. It doesn't make inroads into changing the mentality or culture. If people get up in the morning and are motivated to hate someone who is not part of their community or who doesn't support their team, how do you change their minds or their hearts? You don't do it by bringing in legislation or changing policing methods. Since I left the force the sectarian problem has changed. Before, abhorrent views would often be confined to the pub or between a few people in the workplace, now someone can post these negative beliefs on the internet and that has taken things to a new level.'

Carole is clear that for her the so called Troubles in the north of Ireland and a perceived identification among Celtic and Rangers fans from opposing sides of the political struggle has added to the negative connotations of the term 'Old Firm' in the media, among rival supporters and non-football fans with an equal aversion to both clubs' political associations across the sea. Having married a Rangers supporter from the opposite social and religious background, Carole experienced both sides of the divide over a number of years and has a unique perspective on the peculiarities of the culture. Both partners continued to support their respective teams while journeying through the composite nature of Glasgow life together. Says Carole: 'I've seen both sides of the dyke. My husband Billy died a number of years ago, but he was a card carrying Orange Protestant. Some of his family wouldn't come to the wedding because he was marrying a "Tim". My mother was suicidal. Her response was "can you not find a good Catholic boy Carole?" I think I can safely say that my husband was a bigot. Our marriage was an indication of how much we loved each other, and he mellowed as a result of marrying me, but our life together threw up some interesting situations. My mother passed away on 5 July and was buried a week later on the day of the Orange Walk. He said I was the only person who could get him into a chapel on 12 July.

'One of my best friends was Ross Crichton, a priest in the north of Scotland. He grew up as a Rangers fan, but he had a conversion of faith and became a Catholic priest. I went to his ordination with Billy. He didn't know Ross, but he had arranged our seats in the chapel next to his family, it was at Easter time. The next thing Billy was looking at Ross's dad with shock asking what he was doing there, his immediate response was, "More to the point, what are you doing here?" They knew each other from the Orange Lodge, so to find the other in a Catholic chapel at Easter was quite a scene.'

The idea of a die-hard Celtic fan sitting in the Rangers end at Ibrox is a difficult proposition even as a one-off. Scottish writer and Hibs supporter Aidan Smith provided a fascinating insight into what it was like to support his hated rivals Hearts for a whole season, in his book *Heartfelt* (2005), changing not only his colours but his social world, singing the songs designed to antagonise him. It was a brave, humorous and absorbing social experiment. Significantly Carole McQueen sat in the Rangers end regularly not for the purposes of journalism but for love, she explains: 'I never missed a Celtic home game and Billy was the same with Rangers. In those days going away to places like Pittodrie was like going on a foreign holiday, so we agreed a compromise: he would come with me to Celtic Park one week and I would go to Ibrox with him the next. Obviously we didn't wear colours when standing in the home end of each other's team, but it was still quite difficult. In those days you didn't really have the political associations with Northern Ireland or they certainly weren't as obvious at Celtic, but there was that sense that you didn't like Rangers. As you mature, hopefully you grow out of that, but at the same time I see nothing wrong with a healthy rivalry. I always loved to beat Rangers. It's something special and I don't hold back, that passion is positive; it's part of who we are. It shouldn't hamper friendships or partners, but it's still a huge thing. There are so many religious people who have no faith – it's part of a ritual, but they have no relationship with God, it's a cultural thing. Many who adhere to being Catholic or Protestant have no idea what it means to live out a faith and that's when it becomes dangerous. I think people of faith are misrepresented enough in the media without these abhorrent and hateful associations that have become part of some supporters' identities in the name of religion that somehow being a Catholic or Protestant makes you better than someone else. I want to make it clear that I don't think denomination matters.

'I wouldn't describe myself as a religious person because I think that has negative connotations. Often people are described as religious and it's a put-down. I'm much more comfortable talking about a living faith, which I think is what the roots of Celtic are all about. Brother Walfrid was a Christian who responded with practical love to a situation that was much needed in the community. He responded to a need that he saw in the times in which he was living and that still serves as a wonderful example and inspiration. I think it's a wonderful thing for a football club to have that at its core. As society changes to suit the orthodoxy of the day, Celtic's beginnings continue to serve as a marker for what's important in this life. That has always been a cause for celebration among Celtic supporters.'

For many of us Celtic provide a sense of communion, that vital spark that can only be created when many individuals gather to sing in unison, not just to support a team but to anchor themselves with others where there are common ideas, a shared history and a sense of hope. For many 'You'll Never Walk Alone' is not just a football anthem to be recited without thought or feeling, it's a way of connecting with others through life's storms or struggles and that a better day is always coming. Carole neatly illustrates the point: 'Celtic won the league the year that Billy died. I was at the last league game of the season against St Johnstone and it was do or die for us. I had taken my seat on the halfway line near the press box and was moved to tears by the emotion of the day. During 'You'll Never Walk Alone' I was thinking about Billy and looked round to see a whole stadium in unison with scarves held high. Anyone who has lost a partner knows that relationship between a husband and wife is different from any other. There is devastation when you are separated by death that nothing and no one can replace, the isolation can be overwhelming. That day it wasn't unlike being in a church, I felt my spirit soar, I felt an overwhelming joy and peace all at once and I absolutely know my God was with me because while we might have barriers to God, he has no barriers with us. While my husband had been a bigot, no one knows the rivers and ravines he had crossed in his life. A few years before I took him to Celtic Park to see Billy Graham and it was that day he got there by the grace of God. We were sitting that night and he leaned over to me and said: "Carole I believe in God, I know who Jesus is now ... just don't tell anyone it happened in Celtic Park!" After Billy died I went to see the *Jock Stein Story* at the Pavilion. The last scene was when he was in the dugout and had a heart attack and died. I could feel my brother and sister-in-law cringing because it was a heart attack that took Billy, of course, they hadn't thought about what the end scene might be. I know it's quite a painful thing for people to think of Jock going in that way, but my thoughts turned to my experience in Celtic Park and I felt sure that God was with

Jock in the dugout that day as he was with Billy.'

Labour politician Jim Murphy is former Secretary of State for Scotland and former leader of the Scottish Labour Party. Born in Glasgow he is a lifelong Celtic supporter and season ticket holder. Murphy's first game, or at least the first one he can remember, was the Scottish Cup final victory against Airdrie on 3 May 1975 at the age of eight. There is a certain irony then in the fact that an image search for him on the internet is more than likely to reveal pictures of the keen footballer in the colours of Rangers – a result of his often being asked to trade Glasgow's green and white for the blue of his rivals in charity events. But the Old Firm is a concept that Murphy has grown up with and played a big factor in his agreeing to get involved in brokering talks on Rangers' behalf when it was first suggested they were heading towards administration in 2009, the day before he was due to fly to Rome to officially invite the Pope to say Mass at Bellahouston Park. He explains how the complexities of the rivalry didn't affect his decision to take part in the talks, although it does dishevel some in his inner circle: 'Lloyds Bank owned most of the shares in Rangers and the government owned most of the shares in that bank, for me it was a responsible thing to do. But my dad was angry with me,' he laughs before adding: 'That was the Thursday, on the Friday I was meeting the Pope at the Vatican.'

The total effect of Rangers' decline remains to be seen, but as the severity of the club's problems emerged, Murphy felt their absence would affect the health of Scottish football, leading to severe implications for Celtic. He explains: 'It was apparent Rangers were getting into real trouble. I was Secretary of State for Scotland, I know many Celtic supporters will disagree with me here, but I felt it was in no one's interest for Rangers to go to the wall. A few of my Rangers pals phoned me and asked if there was anything I could do. It was my job and I've no qualms about it. I want Celtic to be successful first and foremost, but I want them to be successful in a league that still means something to people.'

Born in 1967 Murphy grew up in a working-class housing scheme in the southside of Glasgow. He experienced the separatist elements of rival supporters growing up in the 1970s. For decades images of the Queen on the Union Jack were used to represent Rangers' unionist associations while the Pope's image was used by the Celtic support to symbolise their Catholic culture, often as a taunting mechanism. The Pope's visit to Britain in September 2010 was the first to be designated as a State Visit as the invitation came from the Queen rather than the Catholic Church in Scotland or England. It was particularly gratifying for Murphy to see these two symbols of opposition unified in the Christian values of democracy and acceptance. In Scotland herself for the pontiff's visit, the Queen expressed a desire to 'deepen the relationship with Catholicism', while acknowledging the Mother Church's role in assisting those most in need. For Murphy this enthusiasm and what it meant for Scotland is palpable. He said: 'To have the Queen, the head of the Church of England, the Pope, the head of the Catholic Church and the Moderator of the Church of Scotland together in that way; that was more than a photograph. This country has come a long way and it's not going to go back to the way it used to be. It was a historic occasion. For me personally it was a big deal, not just inviting him to the UK, but also trying to get him to come to my home city. I didn't want to mess it up. It went fantastically well. I know the Vatican was overwhelmed at how well it went in Scotland and England. It was an antidote to the opinion that faith doesn't matter anymore. I got six letters of complaint, in the world of internet and email where anyone can complain at any time of the day and in abusive terms if they wish, that was an indication of where this country is at.'

Murphy's involvement was something of a personal mission. For a variety of reasons the former Minister for Europe developed an aversion to inherited beliefs and with that came a capacity to question everything he was taught or told. If Murphy was going to support Celtic and hold on to Catholic belief he would examine the personal motives for doing so, as a result his support and faith would be reasoned from his own conviction. The choice wouldn't come from a precarious or misguided positioning of one cultural allegiance above another. He explains: 'Generally in life I'm against inherited opinions, they can create false attitudes and beliefs that cascade through the generations, and I think that's a pretty unhealthy thing. But you do inherit culture from family and grandparents and if it's tied up with a sense of right and wrong and a way to live your life – as long as it's a good lesson – I'm comfortable about it. I inherited an affinity for Celtic through my family, but as

I've developed I've formed my own views, so it's something which stayed with me and I'm pretty happy about it. I've let my own kids make their minds up within reason and they have stayed with Celtic and Manchester City. City is my wife's team, so it's a decent family compromise. My grandparents are from Donegal; we'd go there every year on holiday. My granddad came over in the 1950s. I guess my kids are the first generation who couldn't claim Irish nationality. I'm comfortable being a Scot with an Irish heritage, that's who I am.'

Another event involving Rangers caused Murphy to question his love affair with Celtic. He had spent a significant number of his developing years in Cape Town, South Africa, where the family emigrated after his father was made redundant. The family returned to Glasgow in the mid-1980s sickened by the racism they had witnessed there. As Murphy himself suggests 'every romance has a tiff', and his tiff with Celtic came on 2 January 1988. He explains: 'That moment came for me during the New Year derby at Celtic Park, the incident involved Mark Walters and Celtic supporters. He was the first black player to sign for Rangers and a small minority of Celtic fans started throwing bananas at him. There is no excuse for the way those supporters behaved, it was shameful. It is right that we romanticise Celtic Football Club, we like to think that we have a philosophical outlook and egalitarian beliefs, but it's also important to recognise these vile and embarrassing moments. For me, having just come back from South Africa and seeing some of the things that were going on, it was a hard thing to take. I was at the game and saw it happen, I wanted to be angry, but I was too upset. When you look at the history of any football club you have to talk about these things because it's part of our history, I know it was a minority of supporters, but you still have to talk about it, of course you do.

'It's the same with any organisation be it a political party, church or football club, everybody has a mixed history of good and bad. Even now I feel angry about what happened that day, things can happen at a football club which are outside your control, we put players on pedestals but they can let you down. When Tommy Burns was manager it was a brilliant and entertaining time; in the best Celtic tradition something always happened. I was at Pierre van Hooijdonk's first game. It was a league match against Hearts at Hampden as Celtic

Park was being renovated at the time. The football was always exciting and we had some eccentric European players who were fantastic for Celtic. I think it's fair to say that fans went off him when he said a homeless person couldn't survive on his wages [£7,000 a week]. Did he ever try to live on the streets with nothing? I think that was a real insult. Paolo Di Canio was emblematic of the unpredictability of that team and the players; there was a romance and drama around them. I remember when Di Canio arrived with the leather jacket and motorbike there was a mystery and extravagance. In my mind he went from a beautiful skilful player to a fascist idiot. I've got fond memories of his football, but a perpetual hatred of what he stands for. I know he said he didn't mean it, but if you stand on the track at a football match and give a Nazi salute to your own supporters; that's a big statement to make.

'Players and even your fellow supporters can let you down that's why it's important to look at the roots of the football club. I think the statue of Brother Walfrid remains a rallying call for the original values that formed Celtic. Why was your football club formed? To entertain, of course, but in Celtic's case it was also to help those in need; that was the driving reason for the club's existence. There are few clubs in Europe, if any, with a more important purpose. If Celtic is important to you then you should know why the club exists. When you look at the stadium today there is the sense that we have moved beyond the era of being a community club for the East End of Glasgow. The statue of Brother Walfrid is important being where it is. It's not tucked away in a quiet corner; it's at the front of the stadium for everyone to see. As long as there is a Celtic it's inconceivable that his image could be lost. I don't think a football club is about one person, but if this club is, then it's Brother Walfrid. I think his image could be re-popularised especially in difficult times such as these, perhaps through a charity dinner with his name on it. It's through initiatives like that you can reach a new generation of supporters by showing them the uniqueness of the football club.

'I think both Celtic and Rangers have done a lot of great work for charity. I've played in charity matches at both Celtic and Ibrox. One match was Church of Scotland ministers v MPs to raise money for the homeless. The deal was they were in Celtic jerseys and we were in Rangers. But we can always do more. I think Walfrid's original idea is a rallying point because today we have eleven extremely well-paid men chasing a ball around a park. Growing up Celtic players were people you could identify with, such as Paul McStay or Roy Aitken, these guys weren't superstars but you related to them in a way that perhaps you might not now. It wouldn't be a bad idea if players were encouraged to give ten per cent of their wages to charities in Scotland or around the world because if you look at the geography of Celtic there is still a lot of need in the area. Walfrid's monument shouldn't just be a statue; his legacy has to be more visible. His idea was a club to serve a community, so how do the club and the supporters become part of that living heritage? I was talking to Billy McNeill about this recently. I don't have the answer because these things aren't easy to do. Brother Walfrid's statue remains an emblem of why the club exists and what the club has done, but it's also a challenge to us as supporters. What can we do, how do we live out that heritage as a football supporter, as a dad, as a politician? That's a challenge to everybody.'

In December 2012 Celtic impressed even their most bitter rivals when the club pledged to replace Christmas gifts for the sick children at Great Ormond Street hospital in London, which had been stolen by thieves. It was a generous gesture that tapped into the very heart of the Celtic story and Brother Walfrid's reasons for forming the club. Perhaps in the true spirit of Walfrid the move also led to messages of goodwill on the various websites that carried the story from supporters of Celtic and, more significantly, Rangers. During the Christmas period and shortly after the club's 125th anniversary it was heartening to see these perceived 'natural enemies' find common values and a sense of goodwill granting us a modern example of Walfrid's vision that Celtic can be a unifying institution in society, not exclusive or superior but strengthening for all.

Murphy's childhood was steeped in Celtic. Even when the family left for South Africa it remained an emotive link to home, family and a sense of knowing where you really make sense in life. Coming from an ordinary working class background had a beneficial impact on Murphy's burgeoning political career as well as creating a sense of confidence. He says: 'Growing up in Glasgow my upbringing was relatively poor but not unhappily so with my mum, my dad, my granny and my great granny. We lived on a housing scheme in the south side. Looking back it would be interesting to get into the head of an eight- or nine-year-old and look at what Celtic meant, but on reflection it was an escape, a sense of drama to me was that the team were famous people that you somehow had a relationship with; you had a sense of ownership. To me the Celtic team were famous and successful and they wanted my help as a supporter. It was a happy time, I couldn't always afford to go, I never paid but my dad and two brothers would go on the supporters' bus and I'd get a lift over. It was a bit like going to a film premiere, you had your film heroes like Kirk Douglas, but these heroes were Glaswegian; they gave you a sense of pride in where you came from.

'My bus was Nitshill, it was like a particular insight into a different world. I'm not saying I was sheltered, but it was a subculture, the men on the bus would be smoking, drinking and playing cards, sometimes they would gamble their gate money. There was an intensity, you'd be sitting there drinking your Irn-Bru with a packet of salt and vinegar watching this going on and thinking, if this guy loses the next hand he's not going to the game. They were from mining communities and heavy industry; the politics were left wing.'

By the age of 12 Murphy was supporting Celtic in exile. The relationship remained intact: 'We weren't cut off from Celtic, if anything it became more important and a link to home. We used to get the *Sunday Mail* and *Sunday Post* sent over from my aunt in Townhead. Those were the days before the internet so it would take six or seven weeks to arrive. I wouldn't know the score for six weeks. I'd have a sense of relief about what was happening six weeks after it happened. Three decades ago coverage wasn't what it is now, but we'd occasionally get videotapes, which would get worn out. The television was really cheap racist and vile propaganda. There wasn't much reason to watch so the videotapes of Celtic were like gold dust. I remember Maurice Johnston's first goal against Dundee United in October 1984, I'd watch the game on the tape over and over, and it was great just to get something from Scotland.'

The SFA invitation to long-serving Conservative British prime minister Margaret Thatcher to the Scottish Cup final on 14 May 1988 remains an idiosyncratic moment in Scottish football history. She was summoned to present the trophy to the winners of the Celtic v Dundee United tie that prompted the 'Show Thatcher the Red Card' protest. Particularly in Glasgow there remains a relentless volume of negative feeling towards Thatcherism and the then prime minister's appearance at a Scottish game during the height of her powers caused both remonstration and complaint. The win for Celtic in their centenary year cemented a much-celebrated double that continues to endure in the memory of supporters, but the appearance of the Iron Lady, one of the most unpopular figures in recent political history particularly in Scotland, was deeply resented. A red card distributed by the Greater Glasgow Health Joint Trade Union in protest at health cuts and hospital closures was handed to both sets of supporters on entering the ground who communally raised their cards to the Tory leader. But even in a city that was smarting from unemployment, privatisation and sustained hardship, Thatcher's unwelcome appearance failed to dampen one of the most memorable days in the club's recent history.

Despite challenges, Murphy believes political protest remains a healthy and essential component of the Celtic support and cites 'Show Thatcher the Red Card' as one positive example of communal power among fans: 'Positive protest and politics have been an essential part of Celtic's history, the Sack the Board campaign in the 1993–94 season was an entirely legitimate protest. I was at the game [v Kilmarnock] when the fox ran on the pitch at half-time and there were only ten thousand supporters in the ground. The Scottish Cup final in 1988 was another game where Celtic supporters made their voices heard in protest at Mrs Thatcher for valid reasons. It was the right thing to do because in this city, lives were turned upside down by Thatcher and her pals. She and Major got 18 years between them and she created a hopelessness... she destroyed the working-class responsibility to work. The right to work is why Labour was founded and why it still exists, it was about provision for your family. When the mines closed it created a huge gulf in society, she created a culture where it was no longer a stigma not to get out of bed and go to work, she stole people's dignity. Thatcher created a sense of people saying "What's the point?" She created the sit-at home, watch TV and collect your benefits mentality. In Britain there are a large number of people who can work, but don't – that's the legacy of Thatcher.

'My sense is that this is a city that has never given up on itself. Out of her destruction came an exceptionally political culture and that comes out in writing, theatre and filmmaking, there has always been an old kind of quasi-Marxist aspect to Celtic supporters and there is still a strong sense of class consciousness. Sometimes it takes adversity to find your true self. I'd rather you didn't have the adversity; we are currently living in the worst poverty since the Second World War. If people don't remember the last recession they are certainly being shaken by this one. Ideology among the Celtic support has been important, that doesn't come from the state or the government, it comes from having a sense of responsibility and this government has walked away from its responsibility. As a result of the present Tory government people's lives in this country are going backwards. Times are tough but the cuts are going too far and too deep, they are going to cut people's life chances and that will have a generational effect. It's important that this crowd don't get the same length of time in power as Mrs Thatcher.'

While Murphy suggests Celtic supporters are naturally supportive of left-wing and socialist politics and that it has been a vital characteristic, he is keen to separate those ideals from more violent causes: 'I'm comfortable about sport and politics, it can be a vehicle for positive change. If you take the sports boycotts in South Africa they were massively successful in ending apartheid. Sport and politics mix because sport and society mix; football is not in a vacuum, but that doesn't mean chanting about the IRA is acceptable, it's pretty sick. My general sense tells me that celebrating violence, discrimination or racism is wrong. Or put it another way, why is it right to celebrate anti-racism or anti-fascism and not celebrate racism? Why do we not tolerate people who celebrate racism at football matches? Well, because one is right and one is wrong, that's my value judgement. I think a lot of it is ignorance. Some fans who sing these songs don't actually understand their context or history. It's a world with one dimension for some fans: I mentioned the Mark Walters incident, diaspora communities have a romance, it's one of the things that hold them together, but there's no romance in chanting about the IRA, celebrating that has no place at a football ground at Celtic or anywhere. I think in the past the football club tolerated it, they were too slow in dealing with the problem.'

Murphy was elected as MP for Eastwood after the 1997 general election. As 1996 drew to a close the imminent parliamentarian took his seat at Celtic Park shortly before Christmas for a league fixture with Dundee United. It was a particularly tense time for Celtic supporters and, while the football was impressive, results were less encouraging. In a post-match interview then manager Tommy Burns in his candid Glasgow vernacular was typically philosophical while asking the fans to rally round the team: 'The attitude of the fans has disappointed me. Being a Celtic supporter myself, I know that we are a hell of a group for arguing among ourselves. It can be a healthy thing sometimes, but when it becomes abusive, then it demotivates people. We are doing everything we possibly can to win this title, but if it's not meant to be then it's not meant to be. The players have been low in confidence and, really, I would like a bit more help and for people to show a bit more optimism than they have been doing in recent weeks.'

While buoyant over a much-coveted Celtic victory Murphy was less encouraged when he appeared in the newspapers the next day celebrating behind the game's scorer Phil O'Donnell. He explains: 'During the Fergus McCann era my season ticket was in the front of the Rangers end. It was a pouring wet Saturday just a few days before Christmas and Celtic were playing Dundee United. We needed a win as we hadn't secured three points for several weeks and were trailing Rangers for the title again. After a beautiful cross from Simon Donnelly, Phil O'Donnell, returning after a period of injury, scored with a sublime header at the back post. The main photo in the papers the next day was O'Donnell, the United goalie [Dijkstra] and me; we were the only three in the picture. At that point my career in politics was beginning and there I was in all the papers celebrating the goal. I know Fergus McCann has had a lot of criticism, but on a personal level he helped me out. I just wanted to take my seat at Celtic Park and be myself and shout at the ref if I wanted to without having to worry about a camera on me all the time. As an MP it wasn't the best seat in the house. I wrote to Fergus and explained the situation and within ten days a new season ticket was delivered in the South Stand behind the journalists.'

The last few years have been eventful for Murphy, it's fair to say he lost popularity after becoming a particularly vocal supporter of the "No" campaign during the Scottish independence referendum – a later chapter will look at the politician's role in more detail. 2015 in Scotland saw the Labour Party almost wiped out as SNP won 56 of 59 Scottish seats at the Westminster election. In the aftermath of Murphy losing his East Renfrewshire seat and stepping down as Scottish Labour leader he admitted that his career in politics was over. Prior to these events Murphy cast his mind back to 2003's UEFA Cup final, while he could have travelled in an official government capacity he chose to journey with fellow supporters and soak up the experience as a fan: 'I went to Seville with mates. We had managed to get tickets because the club looked after the fans that went to the Basel game, which was only about 500 supporters. We paid £13 each for our tickets. In our hotel we had strangers sleeping on the floor, people I had never met before. I got to the stadium early as I had a spare ticket for a mate, but he missed his plane, there was no mobile signal so I had no idea that he wasn't coming. I waited outside until just before kick-off, but I wasn't going to miss the game. There were a lot of counterfeit tickets and they were being rejected going into the ground. I saw one man crying at the gate in the baking hot sun. He started telling me he had come all the way from Australia and was in quite a state. So I said to him, "There you go; there's a ticket." By that point he was getting hysterical, so I said: "Look, if you don't stop crying I'll take it off you."

'Seville was a unique moment in our history and one that shouldn't be forgotten, I really hope it happens again. I remember thinking it might never happen again for a Scottish club then Rangers got to Manchester in 2008. It wasn't quite the same, but in a football sense it was peculiar that we both got there within a few years of each other. Rangers did it with a team less talented and in a different style, but they got there, so I'll never say never again.'

Chapter Seven
Magnificent

'Henrik Larsson played a massive part in Celtic's history, and even now I'm still surprised. I knew him from his time at Feyenoord, he was a good player but he wasn't a regular goal scorer. When he went to Celtic I thought; "He'll do well". But there is a big difference between doing well and doing the things he done at Celtic, he became one of the club's most prolific goal scorers; I never thought that would happen.'
Pierre Van Hooijdonk

'We weren't afraid of anybody!'
Henrik Larsson

IT'S ABOUT AN hour and a half's journey from Copenhagen over the border to Sweden. I'm bound for Landskrona, a once industrial heartland. Leaving the Danish capital and motoring across the Oresund Bridge, the longest road and rail bridge in Europe, it's a breathtaking sight to look out to the sea and watch the sunlight float over the Baltic waves on a crisp summer morning. Oresund's majestic beauty doesn't go unnoticed and a central role in the acclaimed Scandinavian crime drama *The Bridge* has brought the structure even greater prominence of late. It's a feat of engineering brilliance that has to be driven across, with a certain amount of faith, to be believed. Not long after leaving this steel masterpiece time seems to evaporate when driving through Landskrona's scenic streets overlooking the sea. I've arrived at a football ground known simply as 'IP' to the local community. There's a well-dressed gent of about seventy standing outside the ground looking around tentatively. He's clutching the familiar sight of a crumpled green Celtic F.C plastic bag while holding tightly to a small black and white Jack Russell terrier tugging the length of its leash. Feasibly it could be a fan waiting for Henrik to autograph something on his way into training. No, the plastic bag belongs to Kurt Hultqvist, a retired referee now handling press duties for his local team. Kurt has a warmth of spirit and goodwill that is uncommon in the world of sporting press relations. He introduces me to Elvis, the small terrier, and notifies me that Henrik will arrive at the ground later in the afternoon. In the meantime we pass a smattering of tourists and fishermen while heading to the appropriately named Seven cafe.

As the sea glistens in front of me, Kurt talks about the time he refereed Cantona in France, his vast Elvis Presley collection, which includes a rare disc of The King performing with the 'female Elvis' Janis Martin. From the King of Rock 'n' Roll our conversation changes gear to the 'King of Kings'. I explain to Kurt that a favourite terrace number, 'Henrik Larsson', was chanted to the tune of an old school hymn, 'Sing Hosanna', during the striker's ascendency at Celtic. It riled some in the support, who felt that a hymn meant for sacred worship dedicated to a footballer was in poor taste, but to take the song in the spirit it was intended, Larsson was indeed a sovereign in the context of Celtic players and Scottish football. His DNA is now embossed on the No. 7 Celtic shirt ad infinitum. During his time at the club Larsson fashioned a new inspirational level as much for his individual character as for his ceaseless and proficient goal scoring. The final measure of greatness was his team-centred attitude. 'It's much the same here in Sweden,' offers Kurt when I suggest something of the player's magnitude in Scotland. He continues: 'Henrik is a much-loved player not just in Sweden and Scotland, but everywhere.

I just got a request from Holland for a book on Feyenoord's most popular strikers. Requests to speak to Henrik come from Spain because of his time at Barcelona, but also from places like Germany and Ireland ... so it goes on.'

Kurt's relationship with Larsson goes back to when the player was trailblazing as a teenager. 'I tell him how good he was even then, but he just says 'no'. In truth, Larsson begins many a sentence with the word 'naw', using the Scottish turn of phrase to play down anything that sounds too dramatic or sensational. It's one of many Scottish-isms that reveal something of the Celtic imprint which remains from his time in Scotia. There's a palpable affection in the way Kurt talks about 'Henke' as we drive back to the ground. At the time of writing Larsson is manager of the Swedish second division club

Landskrona BoIS. Before talking to me he handles a number of local press commitments. I don't speak the language, but I can discern from his body language and delivery the same punch and fortitude he had in his playing days. Determination is in the air. The decision that he would enter management was made long before he retired from professional football in 2009 at the age of 38. On the pitch today the former Feyenoord, Celtic, Barcelona and Manchester United striker is warming up before pulling on an orange training bib. 'Henrik is going to play today,' announces Kurt with an expression that suggests the manager's appearance on the pitch is more irregular these days. A bright South African centre forward, known only as Surprise (Amethyst Bradley Ralani), displays some flagrant skill in a style not unlike his boss. The ball is secure at his feet; he outfoxes two opponents with ease and finishes by nonchalantly hurling the ball past the keeper and into the white netting.

Exactly fifteen years ago to the day Larsson was considering returning to his boyhood team Helsingborgs after a contract wrangle with his then club Feyenoord. There is something almost supernatural about the circumstances that allowed Larsson to move to Glasgow where he would so dramatically flourish. As a player he had previously prospered under the guidance of Wim Jansen, a former Dutch internationalist and part of the Feyenoord team that defeated Celtic in the 1970 European Cup final. A personality clash with Feyenoord's then manager Arie Haan could have put an end to Larsson's professional aspirations indefinitely. The fact that a sports journalist enlightened Jansen, Celtic's surprise choice as manager in the summer of 1997, about a clause in the player's contract opened Parkhead's gates to the Swedish internationalist for a mere £650,000. It remains one of the most astonishing and ponderous twists in Celtic's long and illustrious history.

Today in a small wooden Swedish cabin Larsson reflects on the circumstances, his relationship with Jansen and his introduction to Celtic at a time when their greatest rivals were attempting to win ten Scottish league titles in a row. He says: 'I was almost on my way home to play for Helsingborgs again. Due to my situation in Holland I had grown a little bit tired. He [Jansen] was the one who took me out of Sweden to Holland

and he knew the way I could play football. So when he got that chance to take me to Celtic with him I wanted to go because I recognised I would get a fair chance with him as the manager. I was aware he had a lot of knowledge: he had played in two World Cup finals, a European Cup final and he played for two of the best European teams – Feyenoord and Ajax.

'He is the coach from whom I learned most about how important it is to rest your body and take care of it because it's my tool and my trade. If I hadn't taken care of myself the way I did after that I wouldn't have had the career that I went on to have. I remember one day not long after I came to Parkhead, it was a Thursday – we had been off on the Wednesday – I had a wee hamstring problem but I didn't go to the physio. When he asked me why I said: "Because it was my day off." He said: "When you are injured you don't have a day off." At first I got a little bit angry because I thought that I needed my day away, but I started to understand where he was coming from which was important for me. If I didn't take the treatment when it was needed it was going to set me back long term.

'I also learned a lot from him about tactics. There was a bit of trouble in the beginning, he wanted to play a 4–3–3 formation, but the team didn't really take to that so we had a meeting. He said: "OK, if you are not comfortable with this then we have to change it because you are the ones that are going to have to go out and do this on the park." That to me is leadership because you have to be able to feel and get where the players are coming from, the majority of the team were used to playing the 4–4–2 system. He took that on board and made the best out of us from there.'

Larsson's first domestic season with Celtic got off to an uncharacteristically rough start. A bad pass on his debut at Easter Road allowed Chic Charnley to score a memorable goal that saw Hibs secure a much-coveted 2–1 victory. But as Larsson suggests, Jansen was fully aware of his ability and, after a slight shift in mentality and formation, the player was like dry timber waiting to be sparked: 'I enjoyed playing at a lot of away grounds in Scotland: Aberdeen and Hearts, I loved playing at Hampden; the League Cup final against Kilmarnock and the Scottish Cup final against Hibs were special, but I never liked Easter Road because of the start I had... but I scored a few there anyway.

'I started from scratch when I came to Scotland. That first match wasn't the best and I said to myself: "Henrik, it can't get any worse now, get on with it." At the time I was training well in the practice games and I knew that I had the skills to do it, so that wasn't any problem, but it was just getting that going in the games.'

Larsson found momentum in late August, away to St Johnstone at McDiarmid Park, heading home his first league goal after picking up a sublime cross from Simon Donnelly. It took until the New Year derby for the atmosphere of doom to be vanquished by something more hopeful when another Jansen signing, Paul Lambert, dispatched a thirty-yard blast that thundered into the top right-hand corner of the Rangers' net in an electrifying 2–0 victory. Aided by several new signings, the side gathered strength and a sense of itself with every passing game. Previous teams had buckled under the pressure of expectancy and the brutal dominance of Celtic's Ibrox rivals, but now new blood and a fresh outlook were about to create a shift, said Larsson: 'I didn't understand it [the Rangers rivalry] at all and that was a very good thing. There were several new players in the team that season and many of us didn't realise what it meant, we had no idea. If we had a team of players who were used to Rangers' dominance year after year then I think they would have got the ten in a row. But with our team you had a few players that wanted to get their careers going again and show that they were good players, we all had something to prove and I think that really gave us strength that season. The pressure that I understood after my first few years in Scotland, to have started with that when we arrived . . . that is a mountain to climb.' Larsson trails off laughing at the thought before adding: 'The manager was always calm and he believed in us, I think he knew what he had going. That pressure comes to everyone at some point, the question is can you maintain a focus and ability when you are under it?'

When Celtic missed an opportunity for league victory in the penultimate match of the season at East End Park allowing Dunfermline to equalise late in the game, an overwhelming tension attached itself to the nerves of supporters that would climax during an unforgettable decider against St Johnstone. One Celtic supporter even made a convincing personal plea to Larsson, a vital moment that conveyed the Celtic spirit of

'We're all in this together'. 'That was when it really hit home for me, after we lost against Dunfermline away from home; we had a chance to win the league there. A grown man came up to me at Parkhead. He was crying, he said: "Win this for us next week; you have to win this!" It was then I understood how important it was for the people, for the Celtic supporters, then you saw it.

'I was nervous before the game against St Johnstone. I had never heard Parkhead that quiet; it was a strange atmosphere. You could feel how important it was and it was important for me; that was my first league win as a professional player. Looking back now I get goosebumps thinking about it because we really didn't understand before that game. After that I stayed for seven years, so you get to know more and more about the support, the club, the history and the teams that used to play there. You get an understanding of the whole situation and what it means for the people. In Holland football was big, it meant a lot, but when I moved to Scotland it was so much bigger. Playing Hibs or St Johnstone at home, you are playing in front of sixty thousand in the stands every game, that wasn't happening when I was in Holland.'

The worth of John Clark, Celtic's long-term kit man and Lisbon Lion should never be underestimated. His motivational talks have become an essential ingredient in lighting up many a player's understanding of what it means to play for Celtic. Said Larsson: 'John Clark was fantastic; he would start telling me a bit about it. I didn't know who he was, but after a while he was like: "Come here wee man, follow me." He would tell me the history and showed me the cup with the big ears. I remember him pointing at a picture and saying "That's me there". From that I would learn about Jinky and what he did for Celtic. It was fantastic, it's like theatre to go out there and entertain like that, but not everyone can be an entertainer, the team wouldn't be balanced. You want somebody like that who has that bit extra, if you have two or three like that in a team then fantastic, but you need at least one of them if you are expected to win every game like at Celtic. What I tried to do was score goals and everybody finds that entertaining, it's as simple as that.'

Wim Jansen's successor, Dr Jozef Venglos, was the subject of some unnecessary derision in the Scottish media around the time of his appointment. But it didn't take the team long to shake off the atmosphere of negativity with some truly memorable and thrilling football. Venglos brought in both dazzling and essential players such as Lubo Moravčík and Johan Mjallby. The team also included a number of rogue Celts whose attitude towards the club at times was contemptible, but who could be captivating in a green and white hooped shirt. Among them were Mark Viduka and the John Barnes transfer Eyal Berkovic. Just four days after signing for Celtic Viduka headed home to Australia stating he was 'too stressed' to play for the club.

It was a move that Viduka never truly recovered from: said Larsson: 'I learned a lot during that time, I didn't know who he [Venglos] was before he came because he had been working in eastern Europe, but I discovered straight away he knew what he was talking about and what he wanted out of me, though I was a little bit older by this time. It was a question of linking me with the other players and he knew how to do that well, I had a great partnership with Viduka.'

If Henrik Larsson's Glasgow story represents anything it's perseverance. During the 1999–2000 season the player broke his leg in a freak accident during a UEFA Cup match in Lyon. To the supporters the injury had the magnitude of a Shakespearian tragedy as Larsson's Celtic career hung in the balance. In truth it was the curtain falling on the first act of a vocation that had begun with great promise. Just days before the trip to Lyon, Celtic had regained an infectious confidence and capacity to thrill which culminated in a 7–0 thrashing of Aberdeen at Celtic Park. Moravčík provided a relentless onslaught of majestic crosses and corners, the trickery and unyielding confidence of Larsson, Viduka, Moravčík and Berkovic blindsided the opposition and left a rousing Celtic support in raptures. But without Larsson the team were incapable of beating Rangers in four league encounters and lost 3–2 at home to Hearts after starting the match with a convincing 2–0 lead. The writing was on the wall before John Barnes's Celtic finally imploded by losing 3–1 to Inverness Caledonian Thistle in the Scottish Cup.

I remind Larsson of the season that John Barnes took over at Parkhead. He recalls: 'I scored twelve before I broke my leg, it was early in the season but it probably would have been different if it hadn't happened. I knew a bit about John Barnes. I had been sitting at home watching him play for Liverpool and England, but I don't think he fully understood what it meant to be manager of Celtic.' As the team dissolved without Larsson, the player had a battle of his own to deal with as he tried to gauge if his time as a professional football player had reached an untimely end. As he suggests, motivation comes from a strange place and the enforced exile only made him more dogged. As doubt diminished strength was regained and his life slotted back into focus: 'The thing is I love playing football, if I still could do it today I probably would. When you are away for such a long time and you are not allowed to do the thing you love the most you want to get back there straight away. I also had great help with a fantastic surgeon, Billy Leach, and my physio Brian Scott, they helped me a lot with rehab. Graham Quinn the masseur at the time also helped and so did Kenny McMillan who is still fitness coach at the club. Brian and Kenny used to run with me on the treadmill for 20-minute intervals. I don't think I've ever been in better shape, before or since. I did strength training a lot with Jim Hendry; we did a lot of squats so I was strong. Without them I don't think it would have been possible.

'While I was recovering I spent a lot of time with my best friend, the couch. I started reading because it was boring watching television all the time. It was mainly to pass the time and get my mind to relax. I started reading Michael Connelly's Harry Bosch books and I read the Kurt Wallander novels by Henning Mankell. I didn't read a lot about football. I like music and those were the days when MTV would play music on television. It wasn't all reality shows like it is today. I like a lot of music, though it depends what kind of mood I'm in, but I don't really have idols outside of sport. Pelé was my first idol and then Michael Jordan. I really loved what he did with Chicago Bulls, also being MVP in all the finals is so demanding and he wanted to be the best. That's something I got a lot of inspiration from, looking up to world-class athletes, because I know what it is they want to do. I recognise the drive and the will to not always look out for your own best interests, to have no self-preservation I think you would say in English, to just completely empty yourself when you get the chance because there is no tomorrow, there are no regrets, you should try to do everything and not think after the game has finished I should have done this or that, you must try to do everything you can. The feeling I get when I look at a basketball player like Michael

Jordan is that it didn't matter how he won ... as long as he won.'

Another player the young Larsson admired was Kenny Dalglish, who at the time had reached his zenith at Liverpool F.C. Sitting watching television with his father in the coastal city of Helsingborg the pair of them were dazzled by the archetypal No. 7 striker. In truth, no goalscorer had surpassed Kenny Dalglish's popularity and accomplishments since his lamentable departure from Celtic in August 1977. It was another strange twist of fate that would see Dalglish pass the baton to Larsson for the second act of the player's Celtic career. Having stepped in as temporary manger from his role as Director of Football in the aftermath of John Barnes's sacking, Dalglish stabilised the club somewhat with victory in the League Cup final against Aberdeen. His next big decision was when to bring Larsson back. After a tentative exchange Larsson was reunited with the green and white hooped No. 7 shirt 65 minutes into the last game of the season against Dundee United.

Larsson recalls: 'I had to speak with Kenny Dalglish before coming back. I'd had a setback against Hearts in an under-twenty one game up in Ayr, I got a kick to my leg and it hurt so much I thought I'd broken it again. So I went away for a few days with [former Celtic defender] Marc Rieper to Portugal. He was injured at the time as well and had been doing some work for Danish television. I could hardly walk, but we played a round of golf anyway just to get out and get away from everything. When I came back I said to Kenny that I wanted to play and that I wanted to have a chance to go to the Euros. He said: "I'm not sure. Come back tomorrow, I'll talk to you then." So I went back the next day and he was in his normal mood. I thought fucking hell he's going to say no to me, but he turned around and said: "I'll give you half an hour tomorrow." I was so happy, it was like getting another shot at that thing you always wanted to do.'

As players both Larsson and Dalglish were able to pierce the Scottish psyche with something more meaningful. They also showed little interest in the media. In contrast to the typical and sensationalist headlines often associated with top-flight professional footballers both these Celtic heroes articulated a family image that set fans an example on the football field as well as in life. Speaking in 2010 on the subject of family Dalglish offered: 'I loved playing football . . . but my family is the most important thing to me and it always will be.

But if someone wants to recognise you that's quite humbling, you go out and try and do your best and if you please some people then fine but the most important thing for me is my family.'

Before Larsson's return to action, Dalglish held a memorable press conference in Bairds Bar. It was not a popular move with journalists and further illustrated his attitude towards the media. If they wanted a quote they would be getting it on his terms among Celtic diehards.

Prior to breaking his leg, rumours of bids for Larsson were estimated at £10 million and Manchester United in particular were said to be keen on the Celtic striker. The transfer stories persisted at various stages throughout his seven years in Glasgow. In truth what Larsson had found at Celtic couldn't be purchased; the player had secured a steady course at the club and a settled home in Scotland to raise his young family. The unique chemistry he enjoyed with the Celtic support shouldn't be underestimated; it gifted an atmosphere of confidence around the club that soared above the narrow confines of Scottish football. In the modern game, where changeability is second nature and moving to a perceived bigger club for vast sums is a fact of life, Larsson displayed an unusual strength of character to see that, for a multitude of reasons, these moves seldom recompense. The player wasn't about to trade his new-found confidence to find out and he would eventually prove his worth to the doubters on Europe's biggest podium.

At Celtic Henrik Larsson found a definitive role that led to him becoming not just one of the most successful and popular players in European football, but also one of the most popular among his fellow professionals. Fathers would point to Henrik as an example to their sons and his choices and conduct is as significant as the goals he scored in a football culture that's often highlighted some of the most unpleasant pitfalls of the human condition. In contrast Larsson strengthened the values that have existed around Celtic since their formation, the synthesis between player and club can be traced back to the Swede's background and the sensibilities with which he was raised from an early age. Born on 20 September 1971 Henrik Edward Larsson grew up in a background fashioned by traditional working-class values twinned with a strong work ethic. His parents worked rotating shifts in order to provide for

Henrik and his two brothers. The instinctual and consequential value system at work in his career began in early childhood, much of which his father passed on through a love of football.

An association with the game was a subject where positive ideas, ambitions and beliefs could be translated. As Larsson points out, he was encouraged to have a ball at his feet from an early age: 'I was always out on the pitch. You didn't have the toys that you have today, I think that was important because rather than sitting on the PlayStation with friends I'd go out and play football. You would always get something from watching tactics and get some ideas; you start to get the feel of the ball at your feet. Today you are losing hours, you can't go out and play for seven hours now, it's very difficult even to go out for an hour or two every day. We lived in flats, my parents did everything in their power to give me a good upbringing with morals and a good home. They both worked in a factory. Mum worked in the morning and came home around two then dad went out to earn more money, but we always had three weeks of holidays to either Portugal or Spain. They worked their butts off to give me and my two brothers the chance to have a good holiday every summer. We didn't always have the best food and things like that, but they gave us love and what more can you ask? They were trying to give us a better upbringing than they had themselves and to give us more than they had. That is part of being a parent; you want to give your kids everything you can and a better chance to succeed. Today you have to have an education: without education you don't get a job and if you don't have a job you can't pay bills, it's simple maths.

'I worked on the floor [packing fruit] and I didn't enjoy it. I said to myself: "This can't be the meaning of your life Henrik", but I didn't have the best education so there was not much more for me to do.' Larsson's next job was as a youth worker. It was an experience he's still drawing on even today: 'If you get the opportunity you take it, I had the chance to do something better than working with fruit. I really learned from that experience because you get to know people, you get to learn things like body language and the things you can't learn if you don't work. I learned to read people and how they really are. Either it's me or something else, but I've never been in a dressing room at Celtic or anywhere where there was a bad atmosphere. You always had players that you didn't like, but you don't need to socialise with them and you can still play with them for the benefit of the team. It's impossible to like and be liked by everybody, but you just have to get on with it. Football is a hobby turned professional so you have a responsibility, you always have to have that attitude, as long as the people you don't get on with leave you be.

'The things I learned in those early jobs are important even as a coach, they help me to see if the players are frustrated and find out what is wrong with them. Is it something at home, is it me, is it the team, the situation they have in the team? That is invaluable experience. I admire people that can work their whole life in a factory as my parents did because we need those people that are able to do a job like that for a long time, not everyone can do other jobs so to speak.'

Larsson's popularity with the Celtic fans is unprecedented. Over 600 of them made the journey to his birthplace when the club were drawn against Helsingborgs in a Champions League qualifier in August 2012 while the man himself was 500 miles away on managerial duties with Landskrona against the green and white of Hammarby. The trip was an evocative one for supporters, loaded with meaning and many visited the site that hosts a bronze statue commemorating the former number seven. Since he left Glasgow there's been a culture of pilgrimage to places and clubs associated with the player by fans keen to keep up their association. There's palpable warmth from Larsson at the thought of the Celtic support: 'They came to see me in Helsingborg, Barca, Manchester ... home and away ... everywhere they came. If I knew they were there I would always talk with them after the game. They love it when you go to supporters' functions and I understand it's important because it's a chance to meet their heroes, but I didn't do too many of them. I remember one which was after I signed for Celtic, I was playing in a friendly with Sweden against Ireland and I went to a Celtic function in a hotel, there was a lot of fans there and it was a strange experience, you know how it can be, sometimes people have one too many and want to sit on your knee or something. It's important to keep a balance. It's like when you see your name and number on the back of someone's jersey, you never get used to something like that, but I feel proud when I see it and I always had a fantastic relationship with the supporters.

'I think it changed around the time when Venglos came. I scored sixteen league goals in my first year and that's OK in your first season, but I don't think they knew how it would be. I think they weren't sure at first because I wasn't the biggest player and there were some doubts whether I could cope with the physical demands of the Scottish League. But in my next season I scored twenty- nine and then something began to change.' Larsson proved that he had one of the most important qualities asked of any Celtic player during the season in question – that he could score against Rangers – and he did it with relish 15 times. Firstly with a brace in Venglos's triumphant 5–1 obliteration of the Ibrox club at Parkhead and again with the equaliser away from home in the New Year derby.

The mid- to late 1990s were generally optimistic times. The honeymoon period under New Labour saw out the century and working class rock 'n' roll such as The Verve and Oasis dominated mainstream tastes and fashions. In Scotland Dolly the sheep made global headlines as the world's first cloned mammal and in the Republic of Ireland divorce was legalised for the first time – the world was going through some dramatic shifts and Celtic was about to go through a vital transformation of its own. With Henrik Larsson the club were granted their first postmodern superstar. When he arrived he looked like the coolest player on the planet, sporting Rastafarian dreadlocks reined back with an Alice band. 'I wondered how this blond Rasta was going to cut it in the SPL,' Simple Minds front man Jim Kerr once remarked. The player also developed the post-goalscoring ritual of sticking his tongue out: 'It just happened and I stuck with it until I got too many letters from upset parents and I stopped. It was a spur of the moment thing, you see yourself and you think why not?' This iconic image of a celebrating Larsson has become an enduring symbol that summons much joy from a particular era in Celtic's history, as permanent as Billy McNeill holding up the European Cup in 1967 or Kenny Dalglish at his peak in the 1970s sporting a feather cut while displaying the number on his shorts. As Larsson himself admits he once carried more than a passing resemblance to the reggae legend Bob Marley: 'I liked the music and I liked the way he looked.' Marley's son Rohan once claimed to be a Celtic supporter, revealing a desire to play for the club, and former Celtic player Dixie Deans also claimed the Jamaican singer was a Celtic fan with an awareness of the values around the team after meeting him during a spell at Adelaide City.

A glance over Celtic's greatest ever team, as voted by fans in 2002, confirms Larsson as the first non-Scottish born player to make the grade, the first and significantly the last player to join this elite category since Paul McStay. Celtic's Wikipedia entry on the subject reveals eleven blue flags, the splash of yellow on the final mini-pennant exchanging St Andrew's white saltire for a Scandinavian cross. But the Swedish flag only tells part of Larsson's story. Shortly before his retirement from playing he travelled to Cape Verde where his father was born. It was the first time he had visited his patriarch's ancestral home. Situated 350 miles from the coast of western Africa the island country is predominantly Christian, 85 per cent of which is Roman Catholic. 'I went there in 2008 with my father. Before that I didn't have a clue what it was like. He is eighty-one this year and I wanted to see where he came from and meet some people who looked like me. I wanted to see how he had it. It was a great journey and experience for me to go see the small village in which he was born and the places where he grew up. I've always felt Swedish, but I knew I had something else as well. It was great to see those things.'

Perhaps not unlike the Celtic supporter who traces his or her Irish ancestry or the club's historical narrative that has promoted the best traditions of both Irish Catholicism and Scottish Protestantism through the merits of iconic men such as Jock Stein and Tommy Burns, Larsson has embraced the influence of the two cultures that shaped him. As our conversation turns to issues away from the game, he admits that the racism he suffered as a boy disintegrated with success: 'It's strange, but when you become good at something people don't see the race anymore. In the beginning I had to fight for it, but if you win the fight they are not going to dare say it to you anymore.' While living in Glasgow he had to deal with some controversial issues such as the intense rivalry with Rangers. Keeping a healthy distance from the press he was aware how quotes could be fashioned and presented by the media, particularly around the Glasgow derby when the entire country could appear flushed with fervour: 'While at Celtic I didn't read the papers and I tried to stay out of the media as much as possible, I had great help from Celtic's PR department. I would do interviews sometimes, but the thing is, when you talk, it's in the papers and it's not right sometimes before a big match. I didn't want any distractions from the game, I just wanted to go out and play and let that do the talking.'

As the most famous player in Scotland at the time, he was sharp enough to withdraw from the majority of press interviews, creating an enigma that eludes most modern footballers. While he did speak out about racism he stayed away from discussing the bigotry that hangs over the Scottish game. But no doubt about it, Larsson was aware of it and he grew to understand the Irish and socio-religious identity of the Celtic support. The culture around Celtic and Rangers matches was something he started to learn about long before arriving in the city. Says Larsson: 'I knew that Rangers fans burnt flags after they signed the Catholic player in the 1990s, but with Celtic, from what I understood, there was never a problem – if you want to come and play then come and play as long as you are good enough. I knew a bit because of Pierre [van Hooijdonk], they would show the odd match in Holland.'

After his arrival Larsson also came to understand the positive values advocated by Celtic's global support: 'The history is important. It is very hard for the foreign player to fully understand, but I think I know a little bit about what Celtic means to people and how it got started. It's great to see something that was started, as I understand, as something to take part in when you are not working, instead of being out and doing things you shouldn't be doing. I don't think the founder realised it would ever be as big as it is and the impact it has on people all around the world. I hear people talk about Celtic not being a big club. I just shake my head. I've never been anywhere in Europe where you don't have Celtic supporters. You go to the States, you go anywhere in the world, you will find Celtic supporters, it means a lot. You have to talk a little bit about religion. Take this club, for example [Landskrona], the city has a bad name so only the negative stuff is written about, the shit. The fact is that everybody does wrong: Catholic, Protestant, Buddhist, show me the man that never did anything wrong, simple as that. The important thing is to get more positives out of it than negatives. I never used to talk about religion when I was there, but I believe in something. Who is that? God,

Allah, Buddha, who is it? I don't know, show me the man or woman who can say who it is . . . but I believe in something spiritual, yes, and I believe there is something up there and I believe in something after we leave here. As long as you don't hurt anybody you can believe and do whatever you want. In Scotland I didn't understand it completely so I could never put myself in the situation when people talked about how the Irish or Scottish had it. I have never been judged for my religious beliefs so I couldn't put myself into that situation. I made sure from the beginning that I didn't get involved.'

The sense of purpose in Larsson's career flowing with Martin O'Neill's managerial knowledge of getting the best of a player's individual skill created the strongest and most popular Celtic team arguably since the days of the Quality Street Gang. In his seven years at Parkhead Larsson cemented his position as one of the most celebrated strikers in the club's soaring history. He showed a conviction of mind and carved out his own expression, niche and personality within the team without trotting out clichés about home fans or the obligatory badge kissing. It was clear he was settled in Scotland and be it east Ayrshire on a wet Wednesday or a midweek glamour tie in Europe he was continually consistent and committed. The appearance of Larsson ensured Scottish grounds would be packed with spectators on both sides eager to feel the charge of loose electricity in the atmosphere. In a climate where opposition players are savaged, Larsson managed to transcend the usual hatred that was dispensed liberally by rival supporters. It's perhaps a stretch to say he evoked admiration en masse, but even the most indignant Rangers zealot would be a liar to himself if he couldn't admit the player's ability to make us all gasp. His was a talent that enriched the health of the Scottish game.

The Scottish Cup is a competition attractive to even the most casual football watcher and Larsson didn't fail to decorate it with goals. Among his personal favourites were a diving header against Dundee United in the 2001 semi-final at Hampden and a left-footed wonder goal against Hibs in that year's final. During the O'Neill years he became a household name in Scotland and his association with Celtic grew as considerable as Eric Cantona's with Manchester United or Lionel Messi's with Barcelona. These relationships are likely to remain undiminished through time not just because of the players' sheer abilities, but also because of the prolonged relationship each player had with his respective club and its supporters, which has left a legacy unlikely to be superseded. In 2008 a Sportingo poll nominated Larsson's move to Celtic as the greatest transfer of all time.

Larsson suggests that the arrival of Martin O'Neill at the start of the 2000–01 season brought about a vital transformation in the behaviour and mentality of the players at Celtic. At a stroke the new manager eliminated the controversial player culture that had allowed Mark Viduka and Eyal Berkovic to put their temperamental natures above the needs of the side. However, despite scoring for Sweden against Italy in Euro 2000, Larsson himself was absent from the Celtic team sheet for a friendly against F.C Copenhagen. His non-appearance was conceivably the new manager's way of showing that the power had shifted. Players had a choice of either yielding or walking, irrespective of their status: 'I knew that physically I was OK, but I didn't know if I would get the chance to play again. Every time a new manager comes in [O'Neill was Larsson's fourth boss at Celtic] you have to prove yourself again. He read out the team and I wasn't in the starting eleven. I thought OK, nothing much to do today. You feel sometimes when people come into the room that you have to listen and I felt that straight away when he read out the team. It took time to get to know him, but I learned so much: how to motivate players, not in the big games because you don't need any motivation there, but the small games, you need to get players focused from the beginning. He had you focused from the second the referee blew the whistle.'

O'Neill created a Celtic squad that had both athletic mettle and the aptitude to thrill. For Larsson a key ingredient of this was a rejection of individualism, much like the team that conquered in Lisbon, egoism was seen as detrimental to the health of the side as a whole. Players with narcissistic tendencies or an inability to tune in to O'Neill's aspiration of building a team in the spirit of the Lisbon Lions were quickly shunted. The former No. 7 striker suggests that the new belief around the team wasn't based on any one individual talent. A rare synergy had taken place that was more than the sum of individual parts: 'For goals Lubo [Moravčík], Chris Sutton and Alan Thompson were all important, but I would also have to add Stiliyan [Petrov] and [Didier] Agathe to the list, the goals all came from combinations of those players. The team we had then with defenders like [Johan] Mjallby and Joos Valgaeren and the midfield with Paul [Lambert] and Lenny [Neil Lennon], I would play with all of them again any day; they were all fantastic players and we were quite a side.

'Lubo was a very intelligent football player, he had such a great touch with his right and left, you link up with good players straight away and you understand each other and connect in a different way. I also had a great understanding with Alan Thompson as well, I mean I would just go off the shoulder of the defender and I knew the ball would come from him and he knew that I would do that run. Under Martin, Lubo was used in a different way, you can't forget he was a little bit older at that time, but he was still fantastic to play with. Martin used to say to him: "Don't go into your own half, stay up there", and if we won the ball we would try to give it to him. I'd do a run or maybe Agathe, it was different, but I think that Martin got a little bit more out of him. Lenny didn't score many goals, but he knew what he was good at and he knew what he was supposed to do in that team. When you get players like that who know exactly what is expected of them then it becomes a self-run team. If he [O'Neill] didn't like some player or thought someone was not playing in the right way, he would tell them and if they didn't listen and better themselves then they wouldn't play and more often than not they would leave the club in the end.

'I didn't mind not to score because if I see somebody in a better position I might as well give him the ball because if the team wins then that is the most important thing. I think the mentality is typical Swedish. There are other situations when you are 4–0 up and you shoot yourself, I think that's natural. I was always involved in team sports growing up. I don't understand wanting to be an individualist; if you want that then go into track and field. It means more to share success with friends. I used to think, for example, if you go on a golf course on your own and hit a hole in one, who do you celebrate with . . . yourself? Fun? No, if you have a few mates it's a much better experience and the more the merrier.'

Under O'Neill, Larsson would become the first and only Celtic player to win the European Golden Shoe, in the 2000–01 season. It was also the first time Celtic had won the domestic

Treble since 1969. O'Neill's Celtic had dealt a serious blow to the atmosphere of superiority around Rangers. Since crushing their ambition of ten league titles in a row, the following two league titles would also be won by the team from south-west Glasgow. The Northern Irishman's side quickly showed it had the capacity to create a durable shift that would prevent Rangers from regaining the confidence of previous eras. Comments Larsson on Celtic's greatest rivals: 'I was never scared of any of them, Craig Moore used to like to kick me and who was the other player . . . Amoruso? I never felt I couldn't score against any of them, they were good football players, but I never felt I couldn't beat any one of them in the air or couldn't muscle anybody off. Even though I wasn't that big, I was quite strong. There was eventually something like fourteen internationals in that Celtic team, we weren't scared of anybody, and we knew we had the quality to beat them. In the 6–2 game it was important for the new players like Chris Sutton. He won his first Old Firm game; I lost mine. After you beat Rangers, you know you've done it and you can do it again. You sow a little doubt in the opponent's head; they saw how strong we were and Chris scored early.

'With Martin, you listen to the man when he talks, Steve [Walford] and John [Robertson] had a lot of knowledge too, but in certain situations you have to just do it yourself. The gaffer can only send you on to the pitch with instructions and then you have to do it, it's down to you; you have to solve the problems yourself. He gave us the freedom to try different things; I think that was great leadership. It was such a great feeling beating Rangers, that team very rarely lost against them during the time O'Neill was there.'

That first season under O'Neill was a career peak for Larsson. The Golden Shoe award had silenced critics who, in the usual repetitive manner, suggested the striker's merits were lessened by playing in Scotland. After scoring a total of 53 goals, that honour would be the first of many European achievements that would fuel the player's public profile while quietening his detractors. Throughout the season it wasn't just competition in Scotland the player was challenging. S.S Lazio's Hernan Crespo also coveted the glittering prize for Europe's most prolific goalscorer. In accordance with the rules, goals scored in non-major European leagues, like Scotland, were worth 1.5 points in comparison to 2 points for each goal scored in Serie A, effectively increasing Crespo's total by 25 per cent. Larsson reflects on the time: 'It was a fantastic season all the way through and we played fantastic football, the belief we had was unbelievable. You sometimes looked at the opposition and thought "They could play anywhere in the world, but they couldn't play for Celtic", that's how good we were and it felt great. With the Golden Shoe, Crespo was the one who was after me. I remember sitting at home on the couch; I didn't play in the last league game of the season because of a problem with my hamstring so I was watching the game on Teletext and he scored . . . but he needed to score two and I saw that I had won the Golden Shoe. After that people stopped criticising me because I scored in World Cups, European Championships and European competitions with Celtic so there was no smoke anymore, everything was out.'

* * *

Today, a little more advanced in years, decked out in a black anorak and joggers with salt and pepper hair and the now familiar moustache and goatee, Larsson looks every inch the football magus. At the time of our interview he is the gaffer to a new crop of players who looked to him for advice and inspiration. If you're over the milestone of thirty and reading this it's likely you were in Seville or will have at least a significant memory of watching the UEFA Cup final in 2003 and the season that led to one of the most significant occasions in Celtic's history. I can't help but wonder if any of the players under Larsson's guidance understand what that match meant or if they themselves will ever experience what it means to play for a club like Celtic and reach the career pinnacle of a European final. Says Larsson: 'When they talk about pressure I tell them I was seven years in Glasgow; they don't know what pressure is. You can reach some level [with talent], but you won't reach your full potential unless you are willing to put in the work. Sometimes when I look at my players, I wonder if they are willing to sacrifice everything to get to where they want to go. It's easy to say it because it's just words, but before you say it you have to think it through. I try to talk to them about my experiences; they all know who I am. Sometimes I wonder if they really understand, they are young kids and not all of them will make a proper living out of it, maybe only one or two.'

In the 2001–02 Champions League, with his long dreads traded for a close crop an inch from the skin, Larsson proved a dangerous presence for European defences. That season he would find the net against Juventus, Porto and Valencia, the latter in the UEFA Cup. Celtic's horizons had widened and their promise was once again visible on Europe's biggest stage against the most reputable and best teams in the world. The events of the following season remain paramount in the living memory of Celtic supporters. It's now over ten years since the final and it remains one of the most considerable European evenings in Celtic's history. You can sense a tangible joy as Larsson reels off the teams Celtic beat to reach their destination: 'The whole road to the final was fantastic, really, really good. I remember us shouting "men against boys" in the dressing room after Blackburn; it was so good to give them a slap in the face. John Hartson was another important player in that team, he wasn't too mobile, but he could make space and he could score goals. I remember before the Liverpool game O'Neill was saying "Make sure you don't have any regrets tomorrow; no regrets."'

Understandably the final is an event that the player has been reluctant to discuss in the past, particularly in the immediate aftermath. Today the grief of not winning has been exchanged for a more philosophical expression. Before he speaks about it, he lifts up the sleeve of his anorak to show the hairs on his arm standing on end. Like the rest of us he remains in awe at the thought, anticipation and hope of what the final represented. It is at the very least a feeling worth recollecting from time to time: 'The club had been waiting for the final for such a long time. We got there and we didn't win, that was just shit. I scored two good goals in the final; it should have been enough to win the game. I don't remember much but I remember the bus going to the game with Chris, Thommo, Jackie [McNamara] and Lenny just sitting and talking. It was a great day for us; one that we had been fighting for, for a long time, not just for ourselves but against everybody who said the Scottish league was shit. To go and win against the teams that we beat and then not win the final ... to wake up the next day without that gold winner's medal ... what a terrible feeling. I don't remember a lot because it is something I more or less erased out of my memory; it was just too painful. I have to admit today that I can talk about it because I am not as angry anymore.

'In the game that first header was fantastic, even if I can say that myself, there is no angle to get the ball in. But to score two goals in the final when it's not expected of you, I can say I scored two goals, I couldn't do anything more, so maybe that gives me a little bit of closure to the whole thing.'

Larsson was granted a second opportunity to show his capabilities in another European final in 2006, this time for Barcelona against Arsenal. The aftermath of this event would be in sharp contrast to the stark sunrise that greeted him when waking in Seville. Three years on Larsson would rise in a Parisian hotel room to hear Barcelona fans singing 'Campeones' safe in the knowledge that he had earned a Champions League winner's medal by setting up two goals from nothing. The echoes of unknown revellers in rapture must never have sounded more satisfying. In the days after the match two of Larsson's fellow professionals honoured him with tributes that clear the scale of his contribution. Reflecting on Larsson's retirement at Barcelona Ronaldinho had this to say: 'With Henrik leaving us at the end of the season this club is losing a great scorer, no question, but I am also losing a great friend. Henrik was my idol and now that I am playing next to him it is fantastic.' In a postmatch interview that was gracious in defeat Thierry Henry added: 'People always talk about Ronaldinho and everything, but I didn't see him today, I saw Henrik Larsson. Two times he came on, he changed the game, that is what killed it. Sometimes you talk about Ronaldinho and Eto'o and people like that. But you really need to talk about the proper footballer who made the difference tonight and that was Henrik Larsson.'

The quotes both from an opponent and a team-mate had Celtic supporters' hearts bursting with pride, there was also a feeling of vindication: 'Two half-decent players as well eh?' laughs Larsson today. 'To get accolades from fellow professionals who are also great football players, it's the best you can get because they know the game, how hard it is and what the demands are on you, it felt great to get that from those players. I was two years at Barcelona; I came there a bit-part player. If you compare Ronaldinho and me, what I was at

Celtic was quite similar and for me it was quite refreshing to see how he would deal with it, he would come in with a smile or a joke every morning and then I saw him on the pitch having a fantastic time. He played at Celtic Park so he knew my status at the club and when we came back he saw it first hand, he was a far better football player than me, but there we connected because we both knew what it meant to have that enormous pressure to always deliver. They all loved to play there [Celtic Park], they would talk about what an atmosphere it was and how fantastic the fans were always singing, you could ask all the players who have been there, they had never seen anything like it before.'

Larsson's seventh season at Celtic was always going to be a poignant matter. The strains of 'You Are My Larsson' sung to the American folk ballad 'You Are My Sunshine', albeit with an expletive about Newcastle striker Alan Shearer, was undoubtedly the most prevalent song about the Celtic talisman during his seven-year tenure and at times you could hear the fans emotionally crack while chanting it in that 2003–04 season. Aside from being the figure on his shirt, seven makes up the number of letters in each of his names and features in the year he signed for Celtic. Larsson's Celtic career had followed a pattern. Hearing the theme to *The Magnificent Seven* soundtracking the player's goals never sounded more affecting than on his final league appearance at Celtic Park when he scored a brace against Dundee United in May 2004. It was also somewhat appropriate that he would bow in opposition to the team he made his comeback against four years earlier. The support, although palpably sorrowful, were accepting that after seven years Henrik's desire to move on was something of a natural end, with Larsson offering that he had taken his role at Celtic as far as he could.

Today he reasserts it was the right decision and felt a relief after shedding the cumbersome expectations of the Scottish media. He wasn't about to watch what he had built into Celtic's history weaken and the player was adamant he would leave the club at a peak with a Scottish League and Cup Double. 'Being under pressure for a long time takes its toll. As well as playing for Celtic it was about being the best player in Scotland, it was a lot of pressure so for me to go to Barca and just be one of the bit-part players was fantastic. Constantly you have to be aware how you play and in the end it wasn't fun. If I didn't score in two games, it was "Ah, it's not the same old Larsson",' he offers with a smile, 'and then I would score a hat-trick. In the end I think the demands from the media became a little bit too high, but I still delivered.'

Even the heightened powers of Martin O'Neill couldn't keep Larsson at Celtic: 'I remember saying to O'Neill that I would not sign my new contract and he said he wanted to have a chat with me. I said I just want to stop while I'm ahead because it's been a fantastic time for me here and it's time for me to move on now and do something else. At that point I didn't know what I was going to do next season, so I was able to be honest and say: "I don't know". I didn't understand the significance of what I was doing at the time; I don't think I understood what being at Celtic meant to me until I was crying on the last day of the season. I almost get tears in my eyes now when I talk about it. I remember walking into Parkhead on the last day of the season and I'm sitting in the corner and thinking "Fucking hell, it's the last time." I started crying and I just put my towel over my head.'

There were scenes of wild emotion as the tears continued to flow at the end of Larsson's last league game at Celtic Park, even less expressive souls whose only immediate concerns were the three points on offer couldn't help but get caught up in Larsson's swansong. It's crucial to remember that we are in one of the world's toughest cities and that while being a romantic football club, Celtic supporters don't have any less machismo than your average football punter. But, that day, every cheek seemed to be glistening. In the Scottish sporting press Larsson had often been described as 'icy' or 'cold', in reality he was simply protective of himself and his family. But he was never going to be the sort of character who would exit Celtic without showing the supporters exactly what they meant to him: 'I wasn't interested in sharing emotions and thoughts outside the pitch. I would show when I got angry about things I didn't agree with, but I don't think I let many people get to know the real me in Scotland. I made some great friends that I still have there, but I had to keep that little bit, something that was just for me, my family and my friends and the fans accepted that. They were happy to see the way I showed my emotions. It felt great to cry, to show them how I felt. This just wasn't something short term – it was a long time and it meant a lot to me. It was a chance to say thank you for everything more or less and I don't think I could have said it any better. It showed what it all meant to me.'

It was a strange feeling seeing Larsson return to Celtic Park for a Champions League match in September 2004, just months after leaving Celtic. At the time Martin O'Neill offered: 'It was probably written that Henrik would score.' The event was as uncanny for Celtic supporters as it was for Larsson: 'It was difficult, I was in Barcelona and Magnus Hedman [ex-Celtic and Sweden keeper] called me and said: "Guess what?" I said "No", because I knew the draw was happening. It was too soon, it was only a few months and then I was back in a different dress; I didn't want to go back there so early.' It was during that game that Celtic supporters witnessed Larsson's killer instincts while playing for an opposition team: 'I can still see the goal today; I'm making a run from the left side because I see Thommo bring the ball down and play it back to the keeper. If you look at the recording of that game you can see it, because I'd seen it so many times in training ... I knew that I couldn't celebrate.' Former Barcelona manager Frank Rijkaard said of the goal: 'The way he didn't celebrate his goal showed you what Celtic has meant to him.'

After two seasons Barcelona found themselves in the same position as Celtic, trying to persuade him to stay. Rijkaard like Larsson believed in the 'theatre' of stylish attacking football and the pair made an immediate connection. In contrast to his playing days the Dutchman cut a tranquil figure in the dugout and there are undoubtedly elements in the coaching style of the former Barcelona manager that Larsson has adopted: 'What I learned from Frank was to be calm in certain situations and to trust in the things that you prepared for, also it's not always about shouting or talking but tapping into the player's mind. He got them to understand what he was getting them to do was not just for him but for their own career. You can have fun with the back-heels or whatever, but you must get the job done first.'

Significantly Larsson's visit to Parkhead with Barcelona wouldn't be the last time the player would come back to haunt his old boss Martin O'Neill. Shortly after honouring his promise to return to Helsingborgs, Larsson signed a loan deal with Manchester United during a break in the Swedish season.

His first game would be an FA Cup third-round tie against Aston Villa where his former gaffer was now at the helm. Says Larsson: 'I was thirty-five when I went to United and I played OK. The game with Aston Villa, I just knew that I would score that day. We all had a hug before the game. With all three of them (O'Neill, Robertson and Walford) there is a special bond, of course. I think he knew [O'Neill] I would score that day as well. Manchester United is fantastic as a club; there is no club better organised or run. They took care of me and my family in a fantastic way. The players knew me and I knew them, but you have to feel your way in the beginning. I was never a joker in the dressing room, but I participated in the talk because it's the best there is. To come there at thirty-five and play with those players it felt like coming home again because Helsingborgs, with all respect, don't have the players. I understand why Sir Alex continued for so long – because he hates losing. It was great to watch him build a team and see his ideas and thoughts get through to players. He could get angry, he made sure the players were on their toes all the time and he let them know what was demanded of them.

'United have a great following, but it's different in Scotland, in what it means to the people. It's so much more than football; it's a way of living. I have one regret: I should have stayed in Manchester one more year. I had moved home and I wanted to play football while I still had it in my body, I didn't want to sit on the bench. I would have played at least one more year, but I promised Helsingborgs and it wouldn't have been fair not to go. Barca weren't happy when I went to United either. My daughter was still quite young, but my son needed a place to call his home. He was born in Holland and raised in Scotland. I wanted to give him the chance to meet his friends because he was at an age where you start making your best friends. I know I sacrificed two or three years of my career doing that, but I'm more than one-hundred per cent sure I did the right thing. I don't have any problem [with him having a career in football] as long as he has his education first and foremost. He loves football and already has achieved things I never did in my career at his age; I hope he will be better than me.' One thing Larsson's son Jordan has already achieved is playing a match alongside his father. On June 19th 2013 Henrik returned again to the professional game turning out for his first club

Högaborgs BK where his son has similarly begun a flourishing career. In October the same year Larsson played again in a further league match for Högaborgs remaining on the park for 66 minutes in a 2–0 win. In June 2015 at the grand old age of 43 years Henrik took part in a 7-1 friendly win for Helsingborgs over IFK Malmo scoring a typically beguiling goal in the dying minutes of the game. Larsson took over as manager at the club in 2015 after a spell as manager of Falkenbergs F.F who he secured to Sweden's top flight.

Henrik Larsson has many football honours. Although he didn't play in the required number of games for an English Premier League medal, he was given a special dispensation for his contribution to Manchester United's league win in the 2006–07 season. In 2004 he was voted the greatest Swedish player of the previous fifty years in the UEFA Jubilee awards. In 2005 he was awarded a doctorate at the University of Strathclyde. Professor Andrew Hamnett, Principal of the University of Strathclyde, said: 'We are delighted that Henrik Larsson has accepted the honorary degree of Doctor of the University. Mr Larsson's tremendous contribution to sport is well known, however, the university believes that his impact on Glasgow and Scotland as a whole went far beyond the football field. His charity work and general demeanour mark him as an ideal role model for our students.' The roll of honour continued: the following year he was awarded an OBE by the Queen and in 2007 Celtic's King of Kings received the King's Medal, the Swedish equivalent of a knighthood.

Although his playing days in football's top flight are now over, Larsson has little time for nostalgia: 'I don't sit at home and look at them [his awards],' he says, 'but I do get a smile on my lips when I hear the Champions League music on the television because I think somebody is getting a medal. I'm happy for all the awards I got, but I've never been too nostalgic. I keep my focus in front of me because hopefully I'll get old and I'll sit back one day and appreciate those things. But for now there is always a new game or a training session. If you slack off a bit mentally then your standards lower too; I never wanted to get into that position. Being happy is important, yes, but it's good to want more in terms of playing better and scoring more goals or whatever it is.'

Since his departure Larsson has visited Celtic Park on a

number of occasions as a supporter and he's also pulled on Glasgow's green and white hoops for charitable causes. Here he reflects on his return to Paradise after some time away to score a hat-trick for John Kennedy's testimonial: 'It's just something strange with me and that ground – I can't stop scoring goals, I mean it, it's unbelievable; it's more or less like being in my living room. I'm at home there. Nobody wants to show anything bad towards me and it was just a great feeling to give back three goals. People paid money for a good cause and it was great to turn back time. I might not be as quick as I was, but I can still score goals. I miss preparing at the Hilton before a game and I can still see my home in Bothwell,' he says, drifting off almost whimsically imagining his former life. Returning to the moment he adds: 'But Celtic is still there, touch wood, and it's always going to be there. I love the club and in Scotland there are fantastic people. I really enjoyed my time there. I just hope that I do more good than bad, I don't think I am anybody special, but I hope the joy I gave to people during my playing years makes up for some mistakes on the way, because nobody is perfect.'

There are one or two Celtic fans that might decline that notion.

Chapter Eight
Rebel Rebel

'Fergus McCann was very direct and he knew exactly what he wanted to do, he had a vision and he carried that through. I don't devalue what Fergus did for the club, but ultimately it was done by the supporters, it gets a little bit lost that the bulk of the money raised was done not by Fergus or the board but them. It was their money that allowed us to sit in this magnificent arena that we are sitting in today.'
Michael McDonald, Celtic director

THROUGHOUT ITS SEVEN years in existence the Green Brigade has proved to be one of the most organised supporter groups in modern football. Its flags, banners, stickers, fashions, logos and statements have manifested in front of television cameras, football grounds, journalists' copy, radio programmes, red telephone boxes, blue police kiosks, websites, forums, playgrounds, offices, lampposts, fanzines and mobile phones. The truth is that most people in Scotland have heard of the Green Brigade and among the Celtic support they have created a framework that now has the cultural power to influence thinking, ideas and opinions on a range of issues among a multitude of people. Not only do have they remained independent from the PLC, they publicly hold them to account. Their banners, which can be humorous, provocative, philosophical or emotional, have at times been succinct at getting to the heart of current issues around the club and its fans. They have also given a contemporary context to the heroes and history of the club as well as the inclusive social values of the support, making young or new supporters aware of recurring themes and ethics associated and expected among fellow fans. They remain the only visible 'ultras' in a British football ground.

Their style and spirit has its roots in a fan protest that celebrated its twentieth anniversary in the same year that the club marked 125 years in existence, 'Back the team, sack the board' was a succinct piece of sloganeering dreamed up in 1993 by Celts for Change, an organised pressure group who changed the course of Celtic's history and kept the club in existence by backing former owner Fergus McCann to take over from the Kelly and White dynasties, among others, who were for many, leading Celtic to the grave.

Not everyone agrees with that perspective. Firebrand politician George Galloway, as well as supporting the Green Brigade, also admits to preferring the original board, he said: 'I was very proud often to see the Green Brigade flags, banners and manifestations of various anti-imperialist positions. I'm totally against the legislation that has helped to silence them and I'm actually not very keen on the people who run Celtic. They have collaborated with the state in silencing an important section of their own fan-base and I deplore that although it doesn't surprise me. It's paradoxical that Brian Dempsey was involved in the overthrow of the old board and I'm still close to Mr Dempsey but looking on back on it, the old board looks rather more attractive to me than the current board and I never thought I would say that. I'm a member of the House of Commons Celtic Supporters club which has MPs, peers and staff members. Fergus came to talk to us one night, he kept referring to us as customers and I had to *say*: "Fergus we are not customers because customers can go to the shop across the road if they don't like your prices, you can go somewhere else but we can't go anywhere else". Fergus was better than what we have now but I rather think the old board was better than Fergus.'

One person who obviously disagrees is Celts for Change group leader Matt McGlone. In February of 2012 he appeared on *Scotland Tonight* alongside former board member Michael Kelly to discuss Celtic's fate in relation to the demise of Rangers, their pairing on the live news and current affairs programme was a considerable one. Kelly and McGlone had been polarised during a period of critical urgency for the club in the early 1990s, and it was clear time hadn't eroded animosity between the pair as palpable tension filled living rooms across the land.

Matt McGlone has been at the heart of the club and its culture since the early 1960s. When he talks about walking along London Road under the floodlights sporting a balaclava, taking his father's hand and chomping on a Macaroon bar, he is unashamedly starry-eyed while capturing some of the promise and mystery that we all continue to feel as we walk into Paradise for those same thrilling European encounters today. The *Alternative View* editor has been involved in a number of Celtic publications over the years and his work has played an important role in offering fans an expression free from the stifling constraints of official club policy. McGlone's brand has lasted for 25 years and counting, it's no mean feat that in the digital age we continue to jump on to planes, trains, buses and boats clutching fanzines such as his. Born in November 1954 the *Alternative View* editor remains a straight-talking guy with strong opinions, passionate ideas and solid contacts in relation to the issues that really matter to Celtic fans. As a working-class Glaswegian with socialist principles and a punk-rock 'do-it-yourself' ethos his ideas still translate to over 22,000 followers on Twitter and the *Alternative View* readership.

Today in the bustling traditional Tennent's Bar on Byres Road he casts his mind back to November 1990 and the formation of the influential *Once A Tim* fanzine: 'It was a basic street magazine. We were influenced by a student paper at the time, the format was cut and paste, this was before computers, we would cut pictures out of the papers, which was the standard of the time, and we'd have typing underneath. We had a different approach from *Not the View*, which was more student and quirky. That's not a criticism, but we'd go for the jugular.' Undoubtedly the fanzine would have a pivotal role to play in the removal of the old board who believed the club was their birthright. They weren't equipped to engage with the challenges of the modern game and espoused the idea that to contest their leadership was to damage the club, making even the idea of protest an emotional issue for many supporters. The board's position allowed impotent egos and outdated opinions to do real harm to Celtic during a time of little promise. To face up to them would have been unthinkable for many in 1990 but when *Once A Tim* began to apply pressure it would forever change how supporters viewed the club.

The irrepressible McGlone drove the point home that the team and the beliefs around the club belong to no man; they belong to us all collectively and as supporters we all have a right to make our voices heard through any means possible: 'The old board were totally inept at understanding the club was going down the toilet. Their view was "Celtic is ours and we can't let this go", but Celtic is no family's right. If I had ten million pounds' worth of shares then my family have the right to own ten million pounds' worth of shares, but they wouldn't own Celtic. The club will never be anybody's in that way; it will always belong to the fans. It's not through shares you own a club like Celtic; it's through mentality, spirit and emotion.'

During the first of two interviews various locals banter about his recent appearance with Michael Kelly: 'It was awkward for me,' says McGlone, 'the man has never admitted or recognised the problem with the way he was running Celtic. To this day he thinks Fergus wasn't the right man. I said he had a cheek to be on the programme because he nearly took Celtic to the abyss where Rangers are today, except we didn't go into liquidation. We had words off-screen; all in all it was a strange situation for me.'

In Matt McGlone the Celts for Change pressure group had a public personality with some much-needed charisma, who, once in his stride, was able to translate the concerns of the ordinary supporter and if they weren't already, he made them concerned by harnessing some robust Red Clydeside energy. His sound bites, interviews and various stunts were broadcast UK-wide as the story went national. The Celts for Change movement is an essential benchmark in the club's story, it's leader casts his mind back to Celtic's winter of discontent in November 1993: 'I put an advert in the *Sunday Mail* that said "If you care about your club come along to City Halls". There were about thirty people at the first meeting. At the second meeting in December the place was full and there were three hundred and fifty people outside in Celtic scarves and jerseys. I've got to tell you from that moment on, what a buzz that was. Five hundred Celtic supporters got behind us that night and the rest is history. After that point the campaign kind of overtook us, we were trying to pull it back and control the energy and emotion of the Celtic support which was like taking a match to ten gallons of petrol and watching it go.'

When the old board rejected an offer from Fergus McCann and former member Brian Dempsey, the movement gained further momentum. There was undoubtedly a synergy between

McGlone and McCann, which proved to be beneficial to Celtic's long-term health. The importance of that relationship was given a fresh relevance under the circumstances that befell Rangers in 2012. McGlone in his prime became the essential catalyst in shifting fan and media opinion towards the belief that McCann was the right man to run Celtic, had he not been the lynchpin it is likely an immeasurably destructive fate would have awaited Celtic. Long before Rangers went into administration in February 2012 many onlookers expected a rally call from a single-minded leader with the capacity to challenge the club's financial behaviour, but as Rangers plunged deeper into crisis no one emerged. 'I've thought about this and bounced it around a few people,' says McGlone, 'and there are a range of opinions, but one main idea is that Rangers still have a strong establishment mentality. I think there was a serious mindset of "This can't happen; we're Rangers – we're too big." The club went into administration and you could see the train arrive. You began to think what does it take to pull the trigger? By and large I think there was a degree of clinical denial. It's not a new phenomenon that people think: "Everything will be fine; something will work out"; it didn't. I'm not just saying this and you can take me out of the scenario here, but it takes a bit of balls to stand up and do something like that because as soon as you put your head above the parapet whether you are the best guy in the world or not - some negative fucker is ready to shout you down.'

As leader of a pressure group McGlone had to strike the right balance between brain and brawn, and he organised some publicity stunts that brought media attention toward just how desperate Celtic's situation was. One of the most memorable was a protest outside the Bank of Scotland that questioned why the bank was backing a debt-ridden company. Undoubtedly McGlone had a gifted understanding as to how the media ticked and what would make news headlines. Painful as it was to a man driven by his love for Celtic, but just as necessary, was the boycott of a game at Celtic Park in March 1994. It was a complex operation that caused a lot of personal conflict: 'Asking fans to boycott was a terrible and horrible situation, but it was for the betterment of Celtic in the long run. We knew that it would only take one game and the board would fall. We asked fans not to go to the stadium because we didn't want any confrontation, and fans observed that. Michael Kelly said to me that it was an orchestrated campaign. I said: "Of course it was." Even to this day he still doesn't get it! It was never against Celtic; it was against the old board that were running Celtic.'

McGlone's role as an organiser led to a position as a columnist at the *Celtic View*. His opinions were popular with supporters and it's worth noting that one of the conditions of the column's contract was free speech. Even today, more than twenty years on, it remains an impressive fact about McCann's time at Celtic that he allowed McGlone a free hand at the club magazine, which was known to the support as 'Pravda'. But the period wasn't without drama and turbulence either: 'McCann got in touch and asked if I wanted to do the column. I said that would be great, but it would never work. Fergus sort of barked, not aggressive, but he was quick in asking me what I meant. I said: "you've got your ideas and I've got mine." I explained that what I would write wouldn't be what he'd want in the *Celtic View*. At that point McCann made it very clear to me he would give me a two-year contract that stated there would be no interference with any of the copy. To get that kind of guarantee was wonderful. I thought I'd give it a go and those two years were good, then I had another two good years and so on. You read some of the things the papers said about McCann, calling him a tyrant and so on, I never found that. He never interfered not once in several years, but later other people did. The main difference in any club magazine is that it's a corporate, strict and sanitised publication, but as society moves on people want to read some free thought.'

While there are suggestions that McCann wanted to sanitise Celtic's Irish image, hiring a writer with the spirit and confidence of McGlone appeared to be a forward-thinking move for the club. 'Fergus was a quirky wee guy. He lived in a tenement flat in Crossmyloof for about three years while he was in Glasgow. I remember David Low [who devised McCann's takeover plan] was driving him back from a meeting with the accountants at Celtic. He said to David: "Take me to Argyle Street, I need a pair of sneakers." You had to explain to him that you couldn't do that in Glasgow; he was too high profile. Prior to the takeover there was a dinner at the Thistle Hotel in Cambridge Street, which was attended by various people involved in what was going on around the time of the takeover.

Everyone had to get up and say a bit about what Celtic meant to them, but what Fergus said that day will live with me forever. He stood up and said: "We should all be proud of everything we have achieved in our lives as Celtic supporters. We have never had to join any secret organisation to get anywhere in life; what we have got, we have got on our own merit." The hairs on the back of my neck just stood on end. It was at that point that I realised that this snappy wee guy had a deep love for Celtic that had stemmed back to when he was a boy running the bus from Croy.'

The balance between supporter and professional can often be a difficult one to strike. As Martin O'Neill strived to build unity at the club during his years at Celtic, there was a conflict of interest with McGlone. It was also a new era of player power at the club and the team closed ranks against him after taking umbrage to criticism in the club magazine. The spirit of protest is a relatively new phenomenon at Celtic and dissent still doesn't sit comfortably with some supporters who believe you should support the team without question. At the same time the former *Celtic View* columnist found most fans he'd bump into around Glasgow identified with his concerns. His time working for the club remains a fascinating and candid insight into the mechanics and mentality of what goes on behind the scenes at Celtic Park: 'Like everyone else I love Martin (O'Neill.) We crossed swords a few times, but he was always fair. There was one occasion when I was asked to interview Lubo [Moravčík] during O'Neill's first pre-season training session in Denmark. I wasn't popular at home as it was my daughter's graduation, but I flew out at six in the morning. When I got there Stephane Mahé [the popular and committed left back between 1997 and 2001] was shouting and balling in French in an aggressive manner. I'm about to start the interview and Lubo gets up and says: "I have to go with my friend." I had written an article about a Celtic player called Stéphane Bonnes, he came over and signed for Celtic, but he never kicked a ball for the first team and still earned himself a fortune. I took umbrage with that and slaughtered him; it was personal. I said he shouldn't be wearing a Celtic jersey. It turned out he was business partners with Stephane Mahé in a Glasgow strip club called Seventh Heaven, so there was some personal interest there.

'I was also told by Celtic's PR that Martin O'Neill wouldn't have time to talk to me either. I reminded him that I had flown across the North Sea, got a taxi to the hotel and then another for the thirty-mile journey to the training ground and back. I told him we had an arrangement. Martin eventually came down. He said: "I always took you as being a straight forward decent guy." I said: "Nothing's changed." He told me no paper or programme representing any club he'd worked at would criticise players and that he couldn't have that. I told him I understood his situation, but I wanted to explain mine. The team had lost the previous season by twenty-one points; not every game was going to be a great performance. When the team deserved it I'd praise them to the hilt, but when it didn't I wanted to point out a few things. We came to an understanding and found some common ground. He asked me if I fancied a beer and I took him up on the offer and so we sat down to do the interview. We talked for an hour and he gave me more than I needed. He explained his side of things; I really appreciated that.

'I had a good relationship with Martin at Celtic Park, though he would occasionally barge into the media room. There was one time when the players went on strike with the club publication because I had criticised their performance in one particular game. It was player power coming to the fore. Not for the first time Jackie McNamara stood right out of it and gave me his support.' The game in question was a 5–1 defeat against Rangers at Ibrox in November 2000, it followed the 6–2 win at Celtic Park the previous August. The *Celtic View* writer found himself under increasing pressure to deliver copy without the support of the team: 'As a lifelong Celtic fan I was being deprived from doing my job by Celtic players. I found that a bizarre situation, it was hurtful as well. I couldn't quite comprehend it because I had pointed things out and then they didn't want to talk to me and we're supposed to be all batting in the same corner. I hadn't spoken to the players for three weeks, feeling like I had this label on my back. I was unhappy and my concentration was going. I could see the politics coming back into things. When politics come into what you are doing it's very difficult because you can't be imaginative and creative when you have all these negatives being thrown at you like spears and harpoons. It was difficult to cope and during that time I took a few days off to figure out if it was all worth it. I had a wife and a boy less than a year old at home and I'd taken out a new mortgage based on the fact that I had a three-year contract with Celtic, so I decided to stick it out.'

With the players on strike Tommy Burns was nominated to summon the Celtic writer for a meeting with the team's captain Tom Boyd and vice captain Paul Lambert. 'When Tommy approached me about it I said: "What's this got to do with you?" which probably wasn't the wisest thing because Tommy could be quick and we had some fierce run-ins too. But he was a lovely guy, he always called you son; he could have punched me ten times in the head and I would have still loved him, he was that kind of guy. He said to me: "I'm here to sort this out son" and led me to this meeting in Willie McStay's office, which was known as the broom cupboard, which really it was. I was lucky if there were two or three feet between the players and me. In reference to the Rangers game I asked them: "What would you like me to write as a fan in the club magazine? How do you want me to explain that?" They couldn't answer me. It was good cop [Lambert] bad cop [Boyd]. Boyd asked me what right I had to talk about it and he asked me if I had ever played, I told him I was pretty guff, that I had a trial for Celtic and was probably rubbish, but I told him I was a fan with a brain and that I could see what was happening. I turned it round and asked him if he'd ever written an article, created a column or written a book; there was a bit of silly banter between us. In the end as a concession we agreed that if somebody made an error he wouldn't be named, just to get the show back on the road. Once again I have to mention Jackie McNamara, who refused to take any part in the meeting.'

McGlone left the *Celtic View* after a difficult and debilitating time amid office politics and personality clashes. While some at the club were glad to see the back of him, his prominence and popularity among supporters remains intact. In May 2013 the organisers of Celts for Change were invited to Celtic Park. Four of the five original members including Matt McGlone witnessed the unveiling of a tribute to the group at the club's entrance. A paving made of stone now honours the immeasurable importance of these ordinary Celtic supporters. Celtic chief executive Peter Lawwell praised the group and posed for photographs alongside them. The fact that 'the rebels' were honoured was further evidence of Celtic's importance beyond the game.

The Celts for Change leader successfully conveyed to a new generation of fans just how powerful an organised, unified and intelligent support can be. In many ways the baton was handed from McGlone to the Green Brigade. The major difference between Celts for Change and the GB is their lack of a public face, but arguably it's also something of a potent mechanism for the group. A sense of mystery about exactly who they are has only made the myths around them grow and has captured even wider public attention. In January 2015 an advert appeared in the Herald newspaper denying Rangers were the same Glasgow club formed in 1872 that would face Celtic in the semi-final of the League Cup. Once again there was a sense of mystery about where the statement came as it carried no name or organisation. Some agreed but many didn't and voiced their opinion on social media. McGlone suggests that organisations, writers and social media users need to be more transparent when making statements on fans' behalf: 'I couldn't argue with anything in the advert, it got quite serious but what perturbed me was that it said it was on behalf of Celtic supporters, I think it was CQN that did it and it took me a few days to find out who it was. Had it been Matt McGlone or Celts for Change, it would have had a name on it. You may be talking for some Celtic supporters but not everyone, I feel there should have been a name or organisation which it represented. If you make a statement about something or someone then put your name to it! In terms of what it was saying I agree with the point, after Rangers went into liquidation the Scottish press ran with headlines such as "R.I.P R.F.C". They can't suddenly be alive again so yes this is a different club as far as I'm concerned. Obviously the rivalry has been diluted and I can see there is a space that has been left, you can still discuss things and take the piss a bit but it's almost like they are too far away. There is no competition, personally I wouldn't like to see Rangers back because they bring nothing healthy to Scottish football. In terms of the apathy the game in Scotland will just have to readjust itself but they will come back at some point. I went to the Celtic v Rangers game earlier this year and listened to ninety minutes of bile. I have a fourteen year old son, he wanted to go and it was his first time. The reason I didn't take him before was because of that, when I took him home he just sat very quietly in the car. So no, I don't miss that. I have to say it still meant a lot to beat them. When Maurice Johnston signed for Rangers I would say it took Celtic, the club and the support, about five or six years to get over that psychologically. It had a seismic effect and something bad hung over Celtic Park for a very long time, there was a really bad vibe. We had to get the monkey off our back. If we had lost the game against Rangers last season it would have been a really low point. It should have been five or six nil but we were playing in a cow field.'

In August 2015 Channel 4 news reported on how a number of English and Scottish clubs including Celtic and Rangers have banned journalists from media access for expressing views which the clubs don't endorse. It's behaviour such as this which is creating a strange and stifling atmosphere where only the sycophantic and grovelling are allowed access. Scottish Union organiser Paul Holleran described it as a culture of 'bullying'. Another problem has been what McGlone describes as 'agendas' from ex-Celtic players now working in the Scottish media. The former *Celtic View* writer felt that current manager Ronny Deila was given unfair treatment by Chris Sutton and John Hartson who were overtly critical of the Norwegian as he adapted to the magnitude of his new role: 'The tone and style of content about Deila when he was going through a period of transition was unnecessary. A legend had just walked out of Celtic Park and someone unknown walked in. Of course there is an emotional bond for supporters. It was clear that patience was required, it was going to take time to see how this new manager could implement things. What he didn't need was a lot of unfair pressure and certain people who had played for Celtic such as John Hartson and Chris Sutton, who in a very agenda driven way, wrote some very unfair articles. They were both great Celtic players but as critics they were talking rubbish.

Hartson said the player: 'did not have a clue' and Sutton described a performance as 'pathetic'. While both former players have since changed their minds, Deila showed his mettle responding with grace and humility. It was around this time the Norwegian headed out to the award winning Jinty McGuinty's bar in the heart of Glasgow's west end with the club's sports psychologist Jim McGuinness. McGlone had popped into the bar to see a friend and on spotting Deila decided to offer a show of support to the new Celtic manager: 'I could see the style and tone in which articles were written. I was a Ronny supporter from day one in print, online and verbally because I believe he has done fantastically well in his first season. I came into Jinty's and Ronny is sitting in one of the booths. I didn't want to annoy him on a night out but I was intrigued to meet him. I remember thinking I wish I had a magazine because we had featured a two page piece looking at the negative media coverage and how well he had done in spite of that. I nipped out, grabbed a copy and then introduced myself while handing it (the *Alternative View*) over to him. I told him I admired the way he had stood up to some of the unfair criticism directed at him and that it was a new culture, club, city and a different way of doing things. He thanked me and shook my hand and I left him to enjoy his evening. He was very approachable, a real gent. A short time later I saw him walking over to the bar, I was like Whistling Dixie facing the other way. He tapped me on the shoulder and thanked me for the piece, what he commented on was the fact that it wasn't vicious but had pointed a few things out. He asked for my number and we've kept in touch since.'

Today I've reconvened with the *Alternative View* editor for a second interview once again in the city's west end in the same bar he first met Deila and was often joined by former manager Neil Lennon. His mind turns to Lennon a year on from his still much discussed exit: 'I love Neil, I know him personally but if I didn't know him I'd still love him because he's got giant balls, he was attacked six feet from where we are sitting now, punched and kicked to the ground by two Rangers fans who kicked him when he was down because he was a charismatic Irish Catholic playing for Celtic. When he left (Celtic) of his own accord I think it was dressed up. My feeling is that Neil and the club probably came to some kind of mutual agreement. He resigned the day before the Celtic season ticket deadline, it left such a short time to get a new manager. If Lennon was going of his own accord then why didn't he go before that juncture, I think things were said in a private conversation on both sides that will never be said to the public. At best it was a mutual agreement.'

During a previous meeting McGlone didn't mince his words concerning the then First Minister Alex Salmond. On the subject of Scottish independence he remained tight lipped for a period as he weighed up the options. He describes himself as a 'disaffected Labour voter' who like many watched in disbelief as they stood beside the Tories in the battle for Scotland. Speaking today he discusses something of his political journey over the last few years: 'In my own ignorance I didn't fully understand the referendum when it came out in its first weeks. I took it as an SNP gig. I soon came to the realisation of what it was really about, that it's about being governed by your own country and not by Westminster. Once I got that out the way and started paying a bit more attention I was all for it and I voted Yes and I'm glad I did. Now that SNP are in, once you get the showbiz politics out the way, let's get down to serious business - I want to see what they can do for the country. The massive mistake Labour made in Scotland was being so high profile with the No vote. People began to wonder what the party were about. To see Labour standing on platforms with unionists and Tories, who are strongly disliked, was too much for most people to bear. I don't like to use the word hate but for many people, myself included, the memories of the miners' strike, shipyard closures and steelworks closures at Ravenscraig still loom large. It always seemed that Scotland was just a testing ground for these policies and actions. The same with the Poll Tax, we were used as guinea pigs, it's not and will never be Tory supporting country. As a Labour man I'm looking to see what SNP can do, the block vote was a real opportunity to put Scotland in a better negotiating position rather than being dictated to by Westminster. I'm not an SNP knocker but for me I feel that Alex Salmond was too drum beaten, I think that Nicola Sturgeon is very conscientious leader and I want to see what she will do now. The last time I spoke about the party was on the back of the SNP offensive behaviour bill. It seemed to be something that affected Celtic supporters rather than support them. I've been called a dirty Fenian bastard at football matches since I was a boy. I've listening to chants and songs that demonised me and my community all my life so to see that community being the ones affected by the bill made me very concerned.' On the subject of the Offensive Behaviour at Football and Threatening Communications Act Neil Lennon had this to say in April 2015: (It) 'punished the supporter more than anyone, it was a bit restrictive to the supporters and in a nutshell I didn't think it worked. We lost a lot of supporters because of that and good supporters too. It's important that they look at that and correct it.'

The then Scottish Labour leader Jim Murphy pledged to scrap the bill. No one would doubt Murphy's standing among many Celtic supporters but Labour's high profile union with the Tories during the referendum damaged a solid reputation and political career, said McGlone: 'I've met Jim a few times and I like him. I actually stayed with Jim's brother on Manhattan beach in California. Like Jim his brother is a big Celtic fan and a member of the Santa Monica Celtic Supporters Club. Jim is a good guy and a big Celtic man but I don't agree with his politics, I didn't like the fact that he stood with the union on the Irn-Bru crate tour.' Undoubtedly the referendum remains a divisive subject among many and the contradictions of Rangers fans voting Yes and Celtic fans voting No are not difficult to unearth. McGlone suggests that many Celtic supporters were still making up their minds late in the process but were likely to vote Yes: 'I think most undecided fans eventually did vote Yes because it was a massive shift in the culture that took people a long time to get to grips with. After the unionist thing began to rear its head, if you were thinking of voting No there was a strong sense that you were voting with people you had opposed your whole life, at the end of the day I couldn't have voted with them. The day of the referendum I went to a few meetings in George Square or Independence Square as it was called for a while. It was a fantastic atmosphere, something special was happening until the other mob pitched up bringing something very ugly with them. I felt very emotional seeing the riots and police on horseback after the goodness of what had went before. It was invaded by these nasty against everything kind of people and I'm sure many of them were not even understanding why they are against it in the first place.'

Chapter Nine
Ride The Lightning

'I think to some degree Neil Lennon is a metaphor. He's a metaphor and symbol for a lot of things, in terms of what he has suffered he is a lightning rod'
Sir Tom Devine

THE CELTIC STORY in the 21st century is unimaginable without Neil Lennon. His effectiveness both in a green and white hooped shirt and as the club's gaffer is associated with stirring displays, high promise and campaigns exuding confidence and unity. In the best Celtic way it was all wrapped in emotion and sentiment. The arrival of the player with cropped bleach blond hair strengthened an already gladiatorial side under Martin O'Neill and he would prove to be one of his mentor's most valuable assets as an enforcing presence in midfield. The boy from County Armagh was a vital cog in the machine during a final dominant era against Rangers and in a team which saw Celtic once again knock on the door of European glory. As a manager he built a consistent reputation for sourcing talent and with great vision and energy he built one of the most convincing Celtic sides since the exit of Martin O'Neill. On November 6th 2012 the club celebrated its 125th anniversary, the following evening they would play F.C Barcelona in an exhilarating contest which proved the Scottish club with Irish roots from Glasgow's East End could still challenge the most indomitable clubs in the world and dazzle neutral observers across the globe while going about it. Today I find Neil Lennon at Bolton's training ground in the north west of England, he is less eminent in these parts than in Scotland but is perhaps the better for it. Today he affirms a calm and reflective presence. He no longer has to field questions about wider problems in Scottish society or discuss political issues. There are no physical attacks in football stadia from the fans of rival clubs or parcel bombs sent through the post. He doesn't get attacked or receive sectarian abuse in the street. But neither is he a spokesman for a large and significant community. At Bolton he doesn't retain the emblematic status that he did at Celtic Football Club. On his days away from the game he plays golf, spends time with family or turns the pages of a history book. Without the extraordinary and grave concerns outside of football to think about any longer you can only imagine where the 44 year old will travel from here in sporting terms. What is clear is that Celtic will always be in the milieu. Significantly he never saw his role as a spokesman for matters beyond football as an obstacle: 'It was important for me as the manger to front-up these questions and not shy away from that because I knew the history of the club. I was aware of what was going on socially within Glasgow and the environment whether it be sectarian, political or football matters. The Celtic support saw me as the leader to front-up on these issues because I had been in the framework of the club for fourteen years as player, coach and manager. I think they could trust me to lead from the front in that aspect. I didn't always want to do it because I got into some areas that were pretty unfamiliar for me. Coming down here and just talking about the football side of things, it's far more secure and reassuring because I'm not going into waters that are unfamiliar.'

The bond between the Green Brigade and the former Celtic manager was a most fascinating and complex relationship. The major bone of contention with the GB has been an association with pro-IRA and Irish Republican chants and songs. While some Celtic supporters are likely to hold Irish nationalist sympathies the majority are keen to disassociate themselves from songs and chants that deal positively with murder, bloodshed and bombing campaigns. Such links have alienated fellow supporters, fans from other clubs and the mainstream media who are reluctant to see the positives the group have brought to Celtic Park. It is also likely in a self-policing group such as the Green Brigade that there is an ever-evolving range of perspectives and opinions. For many in the Green Brigade, Lennon was symbolic of what it means to follow Celtic. The appeal among many was that he had the same social, religious and cultural context. Within the narrative around Lennon was a big city personae and streetwise sensibilities. He reliably fought Celtic's corner on a range of issues and offered a counter- point when perceived bad decisions and prejudices went unchallenged. At least part of his popularity is due to the fact that most supporters can buy into his wider story which for the best part of fourteen years went hand-in- hand with club. As well as relating to the ordinary aspects of Lennon, the fantastical is also part of the transaction. The Green Brigade visualised the notion of Neil Lennon as 'Hero' and 'Celtic To The Core' in colourful flags and banners which depicted the Lurgan born Irishman at various stages of his career as player, captain and then manager but also as a kind of superhero or politician. He created a new kind of Celtic archetype which current captain Scott Brown was able to carry forward into teams long after Lennon's departure as a player. Banners such as 'We Stand Behind Our Leader' conveyed an important message not just to Lennon but to those on the outside that Celtic and it's fans were united or as another famous flag philosophically declared: 'We Are All Neil Lennon'. After being presented with the SPL trophy for the 2011-10 season the manager placed the trophy in front of the Green Brigade's raucous area of the ground- section 111. In an era where fans often feel patronised or remote from the club it forged an authentic bond and made for an improved atmosphere at Celtic Park. Beyond life at Celtic Lennon's affection for the group persists and he is pragmatic about his own history with them: 'I love the Green Brigade. They brought so much colour and life to the stadium which was lacking for a long, long time and it's easy to forget that aspect but latterly towards the end things became more radical and I felt it got a little bit too political. There were certain political banners at Champions League games which were unnecessary. (In December 2013 Celtic were fined £42,000 by UEFA after a GB banner was unveiled featuring IRA hunger striker Bobby Sands). It was my duty as Celtic manager to speak out about that because it did not represent the whole of the Celtic support at the time. Some people within the Green Brigade had their own agendas whether it be against the club or for political reasons but I didn't think Celtic Park was the amphitheatre to bring them publically in the way that they did. They could have done that elsewhere.'

Neil Lennon became a contemporary Mr Celtic among the club's support for the combination of his sporting skills and cultural associations but as Scottish historian Sir Tom Devine suggests he also symbolised an Irish Catholic other to rival clubs. Lennon admits he was 'no angel', he was an emotive and passionate player and manager. All teams possess characters that want to noise-up the opposition - it's part of their game and Lennon won't be the last player to react to hostile fans or bad decisions against his team. But no sportsman should have found himself the victim of racism, sectarianism, public attacks and threats to their life. To publically attack someone because they are Irish, Catholic or have red hair says more about the functionality and mind of the abuser than it does about the person on the receiving end which Lennon was at almost every away ground in Scotland. There are also significant important questions about how civic society treated Neil Lennon. Commenting in the Guardian newspaper journalist Kevin McKenna in the aftermath of Lennon's exit from Glasgow wrote: 'It is time to ask why enlightened and progressive Scotland treated him in such a vile manner in each of the dozen or so years he spent with us. The resignation of a Celtic manager ought only to be the subject of scrutiny on the sports pages, with his success rate and football legacy being picked apart and compared with others who have occupied that seat. Such, though, has been the universal hatred to which this young man has been subjected in every part of Scotland that any interpretation that fails to analyse why is immediately rendered meaningless. Neil Lennon is, quite simply, the bravest man in Scotland.'

The facts on paper seem absurd when you consider that one of Lennon's many attacks was broadcast live to millions around the globe on television. This writer watched the game in Portugal via a live satellite broadcast. Yet even in light of the televised evidence the assailant was only convicted with a lesser charge of breach of the peace, the sectarian element to the attack was found to be not proven. Speaking today Lennon said: 'From what I was told the prosecution made a boo-boo - they charged him with assault and charged him with a sectarian attack aggravated by racial and religious prejudice and the evidence was that there was no evidence of a sectarian attack. Then they said he had done his time by being in custody so there was no more time to do. Basically the four months he was inside - they felt that was enough. But the whole world saw what happened. It wasn't the first time, I remember looking at the death threat story [before a Northern Ireland match against Cyprus] on the ten o'clock news and thinking they are actually talking about me. It's a bit surreal so after the attack at Tynecastle I thought: "there's got to be an outcry, there's got to be something done now." Was there enough done? No, I don't think there was. Did I feel let down? Yes as a player and manager I felt let down by certain quarters of the media and I know Martin (O'Neill) did. Could they have done more about it? It seemed to get to the point where the attitude was: "It's Neil Lennon; he brings it on himself," all that kind of crap. It was imbalanced and secular to the environment we found ourselves in. For instance when I was sent the bullets in the post, you then had this "he brings it on himself" attitude in the press and that I was an aggressive type. But Paddy McCourt and Niall McGinn got bullets in the post too. So what was the real reason behind it? We know what the real reason was, we were Irish Catholics working for Celtic and playing for Northern Ireland. Everyone refers to Scotland's Shame but not a lot of people did a lot about it.'

In the numerous elegies and epitaphs to Lennon after he departed Celtic a great number referred to his decision to make public his struggle with mental health. Many applauded his courage in using his own popular football profile to highlight depression perhaps removing some of the stigma in Scottish society and the sport. You'd be forgiven for the assessment that behind closed doors Lennon was in a private hell as a result of the threats to his life, physical attacks and a sense of the judicial system letting him down. If anything it drove him toward achieving more in the things that granted him life, he looked for answers in his own success: 'No it didn't affect me in terms of the depression, I never suffered with it while I was managing. I didn't go through a phase for a long time, probably because I had too much on my mind. I didn't have time to think about anything else. My motivation was to beat it, I wanted to be successful and I was in my time at Celtic - that was the only way I could beat them because to come back with an answer [to the bigots] they will always have the final say and they will always come back with something else, they were not accepting or listening to what I am saying. If it helped one person [talking about depression] it was worth doing because there is a stigma attached, there's more people in sport coming forward if you look at cricketers, boxers and rugby. It affects the most strong-willed people, not just sportsmen but a great deal of historical figures suffered from the condition. It's a common illness where people need to feel isolated, they lose self-esteem, confidence, they find themselves in a lonely kind of existence and are afraid to speak up about it. I know from my own experience what I went through. But you can get though and come out the other side of it, if you've got a cold you take a paracetamol , if you have a broken leg you take pain killers. If you suffer from depression and want to take an anti-depressant then there's nothing wrong with that.'

Neil Lennon has proved his worth as an effective team-builder and leader of men creating one of the most eminent Celtic sides of recent junctures. The aforementioned 2-1 dismantling of Barcelona was one of the most remarkable achievements in the club's recent history sending shockwaves throughout the European game. The victory brought Lennon's impressive pool of players much attention and was one of the catalysts for the break-up of a fluent side which contained prolific goal scorer Gary Hooper, midfield powerhouse Victor Wanyama and steady central defender Kelvin Wilson. These players and a clutch of others bounded across the border as they have been doing since the mid-1970s to secure colossal wages and a bigger domestic platform. Their exit hung over the following season and Lennon admits he was in need of a fresh challenge when he eventually moved on from the club in May 2014. At Bolton he was joined by his former Celtic teammate and assistant manager Johan Mjallby who had left the club a month prior to Lennon: 'I was ready for the change, four years as manager of Celtic was a great experience but the time had come for a new challenge, we won the league by thirty points in our last season. What are we going to do next year- win it by forty? I had four years at Celtic and it was a good return.' With the Parkhead club he won three domestic leagues and the Scottish Cup on two occasions but it will be the sojourns into Europe that he will be remembered for the most after qualifying for the group stage of the Champions League twice and on one occasion reaching the last sixteen of the competition. Lennon also convinced many that he was something of a diviner when it came to sourcing unknown quantities and turning them into superstars. In Gary Hooper Celtic found their first real talisman since Henrik Larsson. The player would come back to haunt his old boss while he was finding his feet at Bolton during a difficult run: 'It's bittersweet you know, it's a punch in the stomach to lose a goal. He was unknown when we got him from Scunthorpe, we developed him and he turned out to be one of the best Celtic players of the last twenty-five years. It didn't surprise me that when he got into that position he would score, he's a natural. We got him for £1.5 million and sold him for £6 million - we did something right there. When you look at it - Victor Wanyama, Joe Ledley, Fraser Forster, Ki Sung-yueng they are all thriving in the environment of the Premier League. That gives us a huge amount of pride because we were the ones that developed them into the players that they have become. Kelvin Wilson was another one, he was a player who came in on a free transfer and we sold him for £2.5 million. He also could have played in the Premier League but he was quite happy to go to Nottingham Forrest. 'There was a strategy at the club which we followed, a good recruitment policy with figures like John Park in the background. That's what I want to do here [at Bolton] but also we may have to sell them on at some stage due to the economic climate that the club finds itself in.'

Lennon secured the services of Wanyama's commanding presence for €800,000 and sold him for £12.5 million to Southampton. There were suggestions of more dominant English clubs coming in for the Kenyan and a £25 million price tag was slapped on his head, nevertheless it was an extraordinary piece of business: 'You could tell straight away once he adapted to the pace of the game in Scotland that he would be an absolute superstar. He looked very comfortable in the environment of the Champions League and particularly the performance at Celtic Park against Barcelona on the night he scored, his all round game was phenomenal against the best players in the world. We could see the power that he had, the natural physique. For a big guy his technique was fantastic.'

Against the Catalan club the player's understanding of what it meant to play for in green and white hoops was articulated by the number 67 shirt on his back in a game which undoubtedly changed the Kenyan's fortunes and further bolstered Celtic's mythology with a header that motored like a cannonball against the white netting. Also securing a treasured place in the club's folklore that night was 18 year old Tony Watt

- despite his Celtic journey taking a different turn the moment of virtuosity secured the game and a chunk of history for Celtic. Once again the facts in the modern climate are astonishing, earlier in the year the club had secured the former Airdrie player for the bargain sum of £80,000 - the emerging talent from Scotland's Little Ireland, Coatbridge had dreamed of one day pulling on the green and white Celtic jersey. Within months of doing so he scored one of the most talked about goals of the era. Perhaps too much success too soon, subsequent time at Celtic was at best fragmented and 'discipline' and 'unprofessionalism' became associated with his name in a variety of reports, said Lennon: 'Tony would be the first to admit himself that he didn't apply himself well enough in training. His manager at Lierse had similar problems but since then he has come to Charlton and has really knuckled down. He played against us the other night and he looked well, fit and athletic so maybe now the penny has dropped. He should have a good career in front of him because he has the talent, when you are a young player and something like that happens with your name lit up all over Europe it can affect you in a negative way. I remember thinking: "I hope Tony's name is not remembered just for that goal. I hope he goes on to make a positive contribution to the game."' Celtic's towering history is sometimes garnished with tales of self-defeat where fledgling players full of aptitude and flair never discover the deep reserves required to become true champions of the game. Lore such as this throws up more questions than answers and the wonder of possibility endures. The notable talent of Leigh Griffiths is without question and while he has made ill-thought-out choices, it's also fair to say the amount of puritanical aggression directed at the player in his early days at Celtic suggested a lot of first stones were being cast. With that in mind it has been a joy to see him conquer demons and leave the more unsavoury aspects of his past behind. He concedes to rethinking the role his social life, his fitness and his family play in his career. Lennon also came in for some criticism when he secured the former Hibernian and Wolverhampton Wanderers striker's signature: 'He's a natural goalscorer and you can't coach that, his movement was always very good. He's got a bit of the devil in him -you don't want to coach that out because some players need that, it helps them play with an edge. He's been consistent wherever he's gone and we had no qualms about signing him. We were very happy with his contribution, we only worked with him for about five months. He's maybe not at the level of a Hooper but is without doubt a quality finisher and one you could work with and make even better. I've got a lot of time for him and I'm glad things are going well now at Celtic. There was no reason for us to think otherwise, he's a good kid.'

Martin O'Neill has convivially spoke of driving up to Neil Lennon's Stockport residence, described at the time as a 'run down hovel' strewn with half eaten sandwiches and Oasis records back in the mid 1990s. Although the then Crewe Alexandra player was also being pursued by Coventry City [aided by the promise of Premiership football] the persuasive enchantment of O'Neill cast its spell leading ultimately to what was perceived by many as a father and son style relationship, said Lennon: 'It was quite random [coming to the flat to sign him]. He's still a port of call for me in terms of advice now - I was talking to him just the other day. There's no question he was a role model and mentor for me for a very long time. He has given me the best days of my life from a football perspective. I probably wouldn't be in the position I am today without his contribution. Whenever I need any advice I always go back to Martin.' On the subject of Lennon's four years with the Foxes O'Neill in the Foreword of Lennon's 2006 autobiography wrote: 'he bestrode Filbert Street like a colossus, winning tackles, playing the ball, bawling out instructions, cajoling and generally being brilliant. The role of Leicester manager is one job that continues to be associated with Lennon and would undoubtedly be a good fit when his period at Bolton expires. His time with the Premiership club remains among his career highlights: 'Winning the play-off final with Leicester and getting into the Premier League is up there because it was a spring board – a lot opened up for me after that. Obviously getting to the UEFA Cup final, the moment after beating Boavista and to know that you were going was a brilliant feeling - they were the ultimate highs of my playing career. We would have been as revered as the Lisbon Lions if we had got over the line with that. There are too many lows but any Old Firm defeat is emotionally devastating and we lost a couple of league titles on the last day of the season which is pretty tough to take.'

You don't enjoy a fourteen year relationship with a club

like Celtic unless you have something extraordinary to offer. The expectations from the club and its fans are understandably high; passengers aren't tolerated. Neil Lennon's time in Glasgow and what he suffered will undoubtedly be written about, examined and studied by journalists, historians and academics from here to eternity. That it will be regarded as a turning point in Scottish history at best is a rose-tinted analysis, at worst it's a negligible belief. All will be revealed when another player in possession of similar talent and stature from the Irish Catholic tradition makes a contribution in the way that Neil Francis Lennon did. His time at Celtic is awash with permanent memories. As manager of the club that exhilarating contest against Barcelona the day after the club's 125th anniversary will be difficult to eclipse. It's not sentiment to suggest that a known yet bewildering power had engulfed Celtic Park, public houses and front rooms across the globe. Neither is it an extravagant assumption to consider that every player carried something of the founding father's story into the game that night etching a brave new chapter into the walls of Celtic Football Club 'The night before the game it being the club's 125th anniversary, there was just something special about that night [at St Mary's] and you felt like there was something brewing. The following evening you are playing the best club in the world at Celtic Park. You don't get any better than that, it's these events that make a club like Celtic special. The foundation of the club was built on a charitable ethos and that's carried right through today – the club and support are very proud of that history. There would be no Celtic Football Club without Brother Walfrid. I think clubs need history, it's part of the fabric because it provides a substance, it's not a new-age club that has come into new money – that kind of thing doesn't sit right with a lot of football supporters if you know what I mean. The big clubs with a strong tradition like Celtic, Liverpool and Manchester United while evolving with the times they maintain a strong link with the past. Sometimes that past is laced with tragedy but that forms an even stronger bond with the support. Jock Stein's philosophy was about producing your own legends and giving the people something to look forward to. You want to give the next generation something to talk about rather than having to constantly refer to the past.'

For Celtic's Champions League qualifier against F.K.

Quarabag in August 2015. Lennon was reunited with his old team mates John Hartson and Chris Sutton, the spark of chemistry was clear while commentating on Celtic's further European adventures. Even now the press can still be relied on to provide distortions about Lennon when writing about the former Celtic manager. *The Scotsman* newspaper offered a report which studied the three ex-Celts analysis, a confident and articulate delivery didn't prevent a well-known sports writer from describing how 'the Irishman spat at half time' referring to how Lennon delivered his opinion.

He can occasionally still be seen around the old haunts in Glasgow where he retains a number of enduring friendships. Celtic will naturally always be a vital ingredient of his story and he wishes his successor Ronny Deila well. At the same time he is unsentimental about the task in front of him: 'Your first games of the season are your most important, if Ronny can learn from last year hopefully he will get it right because these matches are fraught with pressure and they are dangerous games. A lot of my focus was on preparing for the Champions League because of Celtic's stature they need to get into the C.L. or at least get a good run in Europa. With the Inter Milan game you can see what it means to supporters and the 3-3 draw at Parkhead was a brilliant game. The tie could have went either way, it will have been an significant experience in him going forward. It's important for Celtic to get back on that Champions League stage. Things are not great domestically, last season there was no Hibs, Hearts or Rangers, there's no real competition for Celtic. It will be good to eventually have Rangers and both Edinburgh clubs back but it's not going to happen overnight.'

In the meantime Lennon won't be happy until he has a few players about the place who will set the football world alight and he suggests one or two are already under his guidance. Who knows what gems his knowledge and persistence have unearthed this time. It won't be long until we find out.

Chapter Ten
Swansong

*The most extraordinary recognition of this highly unusual man
was, in the eyes of most football men, that which was accorded
to him on the afternoon of Saturday 14th September. On a
brilliantly sunny, warm afternoon, there was a minute's silence
before kick-off in every football match throughout Scotland at
all levels, in all places. It was absolute silence, nowhere more so
than at Kilbowie Park, Clydebank, where the home side were
playing Rangers.*
Bob Crampsey on the aftermath of Jock Stein's death

IT'S A WONDER that Jock Stein survived a major car crash
at Lockerbie on the A74 after returning from a holiday with
his wife and friends in July 1975. The crash and the previous
development of a heart problem that saw him hospitalised in
December 1972 had understandably diminished the Big Man's
seemingly invincible capacity for greatness. He had created
a team described by Bill Shankly as the greatest club side
in the world citing the European Cup, nine Scottish league
titles in a row and victory over Don Revie's Leeds in Europe
as reasons for his evaluation when pressed by a journalist.
In the aftermath of the accident Celtic players visiting Stein
were shocked to see him in such a vulnerable position. While
reflecting on Stein's singular legacy at Celtic in light of Lisbon
and nine-in-a-row it's easy to overlook the domestic Double he
claimed in the 1976–77 season before his eventual departure
from the club in 1978. The achievement was of momentous
significance for the Celtic manager, on both a personal and
professional level, as the team and football culture in general
had already begun to shift beyond recognition. The car crash
had undoubtedly affected him physically, and more than he
would like to admit. Rangers had quashed Celtic's quest of ten
league titles in a row by the end of the 1974–75 season. During
Stein's official absence throughout the 1975–76 season, Celtic

suffered a barren campaign as Rangers asserted themselves further with a domestic clean sweep. It was with a heavy heart that the Celtic manager saw some of his most-loved players exit Parkhead's gates for the last time in 1975. Stein once joked that his greatest achievement was not winning the European Cup or nine consecutive league titles in a row, but keeping Jinky in the game five years longer than expected. Johnstone's frolics are well documented, but there's no doubt that his eventual exit grieved the gaffer as much as it did Johnstone.

The Quality Street years had provided Celtic supporters with big expectations, but one of the era's greatest hopes, George Connelly, would also make his final appearance in 1975. Connelly was another player the Big Man felt great affection for and despite his best efforts and personal pleas his persuasive powers were unable to yield the desired outcome. Billy McNeill's retirement in 1975 was also seen by many as premature. The player known as Cesar had been involved in the club since 1957 and as Celtic's captain he played a pivotal role throughout Stein's time, his loss was immeasurable. It was also the year in which Kenny Dalglish asserted himself and first handed in a transfer request, though, out of loyalty to Stein, the player agreed to prolong his time at the club. Former Celtic player and Manchester United European Cup winner Paddy Crerand remained close to Stein throughout his time as Celtic manager and was one of the first people to visit him in hospital in the aftermath of the crash: 'The other car had been driving on the wrong side of the road and how Jock survived God only knows; it was a miracle because the hospital had just opened the day before. Jock and Tony [Queen] were the first patients. I had been on holiday with Jock, Tony and Bob Shankly [brother of Bill] and their wives, when I got to the hospital Jock was sitting up with a breathing respirator and Tony was unconscious, they were being treated for various injuries; it was hard to see them like that. When you think of Jock, you think of his strong character and his presence ... really I don't think he was ever the same.'

Despite the accident, associated health problems and a pending court case over the accident, the 1976–77 season was to be Jock Stein's Celtic swansong, his Lazarus comeback and his final opportunity to prove that despite everything, including his own legacy weighing him down, he was capable of one last shot at the title. Journalist and lifelong Celtic supporter Kevin McKenna reflects on the period: 'I remember when nine-in-a-row ended. To us ten was that magic number, but Rangers became dominant during that time. I remember the game on 4 January 1975; Rangers hammered us 3–0. Derek Johnstone and Derek Parlane tore us apart; we were just too slow, you knew the league was gone at that point. Billy McNeill retired after that season and the loss was keenly felt among supporters, he had been an ambassador for Celtic throughout his time at the club and had a big commanding presence for my dad's generation, they felt he was one of them. Because of Jock Stein's accident Celtic were hopeless, there was no leadership and I would doubt if Sean Fallon was given the same control that Stein had. The signing of Pat Stanton in 1976 was crucial to Celtic's renaissance. He had been one of the best players in a fantastic Hibs team that were not unaccustomed to giving Celtic a battering from time to time. Celtic fans would look at Stanton and admire him because he was an intelligent, rock-steady player. The team's frailties were costing us games so when Stanton came in the change was felt immediately.'

Stanton first impressed Jock Stein when he was manager of Dunfermline. Not long after their first meeting he had led the Pars to a Scottish Cup final victory over Celtic in 1961. It was a relationship that would continue throughout Stein's football career. Speaking today at Easter Road stadium Stanton reflects back on their first encounter: 'I was playing juvenile football when I first met Jock, I had a trial for Dunfermline at East End Park and he wanted to sign me. At the time I was training with Hibs and as a supporter I harboured the thought that they would sign me and after a spurt they did, but Jock eventually caught up with me again when he came to Hibs in 1964. Before his arrival managers would come to training in a lounge suit, Jock arrived in a tracksuit; from that moment everything changed. Straight away there was great emphasis on training with the ball, which was unusual. By that stage he was already looking at European styles of management, he had been over to Italy and studied tactics and how the Italians went about things. The club had been in a lull and were slipping back a bit, but within a few games he had players believing in themselves and immediately started building confidence around the team and the club. Before Jock we were dicing with relegation, under him we really believed we were on for the league and cup that season, but it wasn't to be.'

As a boyhood Celtic supporter Pat Crerand had watched Stein marshal Celtic's defence in the way that Stanton would during the 1976–77 season. Crerand suggests that Stein's influence on the club began in his playing days, long before he took on the role of Celtic manager. The Manchester United luminary was another player Stein tried to sign for Dunfermline: 'The way he treated people and his knowledge was second to none, don't forget I saw Jock playing for Celtic. Before the Scottish Cup win in 1951 we were in the doldrums, I saw him win the Coronation Cup final against a great Hibs team in 1953 and I saw him win the league as a Celtic player at Easter Road in 1954. I come from a family of fanatical Celtic supporters and to sign for Celtic was a big deal.

'When Jock retired from playing after injury he trained the Celtic reserves and I got to work with him; it was a delight. Before Jock you had a guy in a white coat smoking a cigarette at the side of the pitch. Jock was a genius and way ahead of everybody; he brought in fresh ideas around passing and movement. I had two years of that and then he got the job at Dunfermline. He asked me to go but I was never going to Dunfermline. Tony [Queen] was the one who told me to go to Manchester United before Jock came back as Celtic manager. Tony was a massive Celtic fan but he said to me: "Celtic are going nowhere, if I was you I would get down to United." Tony and Mike Jackson to a certain degree talked me into it. My time at Celtic was a total farce, the whole situation was a joke. Bob Kelly had too much power. Whatever he said went and it wasn't good for the club; that was the main reason I left. It took Jock coming back as manager to change things at Celtic because practically the whole team that won the European Cup was there when I was . . . and look what he did. I don't think it could happen again.'

In October 1964 Stein's ambitions for the Scottish game were widely revealed when he arranged for Real Madrid to play a friendly against Hibs at Easter Road. Local critics lambasted Stein's aspirations but Hibs comfortably won the game 2-0. During the period Pat Stanton noted Stein's ability to work with players whose lifestyle left the future Celtic boss cold: 'I always got on well with Jock, but some players weren't his cup of tea on a personal level, that didn't mean he'd leave them out of the team. I remember his first team talk, he said very little, but what he said was broad. He said: "Any changes; you'll make them, it's down to you." He used to say: "If God left it out; I can't put it in, I can guide players but they must have desire." He made it clear that everyone would get his chance to be in the team, but you had to listen to him. If you take someone like Willie Hamilton, discipline wasn't his strong point. Let's just say Willie liked to enjoy himself. Jock believed in him and was capable of getting some great stuff out of Willie that others couldn't. By the time he left we were a great side, he had brought in players like John McNamee, who had played for Celtic; he made a big impact here. Stein got Hibs knocking on the door again.'

In March 1965 Jock Stein achieved his lifetime ambition by taking on the role of Celtic manager. Throughout the period Stanton continued to play a pivotal role at Hibs who challenged Celtic for a number of domestic trophies, eventually claiming three: the League Cup in 1972 (with Stanton scoring first in the 2–1 victory) and the Drybrough Cup twice beating Celtic in the 1972 and 1973 finals. Stanton reflects on the period: 'I was always an admirer of players like Bobby Murdoch and Bertie Auld and the wee right winger was quite good too. Rangers also had a strong side and you were playing against the likes of Jim Baxter, John Greig and Willie Henderson. With Rangers and that Celtic team you had to go in with a strong mentality; if you didn't the game was lost before kick-off. These players could intimidate you without saying a word.'

By the summer of 1976 Stanton had fallen out of favour with Hibs manager Eddie Turnbull. He was preparing for a reserve game against Hearts when he received an untypical phone call that would see Jock Stein finally sign the player he originally spotted in 1962. Stanton recalls: 'I'd had two or three opportunities to go to clubs in England during my time at Hibs, but I have to say the club were good to me and I didn't bother . . . but by that time I wasn't in the picture at Hibs and really my career could have just faded out. It was a Wednesday morning when the phone went, my wife said it was Eddie Turnbull, he'd never phoned me for any reason at home. Right away he said: "I've got Mr Stein here to speak to you." Of course, I knew exactly what was going to happen but I hadn't had any inkling before that. He came on and said: "I've got permission to speak to you; how would you like to come and play for the Celtic?" My immediate reply was "I'd love to" because I felt my time at Hibs was at an end.

'For me at that stage in my career to go and play in a team with Kenny Dalglish and Danny McGrain was something great. At Hibs I spent most of my time in midfield, when Stein came to Hibs from Dunfermline he played me at the back in a sweeper position, it was perhaps a role I was more suited to. I had always looked at them as a big club it was always an occasion when the Celtic were coming to Easter Road to play Hibs. My dad enjoyed watching the likes of Willie Fernie and John Higgins in the 1950s, he liked a good player whether it was Jimmy Millar at Rangers or Bobby Evans at Celtic. Immediately the set-up at Celtic was impressive, from the tea lady to the groundsman, you could feel the atmosphere right away and you quickly learned that losing wasn't tolerated. The attitude was "we strive to win everything here" and you had to adjust to that, a lot of good players find an environment like that hard to cope with. I got a warm welcome from the support who I would meet going into the ground for training or on match days. I'd say both Celtic and Hibs supporters are likely to be romantics. My dad's family came over from County Mayo and lived in the Canongate where the Irish people settled in the Old Town. Hibs were formed around St Patrick's Church and my family's roots go back to Michael Whelahan who was one of the Hibs founders. My father was a Hibs fan through and through, but he always had an affinity with Celtic. When I told him I had signed he said: "What?" I said: "I've just signed for the Celtic". He replied: "You can't get better than that son."'

Stanton's departure from Hibs had left fans with an open wound, but after 13 years of service to the club he supported, he found himself in poor form and on the fringes. It was time to move on and the season that followed at Celtic granted a stunning rebirth for the player. Having cemented his place in Hibs folklore it is often overlooked that he also left his mark on a strong Celtic side that had earned itself much respect and admiration from the Parkhead support who themselves were smarting from recent changes. The first game of the season on 4th September 1976 against Rangers was Stanton's first experience of the Glasgow derby. He recalls sitting in an impassioned Celtic dressing room before the game: 'I had never been to an Old Firm game even as a spectator, it was all new to me. I was an experienced player, but the sense of occasion inside the club and the noise just hit you – nothing can prepare you for something like that moment, you are just looking around in awe. My instant feeling was that I didn't want to be the guy who made a mistake because fans tend to remember something like that, but at least we got a draw that day.

'It didn't take me long to settle in the side. I got to play alongside some of Celtic's greatest players; I had Danny McGrain on one side and Andy Lynch on the other and sometimes Tommy Burns. We had to get the ball through to Ronnie Glavin or Big Roy [Aitken], he was only a seventeen year-old laddie, but even then he was like a thirty year-old man, a big powerful player. He played in the centre of the midfield and Roddy MacDonald was centre half. Up front you had Kenny, Paul Wilson, who scored two in my debut, and Johnny Doyle, who had a shot cleared off the line. Jock had teams hemmed in, the team would knock their pan in, but it just took one moment's break of concentration and bang, you've lost a silly goal. Jock made it clear that I had to stop that from happening. I don't think I left my own half all season.'

Suggesting the shifting times, the game was broadcast to millions while 57,000 showed up at the ground. A picture of Stanton congratulating Paul Wilson, the player with his two arms stretched out in defiance while sporting the era's collared green and white hoops implies something of the team's character that season as well as Wilson's remarkable ability to shine in games such as these. The *Daily Record* acclaimed Stanton's role in a Celtic side that had regained its strength and composure with Stein back at the helm, saying: 'Pat on the back: Celts back from the dead to pip Rangers'. The headline also acknowledged that Wilson's second in a brace had silenced premature victory chants with three vital minutes to go in a 2-2 draw.

The season held much promise, and for Stanton especially it wasn't without drama or sentiment. Celtic supporter and journalist Kevin McKenna casts his mind back to April 1977 when Celtic had an opportunity to win the league against Hibs: 'During that time I wasn't allowed to go to the Rangers games, but I was there when Celtic won the league in 1977. The place was rocking and Hibs came at us hell for leather, it's a well-known fact the Hibs chairman [Tom Hart] banned the cameras because he couldn't handle the idea of Celtic winning the league at Easter Road with Pat Stanton. Stanton was outstanding in that game. Danny McGrain, another world-class player, was voted footballer of the year, but I think you could have made a case for Pat Stanton. I don't think Celtic would have won the Double if he hadn't played in that team.'

After a solitarily goal from Celtic's Joe Craig in a hard fought victory, Stanton was the proud winner of a Scottish League winner's medal. Remembers Stanton: 'When Jock Stein spoke to me about joining Celtic someone said to me as I left Easter Road: "You'll be back here to win the league", I laughed. I said "you must be kidding me"; but it actually happened. I was sitting in the away dressing room that day with that medal thinking about a lot of water that had passed under the bridge. The first time I sat in that away dressing room was before a public trial for Hibs as a boy and there I was all those years later in a Celtic jersey having just won the league, it was absolutely terrific. As I was sitting there big Jock came over with a smile on his face, he looked at me and said: "No bad eh?" I said "It's pretty good boss."'

Undoubtedly Stein was aware of the emotional nuances of Stanton's league win. Having recognised his talent while at Dunfermline, managed him for a spell at Hibs and long admired him as an opposition player, that season he finally got to utilise his skill building a strong Celtic team from the back. They finished the season undefeated in five meetings with Rangers. Stein had created an atmosphere of invincibility inside a dressing room bursting with impressive characters both in the side and among the manager's tight circle, which all helped create a winning mentality long before kick-off. Says Stanton: 'Jock had a lot of impressive people around him. Sean Fallon was a smart man and a hardy soul. Jock liked sporting men around him like Jimmy Steel; they would talk about boxing and horse racing. I remember if things got too tense Jimmy used to say: "It's only a game boys."

'Before a big match some dressing rooms are like a doctor's waiting room. It wasn't like that at Celtic; Stein would go the other way and get the boys having a laugh before a big game. I remember when Aston Villa won the European Cup in 1982, Brian Clough was doing the commentary and they asked him what advice he would give Tony Barton. Clough said "Get them laughing". Jock loved Doyley [Johnny Doyle] because he was a bright and breezy presence, he was always up to something - playing jokes on people or upsetting somebody. He used to turn up at Parkhead on match day with his Celtic scarf on, Jock would tell him not to bother with that, but that was Doyley. Kenny [Dalglish] was never slow in offering his opinions either. When you'd see him years later being interviewed on television he often gave one-word answers, but Kenny was nothing like that in reality, he was very quick-witted and always had an opinion. When Danny talked you listened because his comments would only come around once in a while but they were always constructive and straight to the point.

'In that team you had some of Celtic's greatest ever players and in Jock one of the biggest names in football management; the players respected him and he never dismissed anyone's ideas, though you really felt if he disliked you, you wouldn't be there. Tommy Burns was also breaking through. He was a typical Glaswegian character. If you were to ask me from what I experienced who summed up what Celtic was about at that time, it was Tommy Burns, because he was a bright, smart lad but he was also tough. He epitomised the Celtic thing to me. He had his strong faith, but he didn't hit you over the head with it.'

* * *

Jock Stein's final Celtic honour was achieved on 7 May 1977 after a 1–0 victory over Rangers in the Scottish Cup Final. While many supporters fully expected Kenny Dalglish to take a controversial penalty awarded to Celtic, it was Andy Lynch who stepped up to score, cementing his place in the club's history. But in the aftermath of glory things changed rapidly. In a matter of weeks skipper Dalglish had left for Liverpool and on the first day of the 1977–78 season came another watershed as Stanton sustained a career ending injury away at Dundee United. Journalist Kevin McKenna reflects on the sense of the passing era Celtic supporters were already feeling even before Stanton left the pitch for the last time: 'I was there the day he went out injured against Dundee United at the start of the season, we had already lost Kenny and we would lose Danny McGrain that season to injury and I would gladly acknowledge that Stanton's loss was as keenly felt as those two players. In him we had an intelligent and reliable defender who didn't panic at the first sign of trouble. Celtic have always found that kind of player hard to come by and still do. There are very few times when supporters have felt secure about the central defence. But Pat Stanton brought that quality to Celtic Park.' A further blow came in the same game when Stein lost another valuable player in Alfie Conn. Despite returning later that season the player continued to struggle with injury. The former Rangers player had whipped up the Scottish media simply by signing for Celtic after a spell at Tottenham, but once again Stein's common-sense approach profited Celtic while promoting positive ideals in wider Scottish society.

Prior to the fateful injuries both players had made a positive impression on Celtic supporters during a tour of the Far East in the summer of 1977, suggesting realistic hopes for the season ahead. During a 2–0 victory against Red Star Belgrade Stanton displayed some atypical behaviour when he retaliated to a violent challenge, receiving a red card in the process. For a player esteemed as a model of calm it was particularly uncharacteristic: 'I was going for the ball and the guy stuck an elbow in my face so I punched him, he was bigger than me. After the game Big Jock was talking to the team and I'm sitting in the corner not pleased at having been sent off, feeling as though I let the guys down. He said to me: "Imagine a player of your experience falling for that." I was still annoyed from the game so I snapped back: "What would you have done like?" He never said anything, he just turned away and smiled, but out the corner of my eye I could see Bob Rooney laughing. He'd got his palm flat out and he pushed his fist into it as if to say he would have done the same thing; it was brilliant.

'Jock could sum things up without saying a word, or very little. There were certain things he didn't tolerate. I remember the Scottish Cup final, the supporters were whistling for full-time, we were looking to see how long to go. But Jock wouldn't tell you and if someone did he'd let them have it; if you were looking for the time then you weren't paying attention. After the game I was sitting with my Scottish Cup medal, I looked up and there was Jock, he just tilted his head and winked. That said it all to me. Jock knew how to treat people; it didn't matter who they were. There was one occasion when I was heading into training and I got a call from a friend of mine, Ian, who was in Glasgow for the day getting his car serviced. He asked if there was any chance someone could show him about Celtic Park. I told him I'd take him. He was looking around the place in awe; I'm talking about a Hibs fan here. I put the lights half on in the trophy room and we're having a blether, suddenly the lights are hit full and there's Stein standing at the door. I said: "Boss, this is a friend of mine." Right away he said: "No another Hibs supporter ... what do you think of this son?" Ian was a hard-nosed businessman and as I say a diehard Hibs man, but he said to Jock: "You can't fail to be impressed with this Mr Stein." Jock could just sum things up very simply. He said: "That's right son, some clubs buy them; we win them." Even in that short light-hearted conversation Ian got the message; Jock was different class. He didn't have to come in and put off time but that's how he was. Ian passed away a few years ago, but he remembered that moment all his life.'

And so it was that Pat Stanton would end his career at Celtic on the first day of the 1977–78 season, his injury one in a series of misfortunes that would dog Jock Stein's final season in charge of Celtic. With the loss of both Stanton and McGrain in defence as well as Kenny Dalglish, one of the most prolific strikers in Celtic's history, the team went through a period of transition finishing fifth in the league. It was a cheerless footnote that the Big Man's final game in charge was a 3–1 defeat against St Mirren, which also meant the club would lose out on European football the following season. Significantly the Paisley team were managed by a man who would learn much in the coming years as assistant to Stein in the role of Scotland manager: Alex Ferguson. Thankfully there remained a final cause for celebration a day after that defeat. Undoubtedly Stein held great affection for Stanton and took much pride in gifting the player something of a stylish send-off with a testimonial at Easter Road between Hibs and Celtic on 30 April 1978: 'I got on well with Jock and maybe some players during his career didn't, but when I had a big operation at the end of my time he'd drop into the hospital at all hours for a blether. At that point he was very busy and I'd have been quite easy to forget about, but that meant a lot. My testimonial was on a cold miserable Sunday morning. I remember sitting on the old stand at Easter Road and looking at the weather in disbelief. A short time later

Stein walked into the dressing room and said: "Don't worry Pat, the boys are coming through, the buses are on the road." Jock said he wanted Jimmy [Johnstone] to play, but wanted him to train first. He said: "I want folk to see a great player", he didn't want people to see Jimmy any other way.'

The following day's newspaper reports paid homage to Jimmy Johnstone's remarkable capacity to entertain while revealing that two of his Lisbon Lion teammates, Tommy Gemmell and Willie Wallace, also turned out for Hibs. Said Stanton: 'Jimmy was brilliant; it turned into a really special day. After the match we had a sandwich and a drink at the King James hotel, my dad and Uncle Pat were sitting having a blether with Jock. At the end of the night we all got into the car, my dad said: "A very impressive man Mr Stein" to which my uncle, always master of the understatement added: "Aye, and he knows a lot about football."' Today, Pat Stanton's green and white hooped jersey from the Scottish Cup final hangs on his son's wall at home. Not surprisingly he's a confirmed Celtic supporter. 'Give me the boy and I'll show you the man,' says Stanton. 'I took him to Celtic first and now he's a Celtic man. I just thought he can't fail to be impressed with this. His brother, however, is a Hibs fan. I was fortunate to go to a club like Celtic at that stage in my career and I would have played longer had it not been for the injury, but I was very fortunate that I got to play for the club I supported and the team I would've supported if I hadn't been a Hibs fan. It was a long time ago now, but I still get Celtic fans stopping me and they are always very positive. The support was always fantastic to me, from the moment I picked up the phone that day with Jock it was fantastic.'

Significantly Stein continued to seek Stanton out after the player moved into football management with spells at two of the Big Man's previous clubs: Dunfermline and Hibs. Stein's genius at spotting a player showed no sign of shrinking during his final years as Scotland boss: 'Our paths kept crossing. I was involved in a part-time professional tournament, which included lower league international players from Scotland, England, Italy and Holland. Jock phoned me up and asked to come along. It was a great wee tournament and even then Jock was picking out the players who went on to have careers. I remember him saying to me "Have you thought about the wee Ayr United player?" It was Steve Nicol who went on to

Liverpool. I remember a pre-season friendly: Manchester City v Hibs. Jock said to me "You'll be pleased with the wee left back, great tackler." It was John Collins.'

Jock Stein left Celtic garlanded in trophies, but his final exit in 1978 was an unsettled time for both Stein and the Celtic board with both parties concerned about the future. His exit remains a point of much conjecture to this day. After 13 years as manger of Celtic it's not a point of wonder to understand Stein struggling to find the right fit for his talents. He would eventually decline an offer to join the Celtic board of directors and would hastily leave his post as Leeds manager after just 44 days. Pat Crerand remembers events leading up to his appointment as manager of Scotland: 'I never understood why he went to Leeds because he had been offered the Manchester United job years before and he said it was down to his wife Jean that he wouldn't go to England, she didn't want to move. So if it wasn't right before why would it be right then? He phoned me one night to ask if I was going to watch Oldham v Morton in some cup they had at the time. I said: "Jock are you crackers? You're going to drive from Leeds to Manchester to get me and then drive to Oldham and then back to Leeds?" Benny Rooney was managing Morton and his assistant was Mike Jackson. I got the feeling that Jock was a bit bored . . . but anyway it comes over the wireless that Ally MacLeod had been given the sack. I said: "Jock, you'll get that job." By the time you get home they'll be on the phone to you. It was literally days after that he was Scotland manager.

'Jock was very, very hurt about having to leave Celtic. If you look at the picture of the Celtic chairman [Desmond White] trying to shake Billy McNeill's hand [after becoming Celtic manager] with Jock in the middle, it tells you something. My personal thoughts were that there was a feeling of jealousy among the directors at Celtic because Jock was the man and they were never getting a mention. That can happen in football and it can happen in life. It's a very human thing – you are the big star and others don't get the adulation – it can cause a problem. Jock was a Celtic man through and through. Celtic was his team; it was his life – Celtic was everything to him.'

In October 2012 Pat Nevin presented a Radio 5 live documentary *Big Jock* which suggested Stein was the most influential British manager of all time and that his theories, ideas and personal influence continue to reverberate at the highest level of the game. 30 years on from Jock Stein's death there remains a tangible enthusiasm around the stature of the man and his life which continues to grow in literature, supporter websites and media documentaries where much discussion and debate is reserved for his character, legacy and genius which function as a sentinel for the standard continually expected at Celtic and among its support.

Chapter Eleven
Red Skies over Paradise

'The opinion that art should have nothing to do with politics is itself a political attitude.'
George Orwell

THE GREEN BRIGADE'S organised display prior to the Barcelona game 125 years and a day after Celtic's formation was one of the most impressive witnessed in any British ground. Its sheer magnitude and detail right down to the red Celtic cross on the red oval background will loom large in the memory of Celtic supporters for many years to come. During 'You'll Never Walk Alone' Sky Television cameras zoomed in on a James Connolly scarf among the support. It's a strange twist of fate that Connolly is predominantly remembered in his homeland among Celtic supporters. The scarves have always been popular on match days where they are sold outside the ground in an unofficial capacity by vendors.

In times such as these, when fans are questioning which songs are allowed or acceptable in the context of Celtic, it is perhaps time to look at a figure such as James Connolly with fresh eyes. For a start it's significant that Celtic fans would honour a man with such strong associations with a rival club such as Edinburgh's Hibernian. It's worth pointing out too that it's unlikely those same scarves would be seen as appropriate by many Hibernian fans today as the club has a less visible Irish diaspora than Celtic. Hibs historian Alan Lugton explains: 'As a twelve year-old barefoot street urchin, James Connolly would carry the players' kits down to Easter Road, which ensured him of a sixpence and free admission to the match. He carried out hundreds of other odd jobs at the ground too.' When Connolly returned to Edinburgh in his early twenties after deserting from the British Army, he organised fund-raising initiatives for Hibs who were fighting to survive. Letters home written during a trip to America in the early 1900s reveal that Connolly's homesickness was largely associated with missing games at his beloved Easter Road.

He is honoured publicly elsewhere, but in the country of his birth, Connolly is an invisible figure in a cultural dead zone. A question often asked to Celtic supporters not from the Glasgow area is: 'Why don't you support your local team?' It is likely the answer to that question for many supporters is that while not denying Scotland, Ireland dominates in the hearts and imaginations for many who hail from the diaspora. In that context Celtic has and hopefully always will be a place where that identity can flourish in a way that is helpful for individuals, and indeed wider society, who feel an affinity to that way of life and culture while accepting and embracing those who don't. While some might argue having an Irish identity has 'nothing to do with football', it has much to do with Celtic. The reason for the club's existence was helpfully highlighted in the Scottish media on the 125th anniversary of the club's birth. Articles and comment pointed to Brother Walfrid's intentions in creating the club to help the Irish community, as well as native Scots, who were illiterate, starving and living in poverty. With that perspective in mind, it's understandable that a number of politically minded supporters would want to recognise an international figure such as the Scottish-born socialist James Connolly who, like Celtic, has a dual Scottish and Irish nuance as a survivor of a disease-ridden Irish slum in Edinburgh. He went on to become one of the most recognised and honoured political thinkers of the 20th century.

At the same time there are many non-Irish, non-Catholic supporters who feel uneasy about the influence of Irish nationalism because of its association with the dark days of the Troubles. My aim here is to examine how supporters with non-violent democratic beliefs see the influence of Celtic in relation to Irish politics and its influence on their life and work. In 2007 the James Connolly Society had decided to put an end to a parade in which Celtic and Hibs supporters would often march side by side, citing their support of the peace process in Northern Ireland. The event had also developed certain 'sectarian' connotations with pro-violent and extremist overtones during a time of peace. As a result organisers resolved to promote work in communities over a public display which could further harm Connolly's reputation while underlining the need to 'rebrand' Connolly and look at him in the environment of the times in which he was living. In February 2012 calls to revive the James Connolly march in Edinburgh were still causing concern among local councillors and the police.

In truth Connolly loathed sectarianism. As a union organiser in Belfast he successfully managed to unite Catholic and Protestant workers against exploitative employers with the aim of granting them better conditions. Growing up in the extreme poverty of the Irish diaspora in Scotland, Connolly believed in creating a better and fairer society be it his birthplace, Ireland or America; religious background was an irrelevance. In April 2012 the *Edinburgh Evening News* printed a cover picture in homage to The Beatles' *Sgt Pepper's Lonely Hearts Club Band* on its 45th anniversary. The caricature featuring Edinburgh's most eminent sons and daughters found Connolly absent; once again airbrushed out of the city's history, arguably suggesting his inclusion would hit a discordant note. Despite this omission, among Connolly's honours in Dublin are a railway station, a statue and a hospital name in recognition of his role in Ireland's history. For his contribution to political progressive thinking while in America he is recognised with a monument in Troy Park, New York and with a statue in Chicago's Union Park. He was cited in a 2002 BBC poll as one of the 100 greatest Britons of all time, and in 1972 John Lennon named him as the inspiration for his single 'Woman is the Nigger of the World'. In these representations Connolly is seen as a champion of the underdog, but in Scotland he is often viewed as a divisive and sectarian figure. Edinburgh councillor Jeremy Balfour said it's time to break the association with modern-day extremist views, offering the opinion that a statue in Scotland would perhaps give him some kind of official capacity, giving Scots the opportunity to understand more about his early socialist background and views in relation to the land of his birth.

Here Conservative councillor Balfour explains Scotland's difficult relationship with Connolly: 'He is seen as a hero by one side of the community and a hate figure by the other. The [Connolly] march does cause confrontation and raises temperatures within different communities and I'm not sure this is the best way forward. Edinburgh has worked really hard to reduce the sectarian tension that existed in the city and which still does to some extent. Anything that brings tension to the surface like that isn't particularly helpful. I don't think people would want to go along simply because of the trouble that has occurred in the past and if you've got children you wouldn't take them into that environment. Clearly he is an important part of republican history and he came from Edinburgh. Like a lot of people he became more famous when he left the city, but he was born here and he is a part of history and we have to recognise that. If there are people within the city who want to recognise him with a monument or a statue of remembrance and they can raise that money then I think the council should look at marking him in an appropriate way.' The James Connolly march returned to Edinburgh on June 1st 2013. But the original organisers appeared to distance themselves from the event in favour of organising more community based initiatives.

It is no surprise that this historical figure has recently been brought to life by a Celtic supporter. Scottish actor Peter Mullan took on the role for *Connolly*, a biopic that attempts to bring some mainstream credibility to its subject, much like the Hollywood attempt to tell the story of Michael Collins in 1996. The film, which has struggled with financing, will eventually see the light of day on the centenary of the Easter Rising. The actor explains the contradictions of Connolly's life are what attracted him to the role: 'It's a lovely script. I first read a Connolly biography when I was fifteen and the thing that fascinated me was his socialist background. Growing up I thought the Irish tricolour was green, white and gold because of Celtic. I was shocked when I realised how inclusive the flag was, that the green was for Irish Catholic and the orange was for Protestant [the white representing peace]. I loved that idea. I remember going back to what I had read about Connolly, that the flag only became the national flag of Ireland after the Easter Rising. What I found interesting about him as a man is that he was part of a system without being a product of it. He had been part of the British Empire having joined the army at an early age, but he became its biggest enemy. People talk about him being in the army as if that slandered his legacy. I like that dialectic; it's what makes him interesting. While I was doing some research for the part I met his great grandson and

I asked him if there was anything personal that I could bring to his character. He told me he had a problem with the word socialism, he'd had a speech impediment that haunted him his entire life. Of course this produced a lot of sniggers when he was trying to get his tongue around the word – one of the world's great socialists had a problem saying it; that's cool.'

In her book *The Scots' Crisis of Confidence*, Dr Carol Craig introduces her study by telling the story of a young African-American woman who approached her in the aftermath of a talk on Scottish culture and confidence. The woman explained she had been struggling with typical Scots attitudes and a tendency towards negativity. She went on to describe how her husband's outgoing nature and confidence had vanished after returning to his homeland from America saying: 'You see it's different for him here; he's a west of Scotland working-class Catholic.' Undoubtedly, it has been difficult historically for Scots from the Irish diaspora to feel a sense of optimism about being Scottish. But Scotland's denial of Connolly as a son is possibly symbolic of a wider problem, articulating a complex relationship with the land of your birth in Scotland might make sense in your community and perhaps in your relationship with Celtic, but it doesn't necessarily make sense outside of that community. Even in the current crippling economic climate in a country of only five million people, 60,000 supporters chose to pack out a football ground to support their team in Europe. As well as being passionate supporters, this fact perhaps suggests something about the power of Irish identity in Scotland.

Peter Mullan explains his own journey in the diaspora: 'In my case they [the family] were third- and fourth-generation Irish. My great grandparents were Irish on both sides, I think we definitely had hang-ups because my generation were never made to feel Scottish, we felt somehow removed. I imagine that's how some Asian Scots parents would feel; more Asian in the way we felt more Irish. But for the generation beyond me, I don't think they would even question it. I don't think my daughter would ever question being Scottish, if anything I think she would say herself that she feels European. I don't think she would say anything about Irish origins. I learned the hard way. I was filming in Derry, this was sometime in the early 1990s, and one of the make-up assistants said to me: "I love your Scottish accent." I said to her: "I'm actually Irish", to which she replied: "Not another Scot who thinks he's fucking Irish." It was a tough lesson but they were right. Now I'm just pleased to be Scottish and, of course, my ancestors came from Ireland. Take it a step further and it seems ridiculous because ultimately they came from Africa as do everyone's, so ultimately I thought "I'm Scottish, accept the fact." I would hate the idea of someone coming from Eastern Europe to Scotland and not feeling Scottish, that somehow even though they live and work here they don't feel part of it. They deserve the same rights and protection as everybody else regardless of colour, class or creed. Equally I would hate them to forget that their parents came from Poland or Russia.'

Undoubtedly Mullan's ideals come from a socialist tradition that places a strong emphasis on inclusion. He explains that even though the wider culture was unfavourable or held an aversion towards the diaspora, the community resisted changing its identity. But it didn't necessarily mean a rejection of the host culture and instead created an ethnic blend: 'Growing up our house was non-bigoted, I never once heard an anti-Protestant statement, but it was very Irish in that we had JFK on the wall and Brendan Behan on the bookshelf. The only type of thing like that [bigotry] was you would hear talk that was very anti-Japanese because I had two uncles who were prisoners of war. In Lanarkshire I think things were different again because in my generation it was not the same experience growing up a Catholic in places like Coatbridge. What happened there was that people felt under siege by a wider Protestant community. In those places the Irish that scabbed in the mines were beaten to death with stones. It might have happened over a hundred years ago, but the memories are passed from generation to generation.' As a director Mullan has transposed the Catholic inner-city life of his early years to achieve European cinema awards for both *Orphans* (1997) and *Neds* (2010). While he has distanced himself from organised religion in favour of a strong political identity, describing himself as a Marxist, his films retain strong motifs, themes and characters that relate to the faith background he grew up in. Among many Celtic fans the bond between faith and politics of the left remains strong and in tune with Brother Walfrid's purpose in combining faith with action to aid and transform the lives of the struggling and the hopeless. When pressed on whether he retains a sense of belief, Mullan had this to say: 'Probably not, but aye, I'm a Trot, I'm a Marxist. I try to conveniently avoid the question, but so much of it is part of me. I miss going to the chapel on a Sunday, it's nostalgia and the smell of roast tattie Sunday lunch. But when there's a death, you don't go writing letters to the *Socialist Voice*, you go to the chapel and that's when a scientific dialectic lets you down, if you're that way inclined. What happens when someone dies, where do you go to reflect? In my case with my background I go to the chapel.'

Fellow Celtic supporter and scriptwriter Paul Laverty penned one of Mullan's most notable roles in *My Name Is Joe*. At Cannes in 1998 Mullen claimed the Best Actor prize for the role and didn't miss an opportunity in asking jury president Martin Scorsese to sign his Celtic shirt. Laverty is also widely recognised for his partnership with British film director Ken Loach, the pair have made a number of Scottish films concentrating on working-class life in the west of Scotland as well as *The Wind That Shakes The Barley* (2006) concerning the Irish War of Independence [1919– 1921] and the Irish Civil War (1922–23). As a Celtic supporter and republican Paul Laverty explains how his Irish family history shaped the writing of the Palme d'Or winning war drama as well as his own political ideals: 'As a child every summer I'd go to my uncle Pat's farm in Limerick, I remember the shiny golden fields. He and his mates were young strong powerful men in their twenties at the time of the Irish War of Independence. They ran a farm from winter to spring, my grandfather was also in the IRA during that period and I'd heard all the stories about him giving information or hiding guns.' It's not uncommon for Celtic supporters or those from the Irish diaspora to discover relatives who have been involved historically in Ireland's wars. Since the peace process there are many Celtic supporters who retain a republican identity though the overwhelming majority are keen to separate that stance from accusations, often from rival fans, of their support of violent atrocities and sectarianism. It's a subject Celtic fan Des Dillon raised in his play *Singin' I'm No a Billy He's a Tim* in a charged scene between Rangers fan Billy and Celtic supporter Tim:

Billy: We took yees in! An how do yees repay us. By blowing us up!
Tim: I never blew anybody up!
Billy: No? Manchester Birmingham Warrington Fuckin London!
Tim: It wasn't fuckin me but, was it?
Billy: No but I bet ye didn't condemn it either did ye? Did ye? No-none of yees did. Not even your priests.

While this is often a common perception of Celtic supporters among outsiders, the truth is often more complex and obscured, Paul Laverty explains his position: 'I've got a republican identity in every country that I live in; I don't like the idea of royalty, they seem like decent people, but I believe in a democratic republic. The problem is that many people think republicanism is a sectarian thing, which I totally despise with every inch of my being. Many republicans who were executed in Ireland were Protestant, what they believed in was freedom and democracy; you have to take it back to its roots to reclaim it and pull it out of this sectarian cul-de-sac. I've always come at this totally from a human rights perspective; an attack on any civilian is beyond the pale. It's an international and legal principle that I totally believe in. When we look at Ireland it's important to look at the roots, we did that in the film [*The Wind That Shakes The Barley*] and some right-wing journalists went absolutely nuts. If you look at it from the start of the conflict in 1918, a democratic decision was not respected and people were thrown into prison, censored and beat up. These wars were a tragedy and Ireland became a very dark place as a result.'

Undoubtedly for Laverty and other thinking Celtic fans who identify with republicanism it is not their ambition for Ireland to return to the dark days of the Troubles. Laverty was brought up by an Irish mother and a second-generation Irish father. Growing up there was a robust emphasis on education among Irish parents who had worked in gruelling and demanding occupations; they wanted their children to have the best education available to them so their offspring could progress beyond the struggles that had characterised and inflicted previous generations. Laverty is undoubtedly a product of that transformative culture and this mentality continue to reverberate in his screenwriting for feature films such as *The Angels' Share* (2012) in which lead character Robbie, played by real life East End Celtic supporter Paul Brannigan, overcomes a chaotic world of inner-city violence and substance abuse while striving toward a future of hope and possibility.

The late Brazilian philosopher Paulo Freire and his transformative vision for the oppressed shares much in common with Laverty's ideals. He writes: 'It is necessary that the weakness of the powerless is transformed into a force capable of announcing justice. For this to happen a total denouncement of fatalism is necessary. We are transformative beings and not beings for accommodation.' It's this 'denouncement of fatalism' that has been the essence of the Celtic psyche, a determination not to give in to hate, violence, negativity and resentment despite struggles. Undoubtedly these were recurring themes for Laverty growing up: 'My mother's attitude was massively important. With immigrant populations many parents worked in navvying or cleaning and it was heavy work. In those cultures the children are made to study like hell and so the next generation excelled in school because there was a realisation of how important it was. My grandfather apparently left Ireland when he was two and worked on the shipyards, I often wonder what it would have been like to work in that atmosphere of tremendous sectarianism in the late nineteenth century on the River Clyde. I think it would make for another great story one day.'

Laverty first attended Celtic Park after obtaining a philosophy degree at the Gregorian University in Rome. Significantly the culture and irreverent humour around the club's support remained a strong influence on his life and work, particularly in the short film *Tickets*. Laverty discusses his first visit to Parkhead and the significance of Celtic in his formative years: 'The first time I went into the Jungle was against Hibs with mates from Maryhill; it was gobsmacking. For me it ties up with childhood and memories, family and mad days out. The summer of 1967 is ingrained in my mind doing summersaults and spilling cups of tea, there are moments of sadness and tragedy too like Dixie Deans knocking the ball over the bar in the 1972 European Cup, you never forget these times. It's a place full of wonder and excitement, a place of many emotions and also a place to relax and forget. It's much more linked to memories and mates for me now; you look back and remember what you were doing and who you were with when a certain goal was scored or something mad that happened. One of those was when Tony Cascarino famously couldn't get a goal; when he finally scored there was more hearty laughter on the terracing than clapping, I loved those moments.'

There was something of that comical nature captured in *Tickets*, directed by Ken Loach, about three Celtic fans travelling to a Champions League match by rail. Their journey hits the buffers when a stowaway from Eastern Europe steals one of the fan's match tickets. Says Laverty: 'I've got a lot of sympathy for football fans generally. I remember when Celtic went to the UEFA Cup final there wasn't one arrest; the fans were amazing. I tried to capture that sense of celebration and high spirits. A number of European clubs have got that tradition; football brings people together and can help represent people in the minority. I think football supporters can get stereotyped in the media when often all they want to do is travel, try the local food and meet fans of other clubs ... and maybe get up to some mischief. It's hard to be objective [about Celtic], but I told the story about characters and people I would recognise. I wanted them to be the mischievous, slightly dopey scallywags that would be familiar to people. When I wrote those parts they arrived very easily.'

When working with director Ken Loach, Laverty has often used actors without formal training, making room for a more naturalistic atmosphere in their work. Martin Compston brought some terrace craic from Celtic Park for his role of Jamesy in *Tickets* and there is some inner-city Celtic character in a number of his roles from *Sweet Sixteen* to the equally acclaimed performance in *Red Road*. A former professional footballer with Greenock Morton, Compston has found success as a movie and television actor as well as being selected as a games ambassador alongside Billy Connolly for the Commonwealth Games in 2014. He was also a vocal supporter of the Yes campaign during the Scottish independence referendum. Compston explains his pleasure at being asked to portray a Celtic fan on screen: 'It's something in our DNA, the fact that we come from an immigrant community that tried to look out for each other; that's still there. Celtic was set up to help people and that's really what *Tickets* was about,

Paul [Laverty] was influenced by the story of Seville and those eighty thousand fans travelling to another country with no arrests recorded; you won't see that with other clubs. Celtic supporters are all about supporting the team and doing it in a positive way.

'Making *Tickets* was a really great experience for me; I got paid to wear a Celtic top and sing the songs for a few weeks. The best of it was wee Gary [Maitland], who played Spaceman, is a Rangers diehard. We had to get him in the hoops and teach him a few songs to get him into the part, which was brilliant.' The community aspect of Celtic has remained with Compston as an actor travelling wherever the work takes him. It's also helped get him out of a few tight spots, suggesting that sense of helping others remains paramount wherever supporters gather to watch the games: 'My one constant in life, wherever I go in the world, is that I'll find a Celtic bar because you're guaranteed a warm welcome and a friendly face. It's one of the first things I look for, and you always find one which helps when you are far away from home in a strange place. I've watched a few games with Los Angeles CSC in Joxer Daly's; their motto is "You'll Never Surf Alone".

'I've also had some great times with a few other actors: Ross McCall who was born in Port Glasgow, Tony Curran and Eddie Cahill who was in *Friends* and *Sex and the City*, he's absolutely Celtic daft! One of my best moments was when Naka scored the free kick in the 1–0 Champions League game against Manchester United from thirty-odd yards; it was incredible. I watched that game in Toronto with Peter Mullan, we had been working on a film and ended up watching the game in a hotel. I've watched a few games with Peter, most of the actors that support Celtic have that strong socialist thing going on and they bring that sense of community with them. LA is a hard place to be. When I arrived to get work the only person I knew was Tony [Curran], so I phoned him and he told me to come and stay with him. He then got a job out of town and told me his flat was mine for as long as I needed it; to be honest I don't know what I would have done if he hadn't answered the phone. I think that's part of the Celtic thing, you help each other out, that what it's all about.'

There are two ambitions at the heart of Celtic Football Club's reason for being: to be a club of sporting excellence and to engage in a wider community with shared ideas. As Celtic supporters we are always participating in a wider community, whether it's at the ground, in the pub or a supporters' club or in far-off places. As societal behaviour and values shift, the culture around Celtic remains rooted around a response to those in need. The current fatalistic climate around Scottish football and the ugly return of bigotry and racism were both transcended in a season that defied the odds. In the aftermath of Celtic's inspirational victory over Barcelona in November 2012, the *Daily Mirror*'s Brian Reade pointed to the force behind the team suggesting it was: 'Player spirit over ego and supporter passion over presumption. Here is a real team representing a real club with a history and standing that has nothing to do with a stranger's billions.'

The Christian values that inspired a Marist Brother to form the club remain as important today as they did in November 1887. As history reveals it's supporters who have had to act to preserve not only the club but the values that make Celtic unique; it's the very moment when supporters have become frustrated or felt backed up against a wall that they transformed more pessimistic expectations.

As Compston suggests, he has watched foreign opposition and their fans overwhelmed at the sheer irrepressible spectacle of 60,000 people singing 'You'll Never Walk Alone' in unison with scarves held aloft. It's a moment when a community and history transform into the team's mystical 12th man before the opposition's eyes. It's the average Celtic supporter's understanding of the club's history and its social significance that has worked as a communal force, particularly during bad times when there remains the belief that we are all travelling the course together while gaining on a better tomorrow. This idea has elevated the club, team and support when it's been needed most.

Compston reflects on his experiences as a Celtic supporter: 'I think it's easy to forget how difficult it was being a Celtic fan up until fairly recent times. I've had hassle from people calling me a glory hunter and asking: "Why don't you support Morton, your local team?" In Scotland it's different; your team is passed on through your family and your religious background, that's just how it works. When I began to support Celtic, it was one of the darkest times in the club's history. I was born in 1984 so

I don't really remember winning the Double in 1988. What I remember is the barren years between 1989 and 1995 and not winning anything. When I was going to school it was the "Sack the Board" campaign when the reality of Celtic shutting up shop seemed very real, we were on a downward spiral. The first few games I went in the Jungle and I got banned as a jinx by my dad and brother. We had Wayne Biggins up front who never got a goal, Lou Macari was signing soldiers. I remember the joy of reaching a cup final and then getting humped by Raith Rovers ... I was devastated. Stopping Rangers winning ten-in-a-row in 1998 will always be unbelievable to me because I'd never seen Celtic as league winners. Then there was the 5–1 game against Rangers who had been mostly the dominant force. Everybody was cracking up about Lubo being up front because he was an unknown quantity, but when he scored those two incredible goals he went on to become a hero.

'It wasn't really until Martin O'Neill arrived that I saw a winning mentality at Celtic; that was my era, players would have run through brick walls for him. Neil Lennon has the same mentality. It all started with that Champions League qualifier against Ajax [in 2001] when we won 3–1 away from home, there was a belief that had kicked in that I hadn't experienced before. From that point on I relished European nights at Parkhead, especially when we were up against it and written off because that's when we're at our best.'

As well as watching live matches with Tony Curran, the pair also starred together in *Red Road*, the award-winning drama which saw both actors trade LA for Glasgow. Still located on the west coast of America, season-ticket-holder Curran flies home for as many games as his filming schedule will allow. Once again our conversation turned to issues beyond the game and how the structures and beliefs around Celtic gave the club a strength that continues to defy typical football attitudes. Says Curran: 'One of the best experiences for me in recent times was when Neil Lennon addressed the Celtic support in the aftermath of losing the league by a point against Rangers. That day wasn't sentimental; it encouraged us to look ahead. What he gave us was a feeling of what it's like to be a Celtic fan and not be part of the Old Firm, but being Glasgow Celtic.

'A couple of years ago I got the chance to play at Celtic Park in a charity game for Football Aid. I arrived in Glasgow slightly jet-lagged because I'd been filming *Big Momma's House 3*. I had also been told I couldn't leave the country because I was waiting on the result of a pending green card. I got word thirty-six hours before so it was pretty dramatic stuff trying to get to Glasgow from Atlanta, Georgia. I flew in to London and then straight up to Glasgow, off the flight and over to Celtic Park. It was a very last-minute Celtic kind of vibe trying to make this game; like Billy McNeill waving the boys up the park at the end of the Scottish Cup final in 1988, it had that kind of drama and intensity. One of my best friends is a guy called Sean Conaghan. His dad moved from the Gorbals to Brooklyn, New York. When Sean was growing up there was a serious drugs problem in Bay Ridge where the family lived so he was moved back to Scotland and that's how we met. I'm in the dressing room with the Conaghan boys over from New York and a few mates from Glasgow getting ready and in walks Danny McGrain. It was quite a moment because we'd all watched Danny play for Celtic and Scotland and here he was about to give us a team talk before we ran out to play at Celtic Park. You can imagine the energy in the room, the place is buzzing with adrenalin.

'I've got a bit of a connection with McGrain because my grandpa was a scout for Celtic between 1966 and 1974 and he spotted Danny and brought him to play for us. My grandpa was quite a shrewd and stoic Glasgow-born man of a certain generation, he had been involved in promoting big boxing matches with fighters like Alan "Boom Boom" Minter who was a middleweight champion. I asked Danny if he remembered him, at that point everyone is transfixed and he's automatically into it, the patter is great. He says: "Aye son, I remember Tommy Riley". He said to my grandpa: "Mr Riley, can I tell you something? I just want to tell you I'm actually a Protestant", to which he responded: "Danny, I don't care what you are son, as long as you can play fitba you can play for Glasgow Celtic." The rest as they say is history, but when he told us that we all just looked at each other, there was moistness in the old eyes. I felt very proud. I then ask him if there's a team talk. He says: "Aye, that pitch is bigger than you think it is, and I know your adrenalin is going to be pumping so before you go out there, take your time for the first 15 minutes, don't get overexcited." Of course we didn't listen to a word and burst on to the pitch running about daft. We were playing against George

McCluskey; the opposing team's manager was John Kennedy. We won 7–1 and I set up the fourth and scored the fifth; I scored in the Rangers end at Parkhead.'

While many pessimistic critics lamented the loss of Rangers in the SPL and suggested an Armageddon-like scenario for Scottish football, Lennon's Celtic transformed the bleak landscape by creating a different mindset among his team, taking the club and its supporters on a European journey in the 2012–13 season that would have been beyond many supporters' expectations at the start of the campaign. For a new generation of diehards European football after Christmas has been a relatively new phenomenon, but these adventures in particular have offered fans a sense of the club moving forward while tapping into the team's most evocative narratives. Curran explains how the UEFA Cup final gave many supporters a new spirit of confidence and a fresh vantage point of Celtic in Europe: 'After living through the dark times of the 1990s, Seville was always going to be special because our generation had never been on that kind of adventure with Celtic. To go and see them play in a European final was a big deal. I met the Conaghan boys and some other mates from Glasgow at this quaint hotel. There was Spanish guitar music playing at the bar when we arrived. Five of us squeezed into this tiny room because there was "no room at the inn" throughout Spain. Before the game I went up to get changed into this green silk suit I'd bought a few years before in Covent Garden . . . but it had gone. I thought surely nobody's stole it? So I headed down the stair and the first thing I hear is "Graffiti on the wall says we're magic, we're magic"; the boys had persuaded the hotel to put on a Celtic record and the place was rocking, it had transformed from this tranquil hotel into Bairds Bar. Brian Conaghan is wearing a matador hat with a Celtic top and there's Sean bare-chested in the green silk suit with a sombrero. You can actually see Brian on the official Seville DVD at half-time; he has this look of steely determination that says: "we can still beat this mob". That's how we all felt, and it's also worth remembering that we won the UEFA fan award from that season.'

For Curran, like many Celtic supporters, politics and supporting the club are interlinked, but we are living in times when those ideas have to be clearly defined and put into perspective. Says Curran: 'I know there are probably Celtic fans in Ireland that would still like to see a united Ireland. What's interesting is that it's becoming a reality for Scotland. Realistically the Union Jack might not be flying here one day. I think it was significant that the Queen mentioned "the sad and regrettable" events that could have been prevented when she visited Ireland, that is as far as a monarch could have went without apologising. The important thing is we need to pull attitudes out of this "dirty orange bastard" or "dirty Fenian" mentality ... please, because we need respect between the supports. There is a political element and that can be fine, but it's not when it's just an excuse for visceral hatred where you see people berating and hating each other. It may be a minority, but there was a Celtic v Rangers youth cup filmed [in 2011]. The fans were filmed undercover and even at that you heard "Up the IRA" and "We're up to our knees in Fenian blood". There are some supporters driven by hatred, we need to pull them out of the dark ages.'

While the north of Ireland continues to be a thorny subject for many supporters of several Scottish teams, Curran explains his own allegiance with anti-fascist politics in the frame of supporting Celtic. Neil Lennon and Gordon Strachan share the accolade of being the only Celtic managers to lead the club to the last 16 of the Champions League. The 2006–07 season where Celtic first reached that stage remains a significant one for Curran as it also saw supporters honour the veteran of the Spanish Civil War and fellow Celtic fan James Maley, who had fought on the side of a democratically elected government against General Franco's fascist uprising: Says Curran: 'It was a big achievement getting to the Champions League last 16 with Gordon Strachan for the first time and we matched AC Milan over the two legs before we went out of the competition. I was in LA watching the game in Joxer Daly's and had been shouting "No Pasaran" ["They Shall Not Pass"] at the screen, which was the slogan of the International Brigade during the Spanish Civil War. It was devastating when Kaka got the goal in extra time. We got beat 1–0 on aggregate, but it was no embarrassment – AC Milan went on to win the competition. After the game I went outside and someone said to me: "I like your boots". It was Billy Connolly, he had been in watching the game and he's really into cowboy boots. I hadn't met him before, but we exchanged numbers and he called me after the Scottish Cup semi-final against St Johnstone. I picked up the phone and was like: "Billy?" he said: "Aye, Tony, did you see the game against St Johnstone? The Celtic supporters unfurled a banner which said "No Pasaran" in honour of James Maley. I was thinking of you that night against AC Milan.'

An inseparable association with the politics of the left has been important in the work of a number of Celtic-supporting film-makers and actors. It has formed part of both their political and their male identities. Put into context these supporters are able to explain ideas that are not without ethics or morality, they are not trendy slogans to shout or designed as taunts, but instead are ideas that represent something that exists and has existed among Celtic supporters for generations. Film director Michael Caton-Jones (*Rob Roy*, *Scandal*) grew up in Broxburn, West Lothian. He suggests Celtic offered many young men in the 1960s a 'vital affirmation of existence' and tapped into a 'type of masculinity' that continues among supporters to this day. He believes his ambition as a film-maker was directly inspired by the ethos projected by the culture around Celtic growing up in a time when there were few examples of progression and aspiration. He says: 'I was ten in 1967 so I was the perfect age to be impressed and have these guys as my heroes. To me it was vital; it was my whole sense of identity. It was a symbol that I think people still don't understand. People still don't get why Celtic fans are so mad keen on it. They don't understand what it means historically to people in Scotland. To me it was a philosophy on life.

'Like most people I came from a working-class background. It was the tail end of heavy industry so there was a certain ethos among employed working men. It's where Jock Stein came from. A lot of people of my generation, and the one before it, understood the communal aspect of the masculine side of football. You thought that could be elevated to art in terms of poetry in motion. When I talk to people who don't get, understand or like football I feel sorry for them because they are missing the potential beauty of life itself. It was a validation of your own life; work hard, it need not be just a grind – there should be the poetry and beauty in the ordinary.'

As a young film maker Caton-Jones took that very philosophy that merged a certain type of Scottish masculinity and spliced it with a transformative 'swashbuckling romance' to make his most popular film *Rob Roy*: 'For me I was doing what Celtic stood for. I was using whatever position I had to bring some money into the country and to employ some people and make a film that represented a masculinity that I grew up with. That's why the film is dedicated to Jock Stein and the Scottish/American director Alexander Mackendrick; they stood for a maleness that I understood.'

Chapter Twelve
Twee Are Celtic Supporters

'We cannot break free from the past. When you are creative, it manifests itself in every way – it seeps out in every new mark you make.'
Jonathan Barnbrook

TWEE POP IS much like Britpop or grunge, a term created by music hacks to describe the roots of the independent or alternative genres of guitar pop and rock 'n' roll. With its roots firmly in Glasgow's early 1980s post-punk subculture, the original independent music scene was created by a community keen to escape the depressing and distressing dystopia of Thatcher's Britain by creating something fully removed from the capitalist notions of a London-centric pop industry. The creativity was about making music you could feel with every fibre of your being. Seminal groups such as Primal Scream, the Jesus and Mary Chain and The Pastels along with the lauded Postcard bands of the era Aztec Camera and Orange Juice, all played their part in changing the mainstream conventions of popular culture and taste. While the anger of inner-city post-punk and the gloom of Joy Division summoned a vital and necessary response towards the dark and dour reality of Thatcher's Britain, the spirit that heralded the arrival of The Pastels and Primal Scream further suggested you didn't have to be the best musician or most conventional singer, but you could create a new social world by starting a club night, forming a band and making your own records.

This crop of bands carried forth a new optimism in their attitude and in the glorious pop moments they created. Sickened by the purveyors of progressive rock, the punk rock movement's rallying call was to create a musical year zero, striving to wipe out the past. Central to the spirit of the Glasgow bands was a reverence for the 1960s that wasn't confined to rose-tinted nostalgia, but as a sense of building on the roots and aesthetic sensibilities of guitar pop at its most potent, innocent and irreverent, taking its cue from the silver-suit-era Beatles or the sun-kissed harmonies of America's west coast.

Bobby Gillespie and Stephen McRobbie (better known as Stephen Pastel) had grown up on the folklore and spirit of Jock Stein's Celtic teams. Prior to discovering music, Gillespie has previously stated his only ambition was to play for Celtic saying: 'I went to King's Park secondary school and Jock Stein lived about five minutes away. I'd walk past his house thinking "Stein's in there, the man who won the European Cup, what's he planning, what's he thinking?" I used to have so many scarves, the printed imitation silk ones. I also had a scarf with hundreds of metal badges. My walls were plastered with Celtic, I used to buy the *Celtic View* every week and make scrapbooks.'

Stephen Pastel, a friend of Gillespie's on the Glasgow scene shared a love of Celtic; among others they would play a vital role in setting up new foundations that wouldn't just feed into the climate and infrastructure of Glasgow's independent scene, but would also share values and ideas with Manchester's seminal bands and America's emerging alternative landscape. Reviewing The Pastels in November 2012 The Stone Roses biographer and punk veteran John Robb had this to say: 'From Mogwai to Belle and Sebastian to Primal Scream and Postcard to The [Jesus and] Mary Chain to Creation Records, this is a city that put the maverick spirit right into the heart of guitar bands. Sat there right at the heart of the whole shebang are The Pastels – the band that arguably carry that whole spirit and the torch for vinyl music, a music that is one part classic and one part personal and forward looking. Once the kings of the anorak scene – the anti rock 'n' roll macho bluster of self-effacing yet subtly fierce music, they are unlikely refuseniks.'

Undoubtedly part of that 'maverick spirit' could be seen in Jock Stein's Celtic teams who played with a style and substance that ascended beyond the standard precincts of Scottish football. When not playing with The Pastels, Stephen can sometimes be found behind the counter at Glasgow's alternative record shop Monorail, which shares a space with the Mono bar/cafe. It's often the stop-off for Celtic supporters travelling back and forward to Parkhead. Perhaps it's another disappearing trend, but for Celtic supporting music fans, a trip to Gloria's Record Bar during nine-in-a-row or a visit to Rat

Records in Virginia Galleries during the early 1990s was a vital Saturday tradition before the game. It was for Stephen Pastel. I find him sitting in a towering Victorian building designed by Charles Rennie Mackintosh that once housed the *Daily Record*. The central but out-the-road location in Renfield Lane is now the home of Stereo, a necessary cafe/bar and music spot buzzing with Glasgow hipsters and laid-back charisma. Like his old musical associate Bobby Gillespie, Stephen Pastel retains a youthful demeanour, floppy 1960s haircut and a reverence for the captivating period during which Jock Stein led Celtic to two European Cup finals: 'I think his teams in the 1960s and 1970s made most Scots proud that Celtic could represent Scotland in European football in the way that they did. My dad wasn't a hardcore fan but when I was growing up he would say to me: "Watch this team, watch how they play". Instinctively there was something I liked about Celtic without knowing what it was and even today I'm happy without knowing exactly what it is. At its best, Celtic becomes more than the sum of its parts. There is something about the core identity plus the style of football that just connects, like the moment when Nakamura smashed in that free kick against Manchester United at Old Trafford. In those moments Celtic becomes something very complex and three-dimensional and you feel a part of it – that's the great thing. The best Celtic players: Moravčík, Larsson, Nakamura, Dalglish and Johnstone, they tapped into that and carried it with them; it's something magical.

'The Celtic strip always looked good in Europe, and the great Celtic players always had a lot of style about them. If you think of the greatest ever Rangers player it would be a hard tackler like John Greig or a powerful and efficient guy like Brian Laudrup, but these Celtic players we're talking about were very different. Celtic have a great name in world football, there are a number of teams that aren't always at the top table of European football, but they have a history and a mystique, teams like Anderlecht, Ajax or Saint Etienne. When Celtic are playing in Europe you know they belong there; Celtic v Juventus, it has a ring to it, you know that's where we belong.'

Belle and Sebastian keyboard player and Celtic season ticket-holder Chris Geddes suggests Celtic's European Cup win has become a considerable reference point for his band. He notes the association of Celtic's victory and the wider influence it had on popular culture: 'Our band has been inspired by the 1960s and when you think that Celtic won the European Cup when the Beatles made 'Strawberry Fields Forever' and 'Penny Lane' or when all the great Motown records were coming out, it gives the achievement an added significance. It's also one of the things that Glasgow is most famous for. Celtic was a club on the fringes of Europe who won the competition at a time when the game was being dominated by Spanish and Italian teams; this has a huge cultural resonance.'

By the mid-1980s The Pastels and Primal Scream became closely associated with the C-86 fraction of independent music, which had grown from an NME compilation. The Pastels' 'Breaking Lines' along with Primal Scream's 'Velocity Girl' were among the tracks on an audiocassette given away for free with the music weekly. One of the most lauded bands of the era, The Stone Roses, would recycle and build upon the latter track's melody for their song 'Made of Stone' three years later, suggesting the attitude and style of the Glasgow bands would resonate with the Manchester scene's most determined groups. In 2010 Stone Roses' guitarist John Squire had this to say: 'I took a lot of ideas from The [Jesus and] Mary Chain. I remember noticing that Primal Scream were getting off the ground while we were still rehearsing. They were regulars in the NME. I went to see The Mary Chain a few times, I had some Primal Scream records, but didn't get round to going to see them.'

In 2009 The Smiths' Johnny Marr similarly reflected on the era: 'Roddy Frame [Aztec Camera] is still a great musician and someone I considered one of my contemporaries when I was in The Smiths. I wrote 'This Charming Man' as a direct response to Roddy getting his stuff played on the radio. I got out of bed one day and thought "I've got to start writing stuff in a major key, something upbeat and breezy." I hadn't written anything in G before that.'

In 1985 Bobby Gillespie was one of the faces behind the seminal Glasgow club Splash One, which featured gigs by the likes of The Pastels, Primal Scream, BMX Bandits and American art-rock luminaries Sonic Youth. The club also attracted future members of Teenage Fanclub who were similarly inspired by the groundbreaking movement. One of the band's three singer/songwriters and sometime member of

The Pastels, Gerard Love is a season ticket holder at Celtic Park. He explains why Celtic were an important part of the cultural milieu for many of Glasgow's best known groups 'The roots of Celtic are bulletproof in terms of social progress; it's quite appealing to a lot of progressive Scots. The idea of integration with an immigrant population to enhance Scottish culture is quite important. That social chapter and the foundation is untouchable, but the Jock Stein years were like the second phase of Celtic and he was just as important as the Irish potato famine to the history of the club. Perhaps even more important because he was one of the best signings Celtic ever made; it took them into the modern era and made the club more progressive again. For many people the European Cup win was Scotland's contribution to the 1960s. It was a purely Scottish side and one of Scotland's crowning moments for a lot of people. The style and manner in which Stein gained success was very appealing.

'Stein lost a lot of friends by taking the job and made a lot of sacrifices for Celtic. I think he is the most important character in the club's history.' One of the most celebrated figures among Glasgow's indie fraternity remains Lubo Moravčík. Celtic were scolded by the Scottish media for bringing the player to Scotland in October 1998, with the *Daily Record*'s Hugh Keevins indicating nepotism between manager Dr Jozef Venglos and his fellow Slovakian. At the same time he suggested Scottish Chelsea player John Spencer would have been a more suitable acquisition. Keevins was one among a number of sports columnists and writers that had to live down the same mistake during Moravčík's four glorious years in a Celtic jersey.

'The indie thing is often about looking for things that are not as celebrated as they should be and that's what happened with Lubo. He turned up at Celtic looking like someone from a [Jean-Luc] Godard movie; he had that mysterious Eastern European thing and an unbelievable talent. When Lubo and Venglos came to Celtic everybody was laughing at them, but Venglos was a genius and so was Lubo. When he scored against Rangers the papers said "From Zero to Hero", but the guy was never a zero [something Moravčík himself articulated to the journalist who suggested it]. He was absolute quality and his first season was phenomenal. You start reading and you realise that he was a complete star at Saint-Etienne. He was a completely unknown talent in Scotland. People like that have not got what it takes to be an idol or popular with the press, but quality is much more important and he had that in abundance. One thing I remember wasn't the most graceful. It was a high ball from [Alan] Thompson and Lubo took it down on to the touchline with his backside. If he tried to get it with his foot it would have been too tight. Even with one of the most useless parts of the body, he still had great skill. George Connelly is another guy like that who is always talked about; he obviously was on his way to being one of the greats. I've seen some footage of him, but not enough to appreciate the talent that he was.'

Stephen Pastel had already seen Moravčík playing for Czechoslovakia at international level (he would also win caps for Slovakia after the country became independent in 1993). Says Pastel: 'I've always loved Eastern European football; my earliest memories are watching the Polish national side. I remember watching him playing for Czechoslovakia during Italia 90; they were a good side and were runners-up in their group. I've always liked number tens. I thought the media were too quick to rub Celtic's noses in it when he arrived, the fear for me was that would he be like Andy Thom who was technically very good, but would he get stuck in on a wet Wednesday at Tynecastle or Pittodrie?

'The Scottish game is populated with what Graeme Souness called hammer throwers, he was one himself, but I think it's true he [Moravčík] got targeted. However, he could look after himself, like Larsson, they were both strong and could deliver in the big games when it mattered. During that period we gained a lot of flair players and it's a characteristic we love to see, but often with these guys comes a fragile temperament. There was always a question about players like Berkovic or Viduka giving a hundred per cent, there were players around Celtic at that point you didn't get a good feeling about. I think eventually O'Neill marginalised players who were prima donnas. But I enjoyed Venglos's influence on the team, he had an unorthodox style and I was disappointed when he was phased out. I would like to have seen Dr Jo build further. John Barnes is given the credit for Stiliyan Petrov's appointment, but it was Dr Jo who was behind that move, he had the contacts and I would say he was responsible.

'Moravčík and Larsson also developed a great partnership under him; the creativity and movement between them brought something to the play we hadn't seen since the 1970s. What they had was almost telepathic. It wasn't just the flair, there was intensity; they wanted to play for Celtic and that's what fans want to see. Lubo and Henrik really peaked during the O'Neill era because he built strong players around them. Just as you began to think that we'd never have a world-class side like we had under Stein, suddenly everything clicked again. It was one of the most exciting times. After his first season in charge Martin's team gradually became more pragmatic, but that first season when we won the Treble was something special. The 3–5–2 system worked well for him in the first two seasons, it was easy on the eye and it suited us as most teams in Scotland were still playing 4–4–2.

'At the end of his first season I remember we had already won the league and there was a game coming up against Rangers at Ibrox. Gerard [Love] said to me we should just rest the team and put the reserves out, and I was like "Nah, he's got to take the team" because you wanted to see them win in style. Moravčík had one of his best games, scoring two as Celtic won 3–0. His first seemed to come from nothing, again it was a sublime pass from Larsson with Moravčík tearing the defence apart and firing it past Stefan Klos. For the second he took on Fernando Ricksen, turned outside the box and scored. In all my years loving Celtic there are only a handful of players that are as good as he was, I think part of it was his age, he was nearly thirty six and could still do those things.'

That match, played on 29 April 2001, saw the debut of Shaun Maloney in his first spell at Celtic. It was also the game during which Henrik Larsson netted his fiftieth goal for the Hoops. More significantly he notched up his first win at Ibrox; Celtic's first against their Glasgow rivals in almost seven years. Perhaps for the first time since the days of Stein, Celtic had become a power, absolutely battering their biggest rivals in their own back yard and doing it after securing the Treble. Pastel warms to his theme: 'I think generations will look at that team with Larsson and Moravčík as one of the best, because like Stein's team they were brilliant every week, the place was buzzing. The team had the right balance of expressive flair players and hard nuts like the best Celtic teams in the 1960s and 1970s. My first game was [31] October 1970, we were away to Motherwell and it rained all day, the conditions were really bad, the pitch was waterlogged. I went with some mates that were Motherwell fans who were like "Don't go over the top with your celebrations". We won 5–0 and Harry Hood scored a hat-trick [George Connelly and Jinky also found the net].

'Players like Bobby Murdoch and Bertie Auld had a toughness that you needed to win games. They didn't want to play for anyone else and I'm sure it was horrifying for players when Stein started to break up the team; it was like their world was coming to an end. But some did go on to have careers after Celtic. There's a great book by Eamon Dunphy about his playing days at Millwall. He singles out Bobby Murdoch's presence in the Middlesbrough team they used to play against and how he organised the team by slowing things down. Some players bring a steadying influence to a side, the way Stanton did when he joined Celtic and played sweeper. He was a born organiser and natural in that position, he was very creative at the back and hard as nails. That team in the mid-1970s had the right balance. I remember Alistair Hunter [goalkeeper between 1973 and 76] who also played for Scotland. We signed him from Kilmarnock. It's another characteristic of Celtic teams that we have struggled with consistently good keepers. In 1973 we were on for nine-in-a-row, Alistair Hunter had one of his best games against Rangers [September 15th. Celtic won 1–0]. There were a lot of injuries too. But he could also lose confidence. He went to the same church as my parents and I got to meet him. He was a decent guy who aside time.

'Dalglish was also playing in that game, he was just back from injury. As a player he brought a unique magic and glamour to Celtic, especially in those big games. What he gave to Celtic hadn't existed before. He had an edge in that he was always the most dangerous player on the park, I saw him score outrageous goals out of nothing. When he left you could feel a lull and you could see it because the attendances fell. In the late 1970s there were times you could walk around the Jungle, before that it was always jam-packed and that was the best time ever. I used to go with guys from school that were just kind of bams. I was getting into music and would often buy records and then go to the game.

'I don't think it's fair to describe the players that wanted to leave as mercenaries, but people did find it hard that someone could be captain of Celtic and want to leave. Players like

Dalglish and Davie Hay were intelligent guys and at that point had progressed as far as they could at Celtic; they wanted to be the best they could at the highest level. During the 1980s and 1990s you could say that David Murray embodied Thatcherism with the idea that you could spend your way to success and that "loads of money" idea was floating around. It became a bit of a running joke where we would say "At least we've got Paul McStay" because he was a truly world-class player with a lot of talent and he only wanted to play for Celtic. They didn't have the budget, there were some disastrous decisions in terms of management, but the centenary team played beyond their ability because they knew how important it was to win that year and they've remained in people's memories as one of the great Celtic teams for that. After that period the team and the club was quite downtrodden for a while, I remember going with Gerard [Love] the season at Hampden; it was grim.

'We've talked about players coming to Celtic for the wrong reasons; I have to say I didn't feel that with Paolo Di Canio; I think at certain moments the club did mean something to him. He was very Italian and he was passionate at a time when the team and the fans needed it; obviously if you knew someone politically was a fascist . . . I wouldn't turn a blind eye to that, but you have to take someone as they are in the moment and I enjoyed watching him and I enjoyed that time.'

Undoubtedly it's a sentiment worth holding on to; it's perhaps easy to dismiss Di Canio because of certain indefensible political statements and behaviour in his past. But the former Celtic player did share a tacit and powerful connection with Tommy Burns which the Italian has admitted had a positive influence on his life. There are moments even now that he still thinks of how Burns treated him. While other managers might have thrown him out the team, Burns would throw his arms around the player. It's fair to say that, at least for a season, Di Canio seemed to lack none of the essentials that make a Celtic legend. While that might be a stretch with the benefit of hindsight, he left us with some spectacular memories. Perhaps it's also worth remembering his magnetism had a positive influence on the team and the support after many years in the doldrums, it's a point of view his former team-mate Pierre van Hooijdonk articulated: 'Paolo was fantastic, without any doubts he brought a kind of character we had never seen before. He was a massive laugh, he struggled with his English in the beginning and he'd talk with his hands a lot, he had a certain temperament but he always got us laughing. He was accepted by everyone in that team, everybody liked Paolo not just for his personality, you could see his quality; he was a fantastic player and had come to Celtic from AC Milan. He was very close with Tommy, again Tommy was like the father figure to him and he played a huge part in Paolo and other players settling in. Tommy would always have a book or a video trying to get you to understand what Celtic meant and Paolo got it, he understood Tommy. I think Paolo would have stayed if things could have been sorted out upstairs with Fergus, we all would have stayed, I really believe that. Tommy was like the opposite of Fergus; he was one of us. Everything that Fergus didn't have; Tommy had.'

'May you live in interesting times' says the old Chinese proverb; 'interesting times' is perhaps one viable description of Neil Lennon's time as Celtic manager. During his tenure he became the public face of Celtic Football Club and its support, not just on football issues but on events and happenings beyond a normal manager's remit. In December 2012 he criticised one of his players for attending the memorial of a senior figure in the Real IRA. It's just one of many issues Lennon has addressed outside of football and his words have currency with the support, not just those who watched him as a player throughout the O'Neill and Strachan eras, but also for a new generation who see him as their Mr Celtic.

His fourteen year involvement included two essential ingredients for any Celtic manager: success and continuity. What was essential to Lennon on the field was an ability to trust his own instincts under pressure. He has stood by players who were profoundly unpopular with the media and the support; his bond with Georgios Samaras, for example, has been perhaps one of the most significant player/manager relationships at the club in recent years.

Lennon's faith paid off spectacularly when the player scored a brace in the 2–0 victory over Rangers on 2 January 2011. Supporters were left in raptures, though his reputation was somewhat dented a few months later when he missed a penalty at Ibrox in a match that finished 0–0 during a fraught season that would see Celtic's biggest rivals win the league by a point. While Lennon jokingly acknowledged Samaras was the type of player 'who could get me the sack', he continued to stand by him. The Greek internationalist had a reputation for putting aside time for fans, only getting on the bus after every autograph has been signed and he has noticeably only spoken well of the Celtic support. He articulated a deeper understanding of Celtic's meaning beyond the game, telling the *Scotsman* newspaper in April 2012: 'Celtic v Rangers is in the top three derbies in the world. Boca Juniors v River Plate, Real Madrid v Barcelona and Celtic v Rangers. That one [Manchester] is just about football matters, but here it is the whole community, religion, politics . . . everything is part of the game and you can see it in the passion that the fans have and you can see how much depends on it. For them, it's not just a football game; it's more than a football game.'

The player proved his worth in the position Lennon allotted him, an attacking left winger, but his sporting redemption for many began with his last-gasp winning goal against Spartak Moscow in the Champions League. It will go down as one of the great Celtic moments. Back on the big stage and with a point to prove, summoning the 'last-minute Celtic' ethos when we needed it most, Lennon's team recorded a first ever away victory in the group stages. Fully bearded, dangerous and kitted out in the popular pitch-black away kit, Samaras looked every inch Celtic class. Further goals against Barcelona and Benfica would lead to suggestions in the press that others were circling for the player's signature just as Samaras was finally feeling the love among the majority of the Celtic support. To get there Samaras had to tune out his critics, living down the lows of fruitless seasons and missed opportunities. He retained a faith uncommon in the modern game; instead of moving on he stood as an example that things change, that in the best Celtic tradition negative situations can be transcended, even when nobody else fancies the odds. It's an idea that is in the very roots of Celtic's formation. More dramatically, Neil Lennon went from contemplating his managerial exit after threats on his life to becoming one of the most respected young gaffers in British football.

For Stephen Pastel it is essential that the roots of Celtic continue to be validated in the modern era: 'It is really important to relate to where the club came from along with the charity roots. I also feel personally that Scottish society should have moved on in certain ways, with Celtic I'm more interested in the football focus, but it's important to understand that the club also offered hope to an underc lass in Scotland for a very long time. The great Celtic teams expressed themselves in a very joyful, exuberant and passionate way. They became important for those in Scottish society who felt repressed and discriminated against. I feel that there is still discrimination, but things have progressed an awful lot, with the chants at games that are particularly provocative I would like to see Celtic fans rise above that and support the side.

'Neil Lennon is a very intelligent guy. I've seen him walking about in the West End, he's always got his head up and makes eye contact with people, he carried himself very well as Celtic manager. He was a very cerebral player and was the lynchpin of the team under O'Neill and Strachan so it wasn't any surprise when he went into management. As a fan you always like to have a sense of continuity and an understanding of what a great heritage there is at Celtic, you want to see players develop in a team. When Tony Mowbray came in he threw the baby out with the bathwater, by getting rid of players like Barry Robson and Scott McDonald when they were needed. At times it was eleven randoms on the pitch, there was a sense of "Is this Celtic?" For fans Lennon was untarnished by what went on during that time. My take on it was that Mowbray found him quite intimidating, so he was marginalised. Tony Mowbray was a romantic appointment and that's important at a club like Celtic, but again you have to get the balance right. I felt a lot of sympathy for him; he was out of his depth.

'As soon as Lennon came in there was an immediate improvement in team spirit, to get anywhere in Europe you have to have eleven players who are on your side and understand you. In recent seasons you could see that Samaras is someone who always gives a hundred per cent, but he has been wildly inconsistent in his time. Another player like that is Scott Brown. He tries hard for Celtic, though he's far from my idea of a traditional Celtic midfielder in the Paul McStay mould, but he has been an important mainstay in a team where players come and go, that hasn't been good for Celtic.

From Frankie Miller to the Blue Nile, Glasgow musicians have displayed an authentic link with American roots and culture, arguably more than those from any other European metropolis. The history of Irish country and highland migrants blending with big-city working-class swagger makes that link feel particularly convincing. More widely there is undoubtedly something in the attitude, sound and image of many Scots bands that resonates credibly with American culture. True to that lineage is Celtic supporter and Texas/Red Sky July guitarist Ally McErlaine. He explains something about this part of the world's transatlantic exchange with America: 'Scottish and Irish people, as well as the French and the English, took folk music to America where it got mixed with African music to make the blues. I think Scottish and Irish people are into more soulful stuff rather than being trendy.'

A defining experience for the Glaswegian was travelling on a rock 'n' roll pilgrimage to the Mojave Desert. As a lover of mythology and McErlaine journeyed to the Joshua Tree National Park to honour the life of country pioneer Gram Parsons. It was at Joshua Tree that a friend of Parsons's, acting on a promise, made a botched attempt to cremate the singer's body after his death in Room 8 of the Joshua Tree Inn. As a child of the late 1960s McErlaine was raised on 1960s pop, country and folk, discovering glam and punk rock in the 1970s. As he explains: 'My dad was mad on Bob Dylan; my mum was really into the Beach Boys. My aunties and uncles were into country music, which I'd hear a lot at New Year. Then I started listening to Bowie and a bit later The Clash. I got into Led Zeppelin because of the guitar and Jimmy Page; there's a lot of country, folk and open tunings I learned from him. Football came a bit later for me, when I was younger growing up in Glasgow you'd get beat up if you said the wrong team so I didn't have anything to do with it. When I was at school you had skins, punks, mods, rudeboys, new romantics, metal-heads, rockers ... now it's sad, there's not that difference, the High Street is indie now; the whole culture has been X-Factored, but back then there were so many different types of music that young people were into. For some reason now kids are more into computers than a music culture or supporting a football team; the other thing is working-class kids can't afford to support a team every week, it's only rich people that can afford that.

'I first really got into Celtic just after punk about 1978, my uncle was a Partick Thistle fan and he offered to take me to

Parkhead. We got out the car and started to walk to the ground, I was instantly impressed by it; suddenly I heard the fans singing, you could hear the roar from miles away. The game had already started and I was walking towards this edifice, what seemed like the epicentre. Celtic won 5–2, I had been a Thistle fan up until that point, but after the game I said to my uncle: "I'm going to support Celtic."'

It's now almost 25 years since Ally scored his first hit with Texas, the unmistakable blues-driven bottleneck riff of 'I Don't Want A Lover' remains one of the most definitive singles of the late 1980s. Taking the American inspiration further brought him even greater success with Texas for 1997's *White On Blonde*, an album that produced a run of blue-eyed soul hit singles including 'Say What You Want', 'Black Eyed Boy' and 'Halo'. Singer Sharleen Spiteri's star quality ensured expansive television and press coverage while her looks and sultry image became an essential ingredient, appearing on record sleeves and newsstands across Europe. Behind the scenes Ally McErlaine was the quiet, cool guitarist, often sporting a leather jacket and a feather cut while picking out the band's essential riffs and licks.

It's understandable that McErlaine, who shares his Halloween birthday with fellow guitar hero Johnny Marr, has a penchant for Celtic's most rock 'n' roll players, particularly the ones that while looking and behaving like rock stars, had the style and talent to back up the strut. Says Ally: 'The late 1990s was a great time to be a Celtic fan if you liked star quality because of the players that we had. I was at [Jorge] Cadete's first game [1 April 1996]. We were winning 4–0, he picked up a pass from Peter Grant and literally lifted the ball over the keeper's head with almost his first touch. It was one of those moments that you'll never forget and it's one you've shared with thousands in the stadium; the noise was unbelievable. Cadete and Di Canio are still two of the best players I've ever seen at Celtic. The ball would stick to Di Canio's feet; he could get the ball from any angle, trap it, turn and away he'd go.

'Over the years a few Celtic players and managers have came to Texas gigs. Neil Lennon came with Martin O'Neill, we've had Larsson, John Hartson, Chris Sutton and a few of the playboy players like Mo Johnston and Frank McAvennie. One that stands out was when we were playing at Wembley Stadium with Simple Minds in 1989, Frank came backstage, and I just remember him turning round with that famous smile, the platinum blond hair and a glint in his eye before going into one of his famous anecdotes. He's typical of the kind of player Celtic fans love because he's about more than the football; he had great stories and was straighttalking.'

Undoubtedly for the Texas guitar player, there was also that hint of rock 'n' roll folklore that accompanies Celtic's most-loved players: 'Yes, Frank had that quality more than anybody, there was always things happening outside of the football. There's the story where he was nightclubbing in London after playing for Celtic on Saturday and he arrived on Monday for training at Barrowfield in a helicopter. My favourite was the treasure hunt story that nobody ever quite got to the bottom of, when he was allegedly involved in drugs and was found by the police with a bag of money that he said was to fund a treasure hunt in the English Channel. Sitting in the ground I've always enjoyed that kind of humour among the fans. Even when we're in the doldrums there's always good banter. I still laugh when I think about a guy I sat next to in the early 1990s. Steve Fulton was playing for Celtic and he was getting some stick off this guy, it was after Billy McNeill had compared him to Roberto Baggio who at that time was one of the best midfield players in the world. To be fair Fulton was actually a good player, he was passionate, but he had done something daft on the pitch that day and this guy had enough, he shouted the only thing Italian about him was his "Big pizza face!" It was a wee bit harsh but playful, the fans are so quick on things. In the same team we had Paul McStay. He's still my all-time favourite player; I can still visualise him commanding the midfield and organising. This guy that sat next to me used to say some really bizarre stuff; he'd talk about McStay being the best "chester" of the ball in European football. If McStay trapped the ball with his chest he'd be off on one.'

In September 2009 McErlaine was admitted to hospital with a brain aneurysm. He went into a coma that lasted for nine weeks. Sharleen Spiteri held a vigil by his bedside and bandmate Eddie Campbell told the press: 'It's heartbreaking; I just want everyone to say a prayer for him.' Miraculously the guitarist made a full recovery. In 2011 the musician joined Texas on tour as well as taking new band Red Sky July on the road.

Despite surgeons telling the guitarist he would be left mentally and physically impaired, today he looks the picture of health. 'I'm actually fully recovered; at least I keep thinking I'm fully recovered. It's hard to tell because I'm getting older now and you have to differentiate between what's just age and what's part of my recovery. It was a massive deal. I was effectively dead for three months, the staff kept calling my wife to come to the hospital saying: "He's not going to last the night." She was told to make funeral arrangements; it was pretty bad. I wasn't aware of anything, I never suffered. It was only in the recovery process that I suffered because it was so painful.'

During his recovery Ally befriended a priest from the hospital chapel and they have kept in contact ever since. Doctors told him they had only treated one other patient that also recovered from a grade five aneurysm. Those close to McErlaine, including his wife Shelly Poole, with whom he also performs with in Red Sky July, turned to faith and prayer in their time of need and view the recovery as something of a miracle. Says Ally: 'I'm not religious at all, my wife gets quite annoyed with me, she believes in God. I annoy her when I say I know what it's like to die – I died four times, but I don't remember anything about having the aneurysm. After three months it was like waking from a dream. I had that semi-awake feeling that you have when you wake up; I had that for about a month. I didn't know what a guitar was or anything else.'

Significantly among the many well-wishers were some of Ally's Celtic heroes: 'The Ajax 3–1 away win in 2001 was a special game for me, by that point we had been used to a certain standard from Celtic, suddenly under O'Neill you had a team playing out their skin, players like Bobby Petta were completely revitalised. It meant a lot that Neil Lennon and Martin O'Neill left get-well messages on my answer phone when I was really ill. I know Neil is a good guy and a real Celtic man. I was in London when I heard about Neil getting sent the letter bombs and threats. I remember thinking there are some really mental people in Scotland. I mean what sort of person would do that? They don't know anything about Neil Lennon. I live in London full-time now, my wife is English, and people down south often look at the Celtic/Rangers rivalry as a bit backward. One thing that makes people down here embarrassed about Scotland is the sectarian thing, people view us as simpletons because of it;

you get a different perspective down here.

'I hate hearing songs and chants involving the IRA or the Battle of the Boyne. I suppose it's the human condition having to have an opposite, but it's a low form of thinking and it happens all over the world in different ways, hating somebody because there is something different about them, like having one village pitched against another. I remember somebody having a go at our manager Gerry for wearing a tartan scarf at a Celtic game, someone said to him: "What the fuck are you doing wearing that?" I thought: "C'mon Celtic are Scottish", we have Irish roots but we are Scottish. I don't like that weird anti-Scottish thing some fans have got, you can't take the Scottish element away from Celtic. We had four season tickets around the band and I've been to see Celtic a few times with Sharleen. She was quite into it, but when she moved to London she started watching Arsenal. She's still into Celtic; she's just not that much into football now.

'London's a great place to live, but ultimately it is more soulful in Scotland and people are more laid-back, they take time to listen and get into music, maybe that's why so many great bands come from there. When I was growing up in Glasgow country music was always played in pubs and there would always be old guys at the bar smoking and drinking and telling stories. But it has changed, you can't smoke in the pub now and instead of music they're usually showing *X Factor* on the telly. It's true that a lot of the great bands that came out of the music scene in Scotland support Celtic; there's definitely a connection, maybe it's because there's that reputation for inclusiveness around the world ... I think it's all these things we've talked about and more.'

Afterword
A country team for city folks

A FEW DAYS before Christmas 2012 I received a letter from the New York Celtic Supporters Club. I've visited the club a number of times over the years and had interviewed some of its members for my previous book *We Are Celtic Supporters*. I was saddened to read of the passing of Ken Miller after 'a battle with lung cancer'. I'd sent copies of the book out to a number of supporters' clubs that I'd interviewed and was very humbled to learn that the NY club's president had given a copy to Ken's family after the funeral. I didn't know Ken well, I had only met him once, but I was grateful that he and others had spent an afternoon mapping out the story of their club, which formed in 1995, with much gusto while relating their unrelenting enthusiasm for Celtic. The reason for *We Are Celtic Supporters*, *Faithful Though and Through* and this revised version of the latter has been to capture stories such as Ken's before they vanish. I've been fortunate enough to give some talks about my experiences on the road writing the first book. At the end of one Q&A, I was humbled when a teenager asked if I would sign his book. I noticed the copy already had a poignant message hand-written, the lad explained to me that his father gave him the book as a gift shortly before he died. It's moments like this that say so much to me about why the positive ideals, irrepressible spirit and sense of hope that is manifest around Celtic is as important as ever. Over the course of writing the two books I have faced one or two closed doors, but the vast majority have been open ones, through which I would be invited in and asked to sit down by the hearth with a cup of tea and a piece or whatever was in the scullery.

Growing up, the scullery was the place I began most of my Celtic journeys, sitting with my gran before going to a big game. The wireless would be blaring, there'd be something in the frying pan and there was that view of the city from her front window. These were all things that would keep her going when she was unable to get up and down the stairs in her later years.

I remember my sister Jenny coming into the kitchenette just before she went to New York for the first time, not long after the terrorist attack on the Twin Towers. My gran was petrified. In the week before she went there'd be broken sleep and twilight pots of tea where her imaginative mind would create fresh causes for worry. That morning we looked on as the plane flew out from Turnhouse to Newark amid unsullied blue skies; it was as if she was flying into some celestial sphere. 'New York eh son,' my gran said as we wondered what awaited Jenny Wren in 'Manhattan's desert twilight'.

A few years later I was getting organised to go myself, the last-minute cup of tea in the scullery was by now almost a ritual before a transatlantic journey. It was then my gran casually revealed that her parents were married in New York. She always had a talent for producing some new piece of family information when there seemed nowhere else to go. It became a pastime for both my sister and me to mine the family history. My gran, Mary, had been orphaned in childhood and was brought up by Irish nuns, so this was a morsel of gold dust. I managed to do some phoning around and a former teacher put me in touch with a records office in New York shortly before I left, so I phoned ahead. My gran never liked dwelling in the past. Ninety years later here I was trying to get to the bottom of what happened to her mother and father.

When I arrived in Manhattan I had shifted back to my aim of covering The Pogues' first concert in New York for 15 years while visiting the New York-based Celtic supporters that were gathering to join the St Patrick's Day parade on 55th Street. Hearing a communal blast of 'It's A Grand Old Team' and 'Willie Maley' was a convincing pointer to where I should be. Amid the throng I jumped in for a picture with Hillary Clinton who was looking to keep her profile raised among Irish-American voters on the parade. Outside St Patrick's Cathedral a minute's silence was observed for Jimmy Johnstone who had passed away just days previously. This was followed by New York based opera singer Barry Banks singing 'The Celtic Song', turning the number back into its original, thunderous operatic roots before his sell-out performance at The Met. As the Irish marching band began to disperse, the New York Celts gathered for a street huddle before scattering into various pubs and taverns across the city. We would meet again a few days later to watch a victorious Celtic in the League Cup against Dunfermline. Before heading to Toronto for an Oasis gig, I noticed a poster of Noel Gallagher close to the exit of a record store in Greenwich Village. Leaving the shop I saw the real thing; one of the last great quotable rock stars, I handed him a spare vintage Celtic scarf I had on me.

Before I left New York I wondered if there would be time to forge ahead with the search for my great grandparents' wedding certificate. I went down to the New York City Department of Records and Information Services Municipal Archives and asked for the lady I'd spoken to on the phone, Leonora Gidlund. I had to wait for her to come back from lunch and I sat for about half an hour in quiet anticipation. Before long an older lady with undeniable warmth of spirit walked into the room, one of the younger archivists pointed her towards me, and she announced with a smile as wide as the Clyde: 'I've got something for you!' I don't know who was happier, her or me, as she explained she gets a lot of similar requests which turn up very little. The certificate she held in her hand concerned two people who had married in St Jean Baptiste Catholic Church on East 76th Street, Manhattan, on 25 September 1916:

GROOM: William Ryan
BIRTHPLACE: City of Limerick, Ireland
AGE: 23
GROOM'S RESIDENCE: 12 (1/2) Truman Street,
New London, CT
OCCUPATION: Machinist
FATHER'S NAME: Patrick
MOTHER'S MAIDEN NAME: Bridget Kelly
BRIDE: Hannah McGhee
BIRTHPLACE: Port Glasgow, Scotland
AGE: 19
BRIDE'S MOTHER'S MAIDEN NAME: Mary Jane Dougherty
RESIDENCE: 226 East 39th Street
FATHER'S NAME: James

There was another name on the wedding certificate, Maud Ryan, who'd been a witness at the wedding. I subsequently found passenger lists that revealed how a number of my Irish family sailed across the Atlantic for the wedding. It's often an unusual name that speeds up the process or at least provides a vital clue and in this case it was Maud, my great aunt. William Henry Ryan had come from a family of 13 and his mother Bridget and a number of his brother and sisters including Maud had decided to travel and some planned to stay. Within months of his big day William becomes untraceable. We subsequently found his grave at Holy Cross cemetery in Brooklyn. Maud accompanied Hannah on the trip back into Liverpool on Christmas Eve before Hannah headed home to her Irish family in Port Glasgow. My gran was born the following August. As I write these words in August 2015 I have just passed through Port Glasgow on my way to catch a Ferry. With Mary passing away in the early half of this year the journey feels particularly poignant. My gran was one of those Irish mammies who supported Celtic with fervency while listening to the wireless at home, the importance of these women from the community who for generations filled their families with confidence and pride shouldn't be overlooked; even though many of them have never set foot in a football ground their contribution to the culture can never be underestimated. The creation of Celtic also created a space for them to carry hopes, dreams and ideals that went hand in hand with everyday family life.

The memory of Brother Walfrid is one that has been kept alive by the communal efforts of Celtic supporters; the history of the Irish in Scotland is a story of a relentless kick against oppression amid an effort to survive. In his book *The Old Firm* Bill Murray writes: 'The Celtic Football and Athletic Club was founded as a charitable organisation to raise money to provide free dinners, clothing and other relief for the poor in the East End of Glasgow, specifically in the Catholic parishes of St Mary's, St Andrew's and St Alphonsus. At the end of the 19th century Scotland abounded with football clubs like Hibs, Harps, Shamrocks, Emeralds and even Emmets, the most successful of whom were the Hibs of Edinburgh and the Harps of Dundee. It was the success of these two clubs that finally impelled some prominent Catholic citizens of Glasgow's East End, under the lead of Brother Walfrid and his assistant Brother Dorotheus, to set about forming an Irish football club in the heart of the city.' There's no other founder in world football as eminent or honoured as Brother Walfrid, a man who endeavoured to support the struggling when there was no financial security blanket, no welfare and no future. It's worth asking the question why, of the many other Irish teams that were being formed around Scotland, was it Celtic that prospered?

Celtic's Champions League match against Lyon in 2003 allowed me to do some research for an article on the roots of Walfrid that appeared in the *Celtic View* and was latterly published in a commemorative booklet about the founder. The Marist Brothers were formed in 1817 by St Marcellin Champagnat. Ordained as a priest the previous year, Champagnat spent the next few months climbing Mount Fourvière, a shrine to the Virgin Mary, and was inspired to form an order in her name with a focus on education and social justice. While serving as a parish priest Champagnat was asked to help a dying teenager through his last moments on earth. He was struck by how the boy knew nothing about Christianity and resolved to dedicate his life to religious education.

In 1852 the first Marists arrived in Britain and by 1858 were working with the survivors of the Irish famine who were in the midst of building a community in Scotland. As mentioned elsewhere in this book, pilgrimage is an integral part of the Celtic way of life and the birthplace of Andrew Kerins in Sligo has attracted many of the club's supporters. On arrival in the county there's an immediate sense of rural life and life-giving old-world charm that has filtered through into Celtic Scotland, but here it's more potent, like the poitín. Irish bluegrass bands and traditional folk music sessions with the likes of Sligo-born resident fiddle player Steve Wickham from the Waterboys take place regularly in the town's thriving music scene. There's a strong Celtic presence throughout Sligo and they have an awareness of the history and a pride in Walfrid and his pivotal role in creating Celtic Football Club. A taxi driver, dropping me at O'Neill's, unmistakably a Celtic pub (it's painted green with the club's badge on the outside), left me with this parting shot: 'It took a Sligo man'. Perhaps he's right. His comment reminded me of an old school pal's dad also from the area who often said: 'Fuck the begrudgers'. This was the kind of straight-talking advice dispensed to me during my teenage years; I can still hear the echoes of Gerry's lyrical accent offering his insight into dealing with life's bitter or reactionary characters or just downright poor grace. I happily raised a pint to him in his home town. Undoubtedly Andrew Kerins had to adapt something of this dogged but positive mentality when battling the elements that would get Celtic off the ground, albeit without the expletive.

It's a bright autumnal October day when I arrive at Brother Walfrid's home town of Ballymote where he was born in May 1840. It feels like walking onto the set of *The Quiet Man* or *Ryan's Daughter*, albeit with more convivial characters than the latter. The pubs are opening in the small market town when I arrive at midday, passing boxes of bits and pieces for sale on a grassy knoll and an aesthetically pleasing green post box. Suddenly, in the shadows of a castle, church and railway station it looks like I've found my destination. Through green trees the sun glistens on the calm expression of Walfrid, the face on the sculpture is an exact replica of the famous picture of the Marist as a young man that adorns banners, various books and magazine articles. As serenity settles and my objective is reached all that's left is to reflect, pray, talk and be at peace with the world. To quote the poet most associated with Sligo, W.B. Yeats, it's a place to 'Come away, for the world's more full of weeping than you will understand.' The road from Sligo to Parkhead was something like the Camino de Santiago de Compostela when Celtic supporters from the north-west corner of Ireland raised enough money to build the sculpture through a sponsored walk and crossing over the water. They are honoured here with a mention alongside fellow Sligonian, the late Sean Fallon, and former Celtic chairman Brian Quinn who were both here for the unveiling on 24 October 2004.

In some ways the journey to Kerins' birthplace was in sharp contrast to a visit to Walfrid's resting place in Dumfries a few months later. While honours to Robert Burns are expected there's nothing to indicate that this small town in south-west Scotland was the final resting place of a man with significant and vital links to Scottish life and culture. The Globe Inn, a place where the bard drank and slept, is packed with tourists from around the world, but there is no statue commemorating Brother Walfrid anywhere in the town, nor even a sense of mild awareness that he came here to retire in 1911, finally passing in April 1915 just a short time before what would have been his 75th birthday. In March 2013 news broke that Walfrid was the subject of a forthcoming feature film directed by Peter Mullan, it was said to be attracting interest from Daniel Day Lewis. In August 2015 it was confirmed that Scottish novelist Andrew O' Hagan was working on the film's script. The launch of Peter Howson's Brother Walfrid painting also brought the Marist's story into public focus in November 2014. The work which featured the painter's interpretation of the Celtic founder, the crucifixion of Christ and those ravaged by the famine mainlined Celtic back into it's very roots - a football club created for the poor and struggling. You can only imagine the tragic circumstances he lived through and the scars which famine had left on him before he left Sligo for Glasgow in 1855, aged only 15 years. In 1864 he joined the Marist Brothers aged 24, some might say he was late in entering the vocation. He would return to Glasgow after an education in France, taking the name Walfrid after an 8th-century Italian saint. My visit to Dumfries felt a long way from Glasgow and Sligo, the grave itself was not easy to find due to maintenance work at the time of writing, but a janitor at St Joseph's College pointed myself and fellow Celtic supporter Ronnie in the right direction. 'How will we find it?' Ronnie asked. 'I've tied a green ribbon around it,' he said just above a whisper with a slightly knowing smile.

Mount Saint Michael's Chapel is no longer under the jurisdiction of the Marist Brothers, but their former presence is evident in the Catholic statues and iconography in the grounds. The visit occupied much of our conversation on the road home. Perhaps this is how Walfrid would want it, out of view with no mention of his wider influence as the founding father of a world institution. In keeping with the unassuming stature expected from a man of the cloth, on a metal heart below a cross with the Virgin Mary his vow of stability is mentioned alongside his birth and death dates telling us simply that he served 51 years in community.

There are a number of other significant links to Celtic among the graves reserved for the Marists. *The Celtic Story* by James E. Handley (Brother Clare) has become a valuable collector's item among Celtic supporters; he is also buried in the graveyard as is Brother Thomas Aquinas (James Curry) who was the brother of Walfrid's assistant Brother Dorotheus (Henry Curry). You get something of an understanding of the wider framework of the Marists as well as their context and relationship to Celtic. Without doubt coming here and visiting

Walfrid's grave gives some perspective of the peaceful and devoted time he would have had here in contrast to the active life lived in Glasgow and London after the famine years.

The subject of the Irish famine still affects the lives of many today. In Dumfries I reflected on my trip to Ireland, where I had a conversation with a fellow traveller, John from County Offaly. He told me that he had recently been to a mass in remembrance of those who had perished in the famine: 'Everyone had someone who died,' he explained. 'There was a sense of shame among those who survived that they were the ones who had enough to eat, that they could eat what little they had at the expense of others, they carried that sense of guilt. My faith and prayer helps me deal with how the famine affected my family.' To return to Sligo for a minute, the comedian and writer Spike Milligan is honoured with a plaque at No. 5 Holburn Street. A particularly interesting example in the context of the diaspora, his Irishness played out during his lifetime in a number of significant ways. He suggested that both his humour and his battle with depression were because: 'I'm Irish and the Irish see things sideways.' Milligan's absurd, surreal, anarchic and anti-establishment brand of humour is not dissimilar to the kind you would traditionally hear around Celtic Park. Milligan could also be poignant and emotive, perhaps more unusually for a groundbreaking and edgy entertainer such as him, his Catholicism and ethical beliefs also manifested through his work and causes he would speak out on. He passionately supported a number of issues and campaigned against domestic violence and abortion writing the poem 'Unto Us' about the latter. Having the last laugh in his ancestral tongue his gravestone reads: 'I told you I was ill'.

From Spike Milligan to Brother Walfrid, far from being a diluted diaspora, Irishness has become an essential feature in British life. Not just in Scotland, but throughout the world Celtic has had a magnetic appeal for those affected directly and subsequently with Ireland's famine and its historical struggles. I was fortunate enough to cover the unveiling of Brother Walfrid's statue at Celtic Park on 5 November 2005. Once again there was a sense of the divine spark in the air that began when Walfrid, in an effort to aid the helpless and bring joy to the broken hearted, created Celtic. Former chairman Brian Quinn had this to say: 'I did some research on this; a student sent me a report on what conditions were like in Glasgow during the 1880s. It's pretty appalling stuff. By any standards it was dreadful. The main problems were with children; infant mortality rates were very high. Diseases such as measles, pneumonia and tuberculosis were related to conditions and to nutrition. There were ten to fifteen people in a house and they all had outside toilets.'

Out of the hellish vision that the former deputy governor of the Bank of England describes, Walfrid created Celtic as a motivational tool to raise money for those very children. Described as a 'born organiser' and well-connected with the middle-class entrepreneurs and Irish Catholic businessmen of the period, the club was well established by the time he was posted to the East End of London in 1892 to work with the Irish in the aftermath of the famine in that part of Britain. It's not difficult to imagine Walfrid's work during the period. Post-Dickensian London in the late Victorian era continues to influence endless dramatic film and television adaptations. Representations of Jack the Ripper and perhaps less so the Elephant Man characterise the period in public consciousness, most recently the BBC's *Ripper Street* gives some indication of the grisly world of prostitution, murder, poverty, disease and overcrowded slums. As a teacher and educationalist Walfrid's final post would be to a French college near Canterbury. In 1911 he hosted the Celtic team in London after a tour. After being somewhat exiled from the club since his exit from Glasgow life, his affection remained tangible when he said to Tom Maley: *'Well, well, time has brought changes; outside ourselves there are few left of the old brigade. I know none of these present players, but they are under the old colours and are quartered in the dear old quarters, and that suffices.'*

As Sir Willie Haughey suggests, Walfrid's notoriety among Celtic supporters is one that has taken time to develop. In bygone eras the concerns of family life and work would leave little time for much else beyond supporting the team. Today Celtic fans are unique in that many have a thirst for knowledge about the club that encourages them to travel, be it to Lisbon or Dumfries. It also gives them a sense of insight. By comparison other teams often seem inane, without much significance beyond the game itself. It's also worth pointing out that it's the supporters who have funded both the statue outside Celtic

Park and the memorial in Sligo, communities of Celtic fans have always been proactive in symbolising what is important to them about the institution to which they offer an unrelenting, passionate and generous support. Their efforts have ensured that the Brother Walfrid story – his Catholic vocation, Christian beliefs, religious philosophy and his immense social capacities – has grown in stature, defining the football club. During one of the darkest periods of Irish life Andrew Kerins created a reason to believe for the country's Scottish born offspring that were looking to gain something positive from a hellish, troubled and catastrophic past.

The late Irish-American writer, Brennan Manning, was a Franciscan priest and war veteran born in Depression-era New York, he pointed to the examples of faith in popular culture in his now classic book *The Ragamuffin Gospel*. He said: 'Grace abounds in contemporary movies, books, novels, films and music. If God is not in the whirlwind, he may be in a Woody Allen film, or a Bruce Springsteen concert. Most people understand imagery and symbol better than doctrine and dogma. Images touch hearts and awaken imaginations. One theologian suggested that Springsteen's *Tunnel of Love* album, in which he symbolically sings of sin, death, despair and redemption, is more important for Catholics than the Pope's last visit when he spoke of morality only in doctrinal propositions.' For the Irish Catholic community in Scotland and beyond, Celtic remains a popular symbol in our culture of faith in community. Part of that transaction was the formation of a football club whose roots are impossible to deny, hide or criticise. It is certain that Brother Walfrid would not want to be looked upon as a hero, but he would no doubt, celebrate the passion and nature of the support and be glad to see that charity is being carried on in the club's name.

Switching on the radio when driving home from Dumfries I heard that 20 per cent of children in the UK are living below the poverty line. Today in the constituencies of Belfast West and Glasgow North East it's 43 per cent. Glasgow's East End continues to have some of the worst child poverty, health, addiction and violent crime statistics in western Europe. In Brother Walfrid's other former parish, Bethnal Green and Bow, it's 49 per cent. A number of these families have lost benefits or found themselves in debt to doorstep lenders and pay-day loan sharks as a result of Tory welfare cuts which value economic benefit over people. Once again hunger has become common in British life and society. Even among the employed, many have had to resort to food banks. Journalist Paul Mason on the subject of poverty reported that: 'The welfare system is supposed to be a safety net, but on the evidence we've found about half of the hunger being officially dealt with is caused by people not falling through it but being forced through it by the system itself. The real safety net is now churches and charities. And as benefits are cut and rules tightened the food banks expect to be seeing a lot more people soon.' The current political shifts taking place are leaving many of us feeling demoralised and powerless. It is estimated 350,000 children from low-income working families in Scotland will be affected by the working tax credits cuts. For that reason it was heartening to see leading lights in the community voice their opposition and concern by adding their name to an open letter addressed to work and pensions secretary Iain Duncan Smith. 70 leading Catholics including Sir Tom Devine wrote to Smith with the aim of expressing their concern over welfare cuts and the damage they are doing to vulnerable people. Iain Duncan Smith has been less than honest about the statistics concerning people who have died within six weeks of their benefit being stopped or cut. David Cameron announced they would be published after Smith denied they even existed. A petition signed by over 200,000 people put pressure on the government to reveal the figures as well as a ruling from the department of work and pensions. Faith and politics can be radical and a lightning rod for good as Andrew Kerins proved when challenging the system and principles of elitism by creating a football club with gospel values at its core for all in the community. Collective strength played its part in forming a football club that would earn one of the most coveted reputations in the world. Today, 128 years after Celtic's formation, in the areas where Brother Walfrid lived and worked, poverty is once again affecting the life chances, education and well-being of children across the UK. For almost 100 years the charitable aspect of Celtic was at best peripheral, but that has shifted in modern times. Speaking in 2005 Brian Quinn commented: 'The charitable aspect got subordinated not long after the club was founded. There was a big argument in the community as to whether they should carry on as a charity or become a public company.' It was perhaps appropriate that Fergus McCann put in an appearance at the unveiling of Walfrid's statue outside Celtic Park in 2005 having established The Celtic Charity Fund. Even more appropriately in its 125th year the club formed an initiative in conjunction with Celtic Charity under the motto 'Football For Good' which encouraged the supporters to each raise £125 for causes around the world. With initiatives such as this the club continues Walfrid's legacy. It's worth considering perhaps that for many it would have been natural over the years for Celtic's market-driven business minds and corporate entrepreneurs to lose sight of Walfrid and a support who believe in social justice. But those voices have made any attempt to obscure the club's roots impossible. Celtic supporters have also clearly formed links with clubs who offer a wider social significance, particularly in times such as these. Institutions that decline a wider positive resonance or have lost their meaning are in danger of looking like superfluous limited enterprises that benefit only the few. That might not matter to some, but it does to those who follow Glasgow's green and white, the core of which will not be pawns in an out of control capitalist vehicle.

Today my own son Ryan wears the Celtic top; his great-uncle Terry had handed it over just hours out the womb at a family gathering amid much whooping and cheering. Perhaps this is one way I can pass on the same values that mattered the day the club was created in St Mary's church hall on November 6 1887. They have survived two world wars and outlasted the concepts of the moment, be it fascism in the 1940s, the social revolutions of the 1960s or Thatcherism in the 1980s. It is often commentated that we are living in secular times, though some commentators believe we are now in a post-secular environment where existentialism is questioned and faith matters. It's this aspect of the wider culture around Celtic, but particularly the support's relationship with Brother Walfrid that gives the club its character and pulse. The fans have incessantly hammered at the door of the club and underlined that importance. Celtic's essence continues to be tied up with Brother Walfrid's purpose for the club. That is why we are Celtic supporters; keeping the faith.